INDIA UNINC.

Praise for *India Uninc.*

This book provides a much needed analysis of India's vast non-corporate sector. Vaidyanathan offers an excellent overview of previous debates, and writes with clarity and insight on the trends and reforms that have touched this sector, how people within it cope, and what more needs to be done.

Nandan Nilekani, Chairman, UIDAI

Although, the Non-Corporate sector occupies a large space in our Economy, it receives little attention. This book brings out the travails of this sector in terms of poor credit availability and dealing with corrupt government agencies. It provides a new perspective to experts who are otherwise focussed on capital markets and those with access to organised banking.

Sucheta Dalal, Editor, *Money Life* magazine

At a time when Finance Ministers seem to think that attracting foreign investment is the only required reform, Prof Vaidyanathan's book is a breath of fresh air. He is absolutely right in saying that the non-coporate sector in India is among the most dynamic, yet least known and most neglected of sectors. It urgently needs faster clearances, less red tape and more credit.

Swaminathan S. Anklesaria Aiyar, Consulting Editor, *The Times of India*

The beam of a searchlight on a sector we hardly look at—a sector that, Professor Vaidyanathan teaches us, has been and can be one of the most powerful sources of growth in our country.

Arun Shourie, Former Minister, Government of India

The Non-corporate sector high share in national income, in savings, GDCF, in manufacturing /in service sector/in taxation, in credit off take etc. makes it an engine of our economic growth and hence regrettably not adequately focused... Therefore, Professor Vaidyanathan has done yeoman service to the intellectual community by providing a recipe for rectifying the situation and this is timely.

Dr. Subramaniam Swamy, Former Commerce Minister, Government of India

Non-Corporate India makes up around 45% of our GDP and provides employment for the majority of our population. Sadly they are not part of any policy, left to fend for themselves and most often at the receiving end of the inspector raj and State tyranny! For the first time Prof Vaidyanathan has explained their existence in a lucid manner pointing out the need for good policy to enable their growth and contribution to employment.

T.V. Mohandas Pai, Chairman, Aarin Capital Partners

This book is from the other India perspective—or the real India, the unknown India and the India that sustains the Indian economy and providing employment and livelihood to ten times the employment that organised private sector provides.

S. Gurumurthy, Senior Journalist

I would choose India's next tryst with destiny is about the non-corporate sector. This book wonderfully synthesizes the puzzle.

Manish Sabharwal, Chairman, Teamlease Services

R. Vaidyanathan has established with surgical precision that the most dynamic elements in our society are small entrepreneurs who remain unsung heroes.

Jaithirth (Jerry) Rao

Too often, private enterprise is equated with the corporate sector. Numbers will show this isn't true and much of industry and service sector growth since 1991 has been driven by the MSME sector.... India's growth story is about unincorporated India.... Professor Vaidyanathan should be complimented for bringing this sector and its three kinds of problems, entry, functioning and exit, into the discourse.

Bibek Debroy, Economist

INDIA UNINC.

Prof. R. Vaidyanathan

Westland Ltd

westland ltd

61 Silverline Building, 2nd floor, Alapakkam Main Road, Maduravoyal, Chennai 600 095

No. 38/10 (New No.5), Raghava Nagar, New Timber Yard Layout, Bengaluru 560 026

93, 1st Floor, Sham Lal Road, New Delhi 110 002

First published by westland ltd 2014

Copyright © Prof. R. Vaidyanathan 2014

ISBN 978-93-83260-56-0

Typeset by Ram Das Lal

Dedicated to the memory of my parents
Shri. S. Ramamurthy and Shrimathi R. Balambal
who imparted knowledge and culture to me

Contents

Foreword   ix

An Introductory Note   xiii

Introduction   xxiii

Section 1 — India Uninc.: Dominant Role in the Economy

1.   INDIA UNINC.: Understanding the Terminology   3
2.   Largest Contributor to the National Income   15
3.   Significant Role in the Service Sector   40
4.   Low Profile, Big Savers   49
5.   Predatory State, Pauper Households   58
6.   India Uninc. and Capital Formation   66

Section 2 — Travails of the India Uninc.

7.   Growth Drivers without benefit of reforms   76
8.   FDI in Retail Trade: Fact and Fiction   85
9.   The Bias against the Self-Employed   102
10.   The Sorry Saga of Contract Enforcement   111

Section 3 — Credit Delivery to India Uninc.

11.   Bank Lending and Non-corporate Sector   120
12.   The Critical Role of the Non-Banking Financial Sector [NBFS]   129

Section 4 — Taxation and Bribery

13.   Taxation: Coverage Issues   154
14.   Bribery and Corruption   162

Section 5 — Social Security for the Self Employed and the Role of Gold

15. Foolish Governments and Smart Women — Role of Gold in our economy   172

16. Demography is Destiny   181

17. Reverse Mortgage as Old Age Security   190

18. Savings or Consumption Driven Society   206

Section 6 — Stock Markets: Role in our Economy

19. Stock Markets: Are they Barometers?   216

20. The Indian Financial Markets: A *Cul-De-Sac?*   224

Section 7 — Caste and India Uninc.

21. Reservations: Strong Policy and Weak Database   234

22. Job reservations: Make them Entrepreneurs instead   242

23. India Growth: The untold story — Caste as social capital   249

Section 8 — Miscellaneous Musings & Conclusions

24. The NGO Sector   266

25. Decline of the West   282

26. Art of Giving: Warren Buffet to be told   293

27. Leveraging on the Mobile Phone Revolution   298

28. Time to Say Goodbye to the World Bank   305

29. Sports in India — BCCI the largest Uninc.   313

30. Bollywood as Uninc.   319

31. Conclusion   325

Acknowledgements   **331**

References   **335**

Index   **339**

Foreword

I have known Prof. R. Vaidyanathan for nearly fifteen years. He did an exhaustive study on the Non-Banking Finance Sector a decade ago which was in a sense an eye-opener for many of us in the industry. The study established that the Non-Banking Financial Sector involving large companies and small moneylenders plays a very important role in the economy of India. The Non-Banking Finance Sector plays an important role in meeting the credit requirements of the small businesses in timely fashion at appropriate risk adjusted rates. He also showed us that a larger portion of credit requirements of sectors like trade, transport, hotels etc. are met by the Non-Banking Finance Sector.

While most of our discussions used to revolve around Non-Banking Finance Companies or NBFCs, Prof. Vaidyanathan enlarged the scope of his study by introducing the role of UIBs or Unincorporated (Uninc.)

bodies like money lenders, chits etc. to consider Non-Banking Finance Sector or the NBFS as a whole.

Prof. Vaidyanathan has been associated with a number of regulatory bodies and also sits on the boards of many large corporates as independent Director. But he has retained his abiding interest in small and medium businesses and their financing.

Prof. Vaidyanathan is a prolific writer in business journals and magazines. He has consistently highlighted the role of non-corporate India as well as the non-banking finance sector of our Economy. He has also dwelt on the salient differences between the Indian Economy and that of US in terms of structure, employment, institutions, instruments and regulations. He argues that Indian paradigms need Indian answers and not 'solutions' copied blindly from western text books.

In this seminal work, he brings out the salient aspects of the Unincorporated or Non-Corporate India primarily consisting of Partnership and Proprietorship firms, what is termed as the P&P sector.

He estimates their share in National Income — more than 40% — in savings/capital formation and employment. He explains that they occupy a significant part of the service sector and also have greater real growth rates. In a sense, they have been the engines of our economic growth in the last two decades. He argues that they occupy a fairly large space in our economy but get lesser attention due to our focus on the corporate sector. From that point of view he calls for re-focusing our reform process to facilitate the growth of these small and medium enterprises. **India Uninc.** is the victim of corruption and bribery by government agencies and lack of timely availability of credit at reasonable interest rates.

In that context, there is a need to reform regulatory and governance mechanisms at the state level. He also highlights the role of caste as social capital in some clusters of economic activity in India. It provides a refreshing perspective on the role of caste in capital formation, risk taking, facing failures and credit transactions with trust. He brings out the importance of a separate developmental and regulatory agency for Non-Banking financing entities which would go a long way in facilitating orderly and faster growth of the Unincorporated sector.

He brings out the issues of Charity and giving as practised by these small businesses from times immemorial and how without a CSR regulatory framework they have been performing acts of charity as part of their ethos.

An important point about his writing is that he backs up his claims with statistics and a generous dose of wit! I am confident that this book will be in a sense a 'tilting point' in discussions pertaining to our economy and reform process. Hence it is critical that policy planners, bankers, government officials, corporate denizens and academics go through this book to understand the economic issues of real India and its strengths and weaknesses.

I wish Prof R. Vaidyanathan all the best in this endeavour.

Mr. R. Thiagarajan,
Founder, Shriram Group, Chennai

An Introductory Note

It has always been a pleasure to converse with or read articles written by Prof. R. Vaidyanathan of IIM, Bangalore. I came to know him soon after I joined the Insurance Regulatory Authority (IRA, now IRDA) in 1996. IIM, Bangalore was one of the first of institutions to provide a platform to the IRA to mount a series of seminars and technical sessions on the propagation of insurance and pension sector reforms. Two other individuals, apart from Prof. Vaidyanathan, were totally committed to this cause. They were Dr. M.R. Rao who was Director of IIM, Bangalore then and is presently Dean, ISB, Hyderabad, and Mr. Sitaramu, who is no more.

IIM created an insurance research centre and collaborated with the IRA and like-minded institutions in a pioneering venture to carry the message of insurance far and wide. That opportunity gave me a chance to know Prof. Vaidyanathan well. What sets him apart from others is his capacity to display a totally different approach to issues, apart from the traditional one and his ability to think out-of the-box and bring forth arguments both in favour of and against normally accepted views have always impressed me. Of late, I have been reading articles written by him in the Hindu and Business Line on various issues, not limited to financial ones — bringing a breath of fresh air in certain areas and possibly appearing to be radical to some. But one cannot deny Prof. Vaidyanathan the credit of being fresh and innovative in analyzing issues and being candid about his views.

The title of this book may surprise many, particularly in the background of the great hype being built up in the country about the performance of India Incorporated. Newspapers are full of praise for the various achievements of India Incorporated — how high their shares are reigning and trading, how their results have leap-frogged over previous records from quarter-to-quarter and how many of them have implemented the code of corporate governance. Much is being written about corporate social responsibility — how enlightened companies and organizations have taken upon themselves the responsibility to correct social deficiencies. Nothing significant is written about the performance, ideals and objectives of those organizations, which do not form part of India Incorporated. To a large extent, either these institutions have followed a self-effacement course or have not been considered to be important enough to be talked of and written about. It has been conveniently under-played how the number that constitutes Corporate India is insignificant as compared to the total population of organizations. The role and significance of the 'Unincorporated' in the total scheme of things is as important as those of 'Incorporated' if not more.

The learned author has followed the traditional method of distinguishing between Incorporated and Unincorporated. All those organizations and institutions subject to some discipline and jurisdiction under specific laws and which are larger in size and having representative bodies supporting their causes and interests have been classified as India Inc. Their number is very limited. Those organizations, which are not subject to the above prescriptions, fail to be considered as incorporated. The author excludes from his present analysis the large agricultural sector, though it forms part of India Unincorporated. This obviously is due to the reason that factors that deal with the agricultural sector are very distinctive from both 'Incorporated' and 'Unincorporated'. Agriculture in many respects tends to reduce itself into a personal activity (not amounting to any commercial consideration) and to a large extent is subject to the pulls and pressures of nature and God.

In this work, the author has referred to a range of organizations that fail to be considered as 'incorporated'. Many of these have been categorised as proprietorships and partnerships. It is true that a non-incorporated enterprise could only be either a proprietorship or a partnership, as the basic structure will reveal. Such establishments have a flexible structure and a limited scope and reach. To this particular category of institutions, one can, of course, add a large variety of professions like teaching, medicine, law accountancy, engineering, consultancy, etc. (That to a limited extent some of these callings like medicine have been converted into a business activity by establishment of corporate hospitals is a later development). The development of these faculties in the recent past has been so striking and phenomenal that these contribute overwhelmingly to the gross domestic product and their share in the GDP is reckoned at 45%. The contributions of the agricultural and the industrial sectors to the national wealth are secondary. The tremendous growth in the knowledge sector has resulted in the service sector attaining a prominence. If the contribution of the agricultural sector to the national economy is added on to that of the service sector (which is normal since agricultural activities will be considered as part of the non-incorporated sector), the contribution of the Incorporated sector will no longer be in the limelight. However, because of their organization structure and the clout that they have in the upper-reaches of administration, the Incorporated sector has projected itself as the sole champion of economic growth.

This book puts to test that assertion and proves conclusively that it is the Unincorporated sector which has a significant role to play not only in the development of society, but in the deliverance of objectives which has received step-motherly attention so far. The fact is that not many have shown the boldness to make this assertion and bring to public knowledge the role that Unincorporated enterprises have played in the development of the country and how their effective functioning has been stymied by a host of factors. Some of these are: absence of patronage from authority, lack of organizational skills, inbuilt difficulties in structure, and lastly, a lack of public appreciation. In 30 chapters spread over 8 sections, the learned author has strung together a garland bringing out the various facets of the functioning of the non-incorporated sector. While it will be not proper in a foreword to deal extensively with any of the issues under discussion in the book, it will be sufficient to state that the presentation has been made in a convincing manner written in straight and simple language. Even a layperson can understand the concepts dealt in here. I must admit that when I started reading the book, I was impressed by the total felicity which the author has displayed in analyzing the problems and suggesting measures to get over these difficulties. Any reasonable individual with a desire to appraise the role the Unincorporated sector has in the economy of the country would find it difficult to put down the book before he finishes reading all of it. One may find it odd in this presentation for the author to mention issues like caste reservations, NGOs, etc., but taken in the context in which they have been referred to, one must reasonably conclude that a reference to those issues were rightfully made.

The author starts with the premise that a lot of ignorance has characterized the appreciation of the role of the unincorporated sector in the national economy and the benign neglect that it has drawn may be due to many factors- the size of the units forming the sector and the products that they may make (which may not attract public attention and large public investments). Many of these units survive on the strength of internal finances, or support from the non-banking financial companies and to a limited extent from the organized banking sector. The organizational pattern with a diffused liability and a structural plan, which is almost restrictive, makes them poor cousins of the organizations in the incorporated sector. The author makes references to how the role of Foreign Direct Investment (FDI) in this country is minimal as far as these organizations are concerned and how even in the context of the organized sector, the role of FDI and the capital market are minimal. Many of the modern economists and industrialists may not agree with the author's view on the subject. However, the context and the background in which the issue has been discussed by the author will convince any one of the reasonableness of the author's approach and conclusion. References have been made to the factor of globalization in the late 20th century and its effects on the incorporated sector. The direct effects of globalization have been felt by the Incorporated sector because of the reasons of structure, reach, funding pattern they follow by adopting global practices; but the same cannot be said of Unincorporated bodies. However, it cannot be denied that these institutions have also been somewhat influenced by globalization — by something like a sprinkler effect. Incorporated bodies have resorted to having their supply chains supplemented by unincorporated bodies, in the process enhancing the wealth of both the organizations. The second phenomenon worth noting in this regard is the feature of 'out-sourcing' where the basic and fundamental work gets attended to by the bodies belonging to the Unincorporated sector. Probably, we can trace the staggering growth of the Indian service sector to this reason alone — the growth in the knowledge sector and the widespread use of outsourcing. The process of globalization has also enriched the quality of work, enhanced the factor of efficiency and resulted in technological upgradation. To a great extent, these have happened across the board — in Incorporated as well as Unincorporated organizations.

Another issue referred to by the author is the pronounced lack of any welfare benefits which those employed in the Unincorporated sector derive. While workers and employees of the Incorporated sector derive benefits like provident fund, pension, gratuity, medical attention, etc. those in the Unincorporated sector are totally bereft of these benefits and have necessarily to dip into their private resources to meet these. The author makes a particular reference to pension and health benefits as being two vital requirements in the post retirement life of a person and how the denial of these can affect peace and tranquility. The comparison becomes all the more pointed, if we take note of the fact that people who constitute the organized sector are only 11% of the working population, with the balance of 89% coming from the Unincorporated sector. The picture presented is thus one of chaos, capable of leading to social tension and unrest. The author also refers to steps being taken by the government to address these issues, but progress in that area however has remained somewhat tardy. The efforts to establish a pension fund administration based on the defined contributory system have at last taken off. There are endemic problems even in this area. Pension and health benefits are better administered in a group rather than to individuals. In the latter case, the presence of a heterogeneous number will present problems on pricing, coverage and settlement of clauses. Extension of these to the Unincorporated sector, and particularly to individuals, will therefore still continue to be a dream.

The author proceeds to raise the issue on bank financing of the needs of the sector and refers to systemic bottlenecks in the system that causes delay and disappointment. He also refers to the inordinate delay in the conclusion of court proceedings. The other issue relates to an unintelligent approach to taxation. In the early part of the book, the author has established clearly that the Unincorporated sector saves nearly 30% of its income, which are invested in bank deposits, insurance policies and money market instruments. (In fact, he would like to establish a disconnect between the bank deposits and bank lending proving thereby that the very institutions which the non-incorporated sector supports, has let them down by not providing them adequate resources at the time of need). Of late, however, there is a noticeable improvement in meeting the requirements of the small and medium sector. A worry that should be voiced at this stage is about the likely result that may come about if the government were to adopt its threatened shift from EEE to EET in the matter of taxation of certain receipts. We have already noticed now the unincorporated sector is mainly responsible for an appreciable support in the level of savings and how savings have got invested in banks, insurance policies etc. The present move of the government to tax the monies at the point of receipt [insurance policy amounts, bank deposits etc.] will most certainly be a departure from the present accepted philosophy of taxation and is bound to cause discomfort to the people. Such a move will have the long-term effect of affecting the growth of savings and will ultimately result in the denial of resources to proprietorship and partnership organizations, leading to a slow attrition of growth, which, in turn, will affect the economy on a long term basis.

Some very interesting issues are found raised in the chapters dealing with reservations, and one is tempted to agree with the author in his statement that caste can be leveraged as social capital and caste only divides politics but unites economics.

Globalization is being thought of as a universal phenomenon which applies across the board, with no respect to geographical boundaries. However, some of the recent developments expose the falsehood of this fact and make one wonder whether the principle of 'Heads I win, tails you lose' is not being advocated. Along with the author, I also feel globalization should be a two-way street. Thus, if today people from outside India would like to come and use the resources here by setting up businesses, etc. an equal facility must be afforded to Indians to go abroad and set up businesses in developed countries. In one-way or the other, this is not being supported. This therefore gives rise to a fear whether we are in a situation where we should only accept and not extend our hands of cooperation for bilateral benefit.

All said and done, this work is a very interesting one. It raises issues and analyzes them in a reasonable manner. I am sure some of the issues raised in the book and the suggested approaches to solving them may not receive acceptance with everyone. Some are meant to provoke discussion by a decision maker. Others are highlighted to draw attention and ponder over the issue. I am sure that a critical and analytical reader will independently examine the issues that have been discussed here and reach independent conclusions. In most cases, he may agree with the author, and, in some cases, he may not. This should set in motion a train of thought and lead to a further discussion and analysis. That, to my mind, is the essential purpose of a book and this is eminently satisfied in this case.

My congratulations to the author for being original and forthright.

Mr. N. Rangachary,
Former Chairman, Insurance Regulatory and
Development Authority (IRDA)

Introduction

Most discussions pertaining to reforms and growth are focussed around the government and private corporate sectors. There are times when agriculture is discussed particularly in the context of farmer suicides or in the context of writing off of co-operative loans.

The largest component of the national economy namely, proprietorship and partnership firms is not an area of focus for planners and economists. The non-corporate sector is sometimes subsumed as part of household sector as in the case of data pertaining to savings, sometimes considered as the unorganized sector as in the case of service activities and sometimes treated as unregistered sector as in the case of manufacturing. When it comes to labour and employment, it is considered as the informal sector. Since this non-corporate sector mainly consists of Proprietorship and Partnership forms of organizations, we sometimes refer to it as the 'P & P' sector.

The focus of this book is the non–government, non–agricultural, non-corporate activities which are dominant in services like trade, transport, construction, hotels and restaurant and other services. These organizations are also significant in manufacturing activities. With the increase in out sourcing of activities done by large corporates, we find that the so-called unorganized sector is playing a more important role in many areas of manufacturing. The non-corporate sector also plays a significant role in savings and capital formation and is also the largest employer in the country next only to agriculture.

The Unincorporated or non-corporate sector of our economy [consisting of partnership/proprietorship firms and self-employed persons] has the largest share in our national income, manufacturing activities, services, savings, investment, both direct and indirect taxes, credit market, employment, forex earnings etc. It is important that we understand the nature and role of this sector, which as stated earlier is also referred to as the 'un-organized', 'informal' or 'residual' sector. All these terminologies are based on concepts pertaining to Western experiences, which are perhaps not appropriate in the Indian context.

Research shows that the fastest growing activities are those activities in which non–corporate India — Unincorporated companies — is a dominant player. In other words, it would not be wrong to say that India Uninc. is the engine of our economic growth.

An important observation is that a substantial number of regulations and taxation related issues of India Uninc. is in the hands of the state governments and not many reforms have been undertaken in these regulations. Hence, it would not be wrong to say that the growth in our economy is not entirely due to the reforms undertaken by the Central Government in the nineties. They are also due to increased savings rate in the economy substantially due to India Uninc. The reforms have not focussed on the activities of India Uninc. and unfortunately, we find that many policy formulations are not conducive for their growth.

In **Section One**, we discuss the issues of terminology and the share of India Uninc. in the national income, manufacturing and service activities. We find that they have a significant share in national income and manufacturing activities. They are also dominant in service activities. We also bring out their significant contribution to savings and capital formation. In **Section Two**, we focus on the travails of the non-corporate sector in terms of government regulations, level playing field due to Foreign Direct Investment (FDI) and the bias against the self-employed in policy formulations. **Section Three** elaborates on this issue with respect to credit delivery to India Uninc. **Section Four** highlights the issues of tax coverage and bribe rate which also should be considered in considering tax rates. **Section Five** deals with issues of social security and gold which can be used for reverse mortgage in the Indian context which would also benefit the P&P sector. **Section Six** focusses on the stock market and explains how the stock markets are not the barometers of our economy. It highlights how Stock markets dominate our discussions when in fact, the Uninc. is the dominant factor of the economy. It also deals with the issue of liquidity in the market. **Section Seven** pertains to issues of social equity, particularly caste and entrepreneurship. The role of caste as social capital for the Uninc. sector is highlighted. It highlights the importance of making the weaker sections entrepreneurs instead of stressing on reservations in jobs. **Section Eight** deals with different types of issues ranging from the impact of the mobile revolution to the sports sector and the film industry.

The idea of this book is to generate discussion regarding the largest but least focussed component of our economy namely, the non-corporate sector — **India Uninc**. The current stress on globalization has had an impact on this sector and the type of developmental model we choose will decide the future of this sector. Will millions of firms wither away and the current owners/employees become proletariat in the corporatised capitalist activities? Time alone will tell. But it is required for planners and experts to consider the implications of such changes on our savings, employment, social security and other related issues.

The book seeks to provide an initial thrust for such a discussion.

India Uninc.: Dominant Role in the Economy

Chapter 1	India Uninc.: Understanding the Terminology
Chapter 2	Largest contributor to the national income
Chapter 3	A Significant Role in the Service Sector
Chapter 4	Low Profile, Big Savers
Chapter 5	Predatory state, Pauper Households
Chapter 6	India Uninc. and Capital Formation

INDIA UNINC.:
Understanding the Terminology

The unincorporated or the non-corporate sector in India is the largest contributor to national income, savings and investments and taxes and accounts for the largest share in manufacturing and service activities and employment. Yet, it is a victim of the myth of superiority surrounding the corporate sector. Understanding the terminology relating to the non-corporate sector is of crucial importance in understanding the nature of the sector.

It is a sign of our times that the largest segment of our economy requires to be identified by negating something else which is relatively small. It is perhaps part of our tradition to define a thing based on the concept of **Na Ithi** — 'that which is not'. We can perhaps take comfort from the fact that — for instance — under some of the constitutional provisions, a Hindu is defined as any person who is not a Muslim, Christian, Parsi or Jew by religion. Here, too, we are defining by negation.

The focus in this book is on the role, regulations and reforms pertaining to 'India Uninc.' or the unincorporated or the non-corporate sector of our economy. The unincorporated or non-corporate sector of our economy [consisting of partnership/proprietorship firms and self-employed persons] has the largest share in our national income, manufacturing activities, services, savings, investment, direct and indirect taxes, the credit market, employment, forex earnings etc. The terminology is itself based on concepts pertaining to Western experiences, which may not be appropriate in our context. It is from this fact that all the myths emanate.

The focus of the reforms and discussions by experts has all along been directed mostly towards the corporate sector. It is high time now for the unincorporated sector to get the dedicated focus that it deserves. Basically, the sector needs to be studied, analyzed and understood, since its share in national income is significant: it constitutes more than one third of the total. This is an important aspect that has been dealt with later.

Terminology

To understand what exactly constitutes the unincorporated sector, it is very important to familiarize oneself with the terminology first. The National Accounts Statistics (NAS) uses the classification of 'organized' and 'unorganized' sectors in presenting national income data. But what is indicated as 'unorganized' in NAS is not the same as 'Uninc.' or non-corporate forms of organizations.

*"Generally, all enterprises which are either registered or come under the purview of any one of the Acts like the Indian Factories Act, 1948, Mines and Minerals (Regulation and Development) Act, 1957, The Company Law, Central/ State Sales Tax Acts, The Shops and Establishment Acts of the state governments, are defined as part of **the organized sector**. Also included are all government companies, departmental enterprises and public sector corporations. Similarly, forestry, irrigation works, plantations, recognized educational institutions and hospitals which are registered as non-profit making bodies are also classified under the organized sector...all unincorporated enterprises and household industries which are not regulated by any Acts of the type mentioned above and which do not maintain any annual reports presenting the profit and the loss and balance sheets are classified as unorganized."* [National Accounts Statistics [**NAS**]; Sources and Methods; 1980: pp. 69].

A partnership firm may, thus, be grouped under the 'organized sector' if it was covered under any of the statutes mentioned and if it maintained annual accounts. Otherwise, it would be classified under the 'unorganized sector'.

Also according to **NAS,** unorganized is defined as *"All unincorporated enterprises and household industries other than the organized ones which are not regulated by any of the acts and which do not maintain annual accounts and balance sheets."* [**NAS 2012; pp 331**]

Thus, non-corporate enterprises can figure under either of the two (organized and unorganized) sectors in the national income classification. In practice, however, corporate form is treated as organized for estimating purposes, except in the case of manufacturing. This is borne out by the explanation in the NAS of subsequent years. The NAS [Year 2012; pp 317] elaborates the **coverage of the organized sector** in NAS as described below:

1. **Agriculture:**
   Government irrigation system, non-departmental enterprises and crop production in plantation crops of tea, coffee and rubber covered in private corporate sector

2. **Forestry:**
   Recorded production of industrial and fuel wood, as reported by the state Forest departments

3. **Fishing:**
   Non departmental enterprises (public undertakings)

4. **Mining & Quarrying:**
   Major minerals, as reported by the Indian Bureau of Mines

5. **Manufacturing:**
   Registered factories covered under the Factories Act.

6. **Electricity, gas and water supply:**
   Total activity of electricity, public sector part of gas and water supply

7. **Construction:**
   Construction works in the public sector and private corporate sector.

8. **Trade hotels & restaurants:**
   Public and private corporate sector and co-operatives.

9. **Railways:**
   Entire sector

10. **Transport by other means:**
    Public sector, private shipping companies, private airlines and road transport covered under the private corporate sector.

11. **Storage:**
    Warehousing corporations in the public sector and cold storage covered under the Factories Act.

12. **Communication:**
    Public sector and companies covered under the private corporate sector

13. **Banking and insurance:**
    Total activity except commission agents attached to the Life Insurance Corporation of India and unorganized non-banking financial undertakings, including professional moneylenders and pawnbrokers.

14. **Real estate, ownership of dwellings and business services:**
    Real estate companies in the private corporate and public sector.

15. **Public administration and defence:**
    Entire sector
16. **Other services:**
    Public and private corporate sector medical and sanitary services, television and radio broadcasting and other services and public and recognized educational institutions in the private sector.

Thus, the **organized sector** is the same as registered factories under the Factories Act in the case of manufacturing and the public and private corporate sector [that is, companies governed by the Companies Act 1956] in the case of all other activities. But there are large partnership/proprietorship firms having regular accounts in trade type service activities. They are part of organized services but unincorporated. Hence, the unincorporated sector is much larger than the unorganized sector.

From these definitions, it is clear that all unregistered units in the manufacturing sector [unregistered units in manufacturing would typically be partnership/ proprietorship organizations] and partnership, proprietorship firms in trade, transport, construction, hotels, restaurants and other services belong **to the unorganized sector.**

It has also been pointed out by the National Statistical Commission (NSC) that *"Direct estimates (of national income) mostly relate to the public sector (of which the government proper is a component) and the private corporate sector so that the estimates relating to them usually constitute what is usually referred to as the 'organized' sector or segment of the economy. Indirect estimates mostly relate to households (including non-profit institutions serving households) and constitute the residual 'unorganized' sector or segment of the economy."* [**National Statistical Commission 2001**: pp 357]

Informal Sector

From the point of view of mode of production or economic activity, the distinguishing features of the informal sector are as follows:

- Low level of organization; small in scale usually employing fewer than ten workers and often from the immediate family;
- Heterogeneity in activities;
- Entry and exit easier than in the formal sector;
- Capital investment usually minimal; little or no division between labour and capital;
- Work is mostly labour intensive requiring low-level skills; there is usually no formal training as workers learn on the job;
- Labour relations based on casual employment and/or social relationships as opposed to formal contracts; employer and employee relationship is often unwritten and informal with little or no rights;
- Due to their isolation and invisibility, workers in the informal sector are often largely unaware of their rights, cannot organize themselves and have little negotiating power with their employers and intermediaries. [ILO 2000]

The informal sector consists of all economic activities that remain outside the official institutional framework (Statutory Control and Implications and Governmental Regulation). Consequently, the government has little control over the quality of employment. Generally, agricultural activity does not come under the purview of the informal set.

Actually, the term 'informal sector' has not been used by NAS. The first nation-wide survey on the informal sector under the National Sample Survey [NSS] was conducted during the 55th round [July 1999-June 2000]. Here, all unincorporated, proprietary and partnership enterprises have been defined as informal sector enterprises. From the above-mentioned discussion on the informal sector we can conclude that it is a **sub-set of the non-corporate sector** if we consider all non-company forms of activities, **Uninc.**

The diagrams on the next page explain the terminology issues in a graphical form.

In **manufacturing activities,** we find that all unregistered units [also called unorganized units] are a sub-set of the non-corporate sector. If an unit is unregistered [not having ten or more workers with power and twenty or more without power], then the unit cannot be said to have the status of a company form of organization since the cost of having a corporate form is significant for such entities. The registered manufacturing units [organized sector] can be either corporate or non-corporate units. A partnership firm can be a registered unit fulfilling the criteria.

In **all other activities** we can say that the unorganized sector is part of the non-corporate sector. But in practice, as already mentioned, in the case of many service activities the Central Statistical Organization (CSO) considers only the government and the private corporate sector as part of the organized sector and to that extent, the non-corporate and the unorganized sector is the same in these activities.

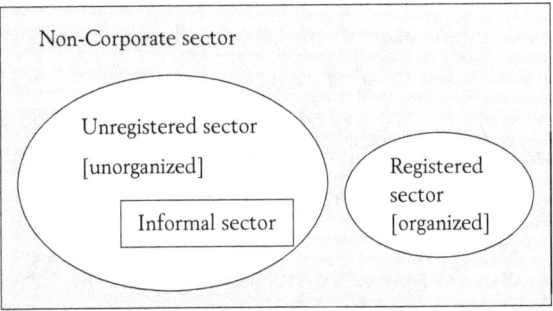

Fig. 1 — Manufacturing Activities

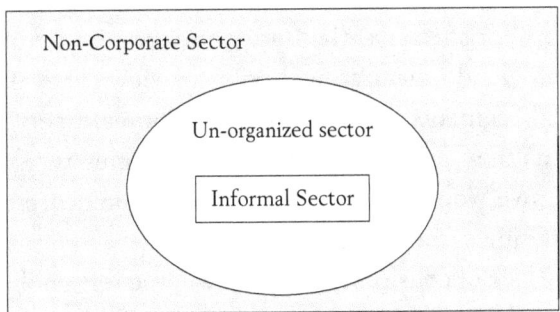

Fig. 2 — Other Activities

Hence, we can define Uninc. or the non-corporate sector as those non-corporate entities which belong to non-agricultural and non-government [departments and non-departmental enterprises] activities. It excludes company forms of organizations in the private sector and also in the public sector. It consists of partnership/proprietorship forms of organizations and other self-employed persons like barbers, cobblers, carpenters, plumbers, electricians, commission agents, cycle-rickshaw pullers as also chartered accountants, architects, lawyers, priests etc. Co-operative forms of organizations, which are not under the government, are also part of this. For tax purposes, the non-corporate form of organization could be individuals, proprietorships, partnerships, Hindu Undivided Families (HUFs) etc.

The non-corporate forms of organizations are major players in activities like manufacturing, construction, transport, trade, hotels and restaurants, business and personal services. Referring to them as 'un-organized' is inappropriate since they are well organized from the economic and organizational point of view. They are not residual segments of the economy. They are very much part of the 'formal' system of laws/rules/regulations. Hence, we would use the term 'Uninc.' [unincorporated] or sometimes, the non-corporate sector.

The lack of consistency or clarity in the terminology is a big impediment in India. *It would be useful for purposes of consistency and clarity if the Central Statistical Organization (CSO) publishes a comprehensive list of all activities and indicates the form of organization and classification*. For instance, in the context of savings data, Uninc. is considered as 'household' — like yours and mine. We will explore Uninc. from various other dimensions and explain how the corporate tail seems to be wagging the dog of the Indian economy.

Without simple and reliable numbers pertaining to national income, savings, labour and so on, it would be a Herculean task to plan for a large country like India.

Many of the assumptions pertaining to the 1950s and the 1960s may not be appropriate now, in the early 21st century. *POTA* data (i.e., **P**ulled **O**ut of **T**hin **A**ir) will be more harmful since resource allocation could get distorted!

With such a weak database, policy-makers try to formulate Five-Year Plans, Annual Budgets and socio-economic legislations. The situation at the State level needs substantial improvement as they constitute the building blocks for the national statistical system.

The Department of Planning and Statistics is dysfunctional in many States and the person appointed as Minister in such a department feels he has been given an 'unimportant' portfolio. Data collection by many of these departments requires significant improvement with the introduction of modern sampling techniques and improved training.

The lag between data collection and dissemination which, in many areas, is nearly two years needs to be minimised. For, with such lag, the numbers that emerge are neither useful to policy formulators nor to researchers for forecasting purposes.

In the current context, many a time, 'quick/provisional estimates', 'tentative figures' or 'preliminary numbers' are used for long periods of more than one year. It is rather unfortunate that the country should aspire to become a major power with such weak databases. It is told in studies pertaining to databases that when the past is imperfect, the present is tense and the future uncertain. There is quite a task cut out for the CSO and the challenges are enormous. One hopes it is able to oversee the building of a vibrant, robust, reliable and timely statistical base for the economy. That would be the best tribute to the doyens of statistics who built fine institutions for research and training in the field.

As pointed out by the National Statistical Commission chaired by Dr. C. Rangarajan, the mission statement of the statistical system should be *"to provide, within the decentralized structure of the system, reliable, timely and credible social and economic statistics to assist decision-making within and outside the Government, stimulate research and promote informed debate relating to conditions affecting people's lives."* (Report of the National Statistical Commission; Volume 1, p82).

India deserves a better database and this is something India can and should achieve as it is a *sine qua non* for orderly growth and meaningful policy formulations.

CHAPTER 2

Largest Contributor to the National Income

The unincorporated sector in India contributes about 45% of the national income, which, by far, surpasses the corporate sector's contribution of around 15% and yet its contribution remains unacknowledged. Also it is important to note that the estimates of this sector in manufacturing and services need to be made more accurate.

The share of the non-corporate sector consisting of P&P firms and household enterprises, etc. constitutes a very large portion of our economy. We shall now look at the share of Uninc. in national income and the manufacturing sector. Traditionally, economists discuss the share of national income as pertaining to the primary sector [Agriculture and Mining], the secondary sector [Manufacturing] and the tertiary or service sector [trade, transport etc.]. We will look at it from the point of view of ownership, namely, government ownership, private corporate ownership and the ownership of Uninc.

Virtually, the whole of the agricultural sector is unorganized. Table — 2.1 reflects the share of different sectors like agriculture, the government, and the private organized and unorganized sectors in the national income measured as Net Domestic Product [NDP].

Table — 2.1 Share of Various Sectors in Net Domestic Product — NDP (%)

Category	1980-81	1990-91	2000-01	2004-05	2010-11	2011-12
Organized						
Government	17.50	23.90	22.7	21.6	20.0	19.8
Private sector	12.50	12.30	18.7	19.5	22.6	22.9
Un-Organized						
Agriculture	38.08	31.46	25.1	18.9	17.8	17.3
Other activities	31.92	32.34	33.5	40.0	39.6	40.0
Total	100	100	100	100	100	100

Note: 1. Agriculture does not include Government and Corporate Agriculture. They are included under respective shares as part of organized. These are based on NDP at factor cost and current prices.

Source: St 24, St 76.1 National Accounts Statistics [NAS], 1997 & 2013 Central Statistical Organization [CSO] –New Delhi.

It may be noted that agriculture here excludes government owned agriculture and private corporate sector owned agriculture like huge plantations in corporate form. These are included under the government and the organized private sector respectively.

This table provides an insight into the importance of the *Non-Corporate* sector in our economy. The share of the government (central, state and all public sector undertakings) in the NDP in 2011-12 was around 20% and that of the *unorganized* agricultural sector around 17%. Of the remaining 63% the estimated share of the unorganized sector was 40%. This is clearly an underestimation, in terms of understanding the non-corporate sector, since the non-corporate sector is also a part of the organized sector. *One needs to remember that the unorganized sector is only a large subset of the non-corporate sector.* As we will see later, according to the Annual Survey of Industries, the non-corporate sector has a share in the registered portion [organized], even in manufacturing activities. The share of the 'Non-corporate sector' in organized manufacturing is around 10%, as indicated later [see Table — 2.4]. Organized manufacturing has a share of around 8% in the NDP, and so the share of *'non-corporate'* manufacturing from the 'organized' sector for the NDP would be about 10% of 8% namely say 1%.

It is to be noted that in practice, the organized portion of the service sector is private corporate and government activities and the unorganized part is partnership and proprietorship firms. This has been discussed in Chapter 1. Even in the case of service activities large partnership/proprietorship firms who keep account books and are subject to certain regulations are present. They would be part of the non-corporate but organized sector. That will increase the share of non-corporate in NDP by at least 4% to 5 %.

Hence the share of the non-corporate sector in the NDP would be around 45% [the unorganized share of 40% plus the organized part of manufacturing and services]. The share of 'corporate' in NDP would be nearly 18% [that is, 23% of the private 'organized' sector, less the non-corporate portion of the organized sector in manufacturing and services] .

Some attempts have been made by other economists to directly estimate the value addition by the corporate sector, using what is called the 'blowing' up procedure using the paid up capital figures of Department of Company Affairs [DCA] and sample company data available from Centre for Monitoring Indian Economy [CMIE] corporate data base or the RBI sample of large and medium public and private limited companies. But this type of estimation does not take into account the leverage aspects of corporate finance. Hence, I have not followed such a procedure.

Developed economies like the US derive a significant portion of their national income from the corporate sector. Table — 2.2 provides the share of the business (farm and non-farm) in the Gross Domestic Product of the US economy for the past few years. Earlier the categories used to be corporate and others. But the role of partnership/proprietorship is relatively small. We find that the corporate sector dominates the US economy to the extent of having around 70% of the share of GDP. This is in contrast to our country where the corporate sector has around 18% of the share in the national income.

Table — 2.2: Share of Corporate Business in the GDP at current prices in the USA — Bil. USD

Category	2005	2009	2010	2011	2012
Corporate Business *	9921.6 [76]	10596.7 [74]	11054.8 [74]	11559.5 [74]	12195.4 [75]
Non Corporate Business	1599.5 [12]	1913.6 [13]	1927.5 [13]	1971.9 [13]	2025.4 [12]
Government	1574.3 [12]	1907.6 [13]	1975.9 [13]	2002.4 [13]	2023.7 [13]
Total GDP	13095.4 [100]	14417.9 [100]	14958.3 [100]	15533.8 [100]	16244.6 [100]

Note: * farm and non farm business, Figures in brackets are percentages to total.

Source: Table 1.3.5 Bureau of Economic Analysis –US Department of Commerce

Share in Manufacturing

Data is available pertaining to the manufacturing sector for registered (under the Factories Act) and unregistered categories. The former is considered as organized and the latter as unorganized by the National Accounts Statistics [NAS].

I have provided the share of registered [organized] and un-registered [unorganized] sectors in manufacturing for recent years in Table — 2.3. It is revealing to see that the share of the Un-organized sector in manufacturing is nearly 35%.

Table — 2. 3 Share of Organised and Unorganised sector in Manufacturing NDP at Factor Cost (at current prices)

Category	2004-05	2005-06	2006-07	2007-08	2008-09	2009-10	2010-11	2011-12
Registered	205844 [59]	246015 [62]	311499 [63]	357748 [63]	407017 [64]	463886 [65]	553152 [66]	612068 [66]
Un-Registered	140651 [41]	153513 [38]	181928 [37]	212317 [37]	225214 [36]	245251 [35]	281378 [34]	312477 [34]
Manufacturing-Total	346495 [100]	399528 [100]	493427 [100]	570065 [100]	632231 [100]	709136 [100]	834530 [100]	924545 [100]

Note: Registered is organised [as per Factories act] and unregistered is unorganised sector. Figures in brackets are percentages to column totals

Source: St.12, National Accounts Statistics , 2013 — Central Statistical Organization [CSO] New Delhi

Table — 2.4 gives the share of the non-corporate sector within the registered manufacturing sector. It is to be noted that the net value added figures for registered manufacturing of Annual Survey of Industries [ASI] is smaller than that of National Accounts Statistics [NAS], since ASI does not take into account defence production which is collected independently by NAS. Also, the estimates of value added obtained from ASI include banking charges paid by the manufacturing establishments and the value of such services according to NAS forms part of the income originating in the banking sector. NAS does the adjustment for the imputed bank charges at the aggregate level. Also, NAS adjusts for the non-responses in the ASI data. The non-corporate sector, as per ASI, consists of partnership, proprietorship, Joint Family [HUF], Khadi and village industries, handloom industries, co-operative societies and others. We see from Table — 2.4 that nearly 10% of the registered [organized] value addition is due to the non-corporate sector.

Since the registered sector constitutes around 66% of the manufacturing activity [see Table — 2.3] we can say that nearly 7% of manufacturing in the organized sector is due to the non-corporate sector. **This, combined with the unorganized sector [all non-corporate], of 34% [table-2.3] gives us estimation that nearly 41% of the value addition in the manufacturing activity is due to the non-corporate sector.**

Table — 2. 4 Share of Non-corporate Sector in Value addition of Registered Manufacturing

Category	2000-01	2004-05	2008-09	2009-10	2010-11
Corporate Sector	123681 [86]	235019 [90]	472194 [89]	531511 [90]	63393236 [90]
Non-Corporate sector	19940 [14]	24888 [10]	55572 [11]	60603 [10]	7064345 [10]
Total Net Value Added — Registered Manufacturing	143621 [100]	259907 [100]	527766 [100]	592114 [100]	70457581 [100]

Note: See text for details. Figures in brackets are percentages to Total.

Source: Annual Survey of Industries — Factory Sector — Various Issues –CSO New Delhi.

At this juncture, it is pertinent to point out that the estimates of the 'unorganized' sector in many of these activities, including manufacturing, needs improvements to reflect the actual national situation. For instance, it has been pointed out by the National Statistical Commission [NSC] that the issue of 'non-inclusion' is a serious problem. The National Sample Survey [NSS 51st round]—1994-1995, considered only those units that were not included in ASI, that is, units outside the ASI frame.

The findings are:

(a) In 1994-95, as estimated by the NSS 51st round, about 1.45 lakh eligible units [i.e. employing 10 or more workers and using power or 20 or more workers but not using power] were not included in the ASI frame; and

(b) Of these 1.45 lakh missing units, about 1.19 lakh units belonged to the employment class 10 to 19 and the rest [i.e. about 0.26 lakh units] belonged to the employment size class 20 or more.

Hence, the 'actual' share of 'non-corporate' manufacturing units may be much higher than suggested by our estimates. [NSC 2001 pp149-150]

We provide below three major surveys conducted by the CSO [Economic Survey], the Census of Unincorporated Enterprises by NSSO and that of the Development Commissioner, MSME sector. **These surveys provide a clue to the significance and size of the Non-Corporate sector.**

I. 5th Economic Survey, 2005

The following are the main highlights of the 5th Economic Survey conducted in the country during 2005 by Central Statistical Organisation [CSO].

1. As per Economic Census 2005, 41.83 million establishments — 25.54 million in rural areas and 16.29 million in urban areas operated during the year 2005.

2. While the non-agricultural establishments accounted for 35.75 million, the agricultural establishments (excluding those engaged in crop production and plantation) accounted for 6.08 million.

3. Establishments registered a growth rate of 4.69% per annum (5.37% in Rural and 3.69% in urban)

during the period 1998-2005 as their number increased from 30.35 million in 1998 (EC1998) to 41.83 million in 2005 (EC2005).

4. Non-agricultural establishments grew at the rate of 4.16% per annum (4.56% in Rural and 3.67% in Urban). At the same time, agricultural establishments grew at the rate of 8.32% per annum (8.62% in Rural and 4.42% in Urban) during 1998-2005.

5. 26.94 million (64.41%) were Own Account Establishments (i.e. establishments without any hired worker) and the remaining 14.89 million (35.59%) were establishments with hired workers. Own Account Establishments grew at the rate of 3.36% per annum (4.18% in Rural and 1.83% in Urban) while the growth of establishments with hired workers was of the order of 7.50% per annum (8.83% in Rural and 6.30% in Urban) during the period 1998-2005.

6. Out of 41.83 million establishments, around 39.61 million establishments were under private ownership.

7. Around 7.54 million (18.03%) worked without any premises i.e. floating establishments, around 2.22 million (5.3%) were seasonal establishments. 76% of the establishments (31.74 million) worked without any power.

8. While Farming of Animals was the major economic activity (87%) pursued by the agricultural

establishments, 'retail trade' (41.8%) followed by manufacturing (23.3%), and other community, social and personal services (7.3%) were the dominant activities of the Non-Agricultural Establishments.

9. Around 100.9 million persons, 52.1 million in rural and 48.8 million in urban, were working in these 41.83 million establishments.

10. While employment in own account establishments were of the order of 35.7 million, the employment in establishments with hired workers were of the order of 65.2 million.

11. Agricultural establishments provided employment to around 10.9 million persons. At the same time, the non-agricultural establishments provided employment to around 90 million persons.

12. The growth rate of employment during 1998 to 2005 was of the order of 2.78% per annum (3.88% in rural and 1.70% in urban). This is considerably higher than the growth rate (1.75%) observed during 1990 to 1998.

13. Out of the total employment of 100.9 million 78.3 million (37.6 in rural and 40.7 million in urban) were male, 20.2 million (13.0 million in rural and 7.2 million in urban) were female and around 2.4 million (1.5 million in rural and 0.9 million in urban) were children.

14. Around 54.4 million persons (53.9%) were hired workers and the remaining 46.5 million were own

account workers. Out of these hired workers, 41.3 million were male, 11.6 million were female and 1.5 million were children.

15. Manufacturing sector was the largest employer providing employment to 25.5 million (25.25%) persons. This was followed by 25.1 million persons (24.91%) in retail trading activity and 9.2 million (9.13%) in farming of animals.

16. Average employment per own account establishment was 1.33 and that per establishment with hired workers was 4.38. Overall, average employment per establishment was 2.41 persons. Average employment per establishment which was 2.88 in 1990 had come down to 2.75 in 1998 and further gone down to 2.41in 2005.

17. Distribution of establishments by size class of employments revealed that around 95% of establishments were having 1 to 5 workers, 3.42% of establishments employed 6 to 9 workers and only 1.51% of establishments employed 10 workers and above.

18. Among the States, maximum growth rate of establishments during 1998-2005 was observed in Mizoram (9.71%) followed closely by Tripura (8.88%), Kerala(8.69%) and Tamil Nadu (8.44%).

19. Highest growth rate of employment was however observed in Jammu & Kashmir (6.82%) followed by Andhra Pradesh (5.87%), Kerala (5.86%) and Haryana (5.35%).

20. Out of total 41.83 million establishments in the country 37.63 million establishments (89.97%) were found to be self-financing.

II. NSSO survey results on the Unincorporated Sector

The National Sample Survey Office [NSSO] of the Ministry of Statistics and Programme Implementation [MOSPI] carried out an all-India enterprise survey on economic and operational characteristics of unincorporated non-agricultural enterprises in manufacturing, trade and other service sector[excluding construction] during the period 1st July 2010 to 30th June 2011 [NSS 67th Round].

The main objective of the unincorporated non-agricultural enterprise surveys conducted by NSSO was to get estimates of various economic and operational characteristics of unincorporated non-agricultural enterprises in manufacturing, trade and other service sector areas (excluding construction) at the national and state level.

The coverage of NSS 67th round (July 2010 — June 2011) was non-agricultural unincorporated enterprises belonging to three sectors viz., Manufacturing, Trade and Other Services. The survey considered the following broad categories of enterprises:

(a) Manufacturing enterprises excluding those registered under Sections 2m (i) and 2m (ii) of the Factories Act, 1948.

(b) Manufacturing enterprises registered under Section 85 of Factories Act, 1948.

(c) Enterprises engaged in cotton ginning, cleaning and baling (code 01632 of NIC- 2008) excluding those registered under Factories Act.

(d) Enterprises manufacturing bidi and cigar excluding those registered under Bidi and Cigar Workers (Conditions of Employment) Act, 1966.

(e) Trading enterprises.

(f) Other Service sector enterprises excluding construction.

The Ownership categories of enterprises under coverage in (a) to (f) above was (a) Proprietary and partnership enterprises. (b) Trusts, Self-help groups (SHGs), Non-Profit Institutions (NPIs), etc.

The following ownership categories of enterprises were excluded from the coverage of the Survey:

(a) Enterprises which are incorporated i.e. registered under Companies Act, 1956.

(b) Government and public sector enterprises.

(c) Co-operatives.

Highlights

The survey was conducted in 8296 villages out of a sample allocation of 8380 villages selected from 647970 villages as per Census 2001 and in 7602 urban blocks out of a sample allocation of 7620 urban blocks selected from 441538 urban blocks as per Urban Frame Survey [UFS] frame. Information was collected from about 3.34 lakh enterprises engaged in the manufacturing, trade and other services activities throughout the country. All unincorporated non-agricultural enterprises, excluding construction, were listed, of which a total of 334474 were selected for data collection.

Operational Characteristics

1. Of those 334474 enterprises, 162375 were in rural areas and 172099 were in urban areas. About 49% of these enterprises surveyed belonged to the rural sector.

2. Moreover, 66% of the total surveyed enterprises were Own Account Enterprises (OAEs). An enterprise which is run without any hired worker employed on a fairly regular basis — that is for a major part of the period when operations of are carried out during a reference period — is termed as an own account enterprise.

3. An establishment is an enterprise which is employing at least one hired worker on a fairly regular basis. Paid or unpaid apprentices, paid household members, servants, resident workers in an enterprise are considered as hired workers.

4. During 2010-11, 5.77 crore unincorporated non-agricultural enterprises excluding construction were estimated at the all-India level. Out of them, 30% enterprises were engaged in manufacturing, 36% enterprises were in trading and 34% enterprises were in the service sector.

5. Of the total number of unincorporated non-agricultural enterprises estimated, about 54% were located in rural areas and 46% were located in urban areas.

6. OAEs had the dominant share (85%) of unincorporated non-agricultural enterprises under the survey coverage. At all-India level, OAEs outnumber Establishments in all the three broad activity categories namely 'Manufacturing' (84%), 'Trade' (86%) and 'Other Services' (84%).

7. Out of 4.9 crore OAEs, 58% OAEs were in rural sector against 42% OAEs in urban areas. However, Establishments were higher in urban areas. Out of 89 lakh establishments under survey coverage, urban areas had a share of 70% establishments against 30% in rural areas.

8. 'Trade' had the highest percentage of enterprises for rural (34%) and urban (38%) sectors and also for the combined sector (36%). 'Other Services' had the next highest share (34%) of enterprises among broad activity categories followed by 'Manufacturing' (30%).

9. The survey revealed that Uttar Pradesh had the highest share (14.5%) in total number of unincorporated non-agricultural enterprises followed by West Bengal (12.6%), Andhra Pradesh (9.7%), Maharashtra (8.9%) and Tamil Nadu (7.8%). These five states accounted for 53.6% of unincorporated non-agricultural enterprises at the all-India level.

10. About 10.8 crore workers were engaged in unincorporated non-agricultural enterprise activities excluding construction during 2010-11. Out of the total estimated number of workers, 51% were located in urban areas and 49% were located in rural areas.

11. OAEs had dominant share of workers under survey covered in rural India. At all-India level, workers engaged in OAEs outnumber those engaged in establishments in all the three broad activity categories namely, manufacturing (60%), trade (72%) and service (63%). However, urban areas recorded slightly higher share of workers in establishments over OAEs in 'Manufacturing' (53%) and 'Other Services' (51%).

12. The sector 'Other Services' had the highest percentage of workers (36%) for rural, urban and also for rural & urban combined (36%) areas. At all India level 'Trade' and 'Manufacturing' had almost equal share (32%) of workers.

13. Uttar Pradesh had the highest share in total number of workers (15%) followed by Andhra Pradesh (11%), West Bengal (11%), Maharashtra (9%), and Tamil Nadu(8%). These five states accounted for 54% of total workers of the unincorporated non-agricultural sector excluding construction.

14. Proprietary enterprises (i.e. enterprises owned by a single household) had the highest share (96%) of unincorporated non-agricultural enterprises, out

of which only 17% of the owner proprietors were females and the rest were males.

15. Only two per cent of enterprises were operated on a partnership basis.

16. Perennial enterprises are those which worked less regularly throughout the year. About 99% of the total unincorporated non-agricultural enterprises were perennial while the seasonal and casual enterprises together constituted a little more than 1% of the total number of enterprises. The distribution of unincorporated non-agricultural enterprises in respect of nature of operation does not differ significantly between rural urban areas, or between OAE and Establishments.

17. About 93% of the unincorporated non-agricultural enterprises had worked for 9 months or more during the last 365 days while about 2% of the enterprises under survey coverage had operated for less than a quarter of the same period.

18. About 67% of all unincorporated non-agricultural enterprises had worked more than 8 hours in a normal day. In urban areas, 75% of unincorporated non-agricultural enterprises worked more than 8 hours in a day while in rural areas, 61% of them worked more than 8 hours a day. Only 5% of unincorporated non-agricultural enterprises had worked less than 4 hours in a normal day.

19. 85% unincorporated non-agricultural enterprises run the business at fixed location either within

the household premises or outside and about 15% operated their businesses without any fixed location. Around 2% of the enterprises under survey coverage operated without any structure but had a fixed location while 10.8% unincorporated non-agricultural enterprises were operated as street vendors and 4% were operated in mobile markets *(haats)*.

20. At an all-India level, about 90% of unincorporated non-agricultural enterprises were not maintaining any sort of accounts. This proportion was nearly 94% for OAEs and 68% for establishments.

21. 62% of unincorporated non-agricultural enterprises were owned by persons belonging to Scheduled Tribes (ST), Scheduled Castes (SC) and Other Backward Classes (OBC). This proportion was more in the case of OAEs (65%) than establishments (47%). Again, more OAEs in the rural areas (69%) were run by entrepreneurs from the backward sections than OAEs in urban areas (54%).

22. Private Non Profit Institutions constituted roughly 1% of all establishments at all-India level and their presence among OAEs was very low (0.3%).

23. 29% of all enterprises under survey coverage were not registered under any Act or with any registration authority. The overall proportion of registered enterprises under survey coverage was higher in urban areas (39%) as compared to rural areas (21%). 'Manufacturing' sector (86%) had

the highest percentage of unregistered enterprises followed by 'Trade' (68%) and 'Other Services'.

24. 66% of all unincorporated non-agricultural enterprises reported to not having faced any specific problem in their day-to-day operation. 'Shrinking or fall of demand' (11%) and 'non recovery of financial dues' (9%) were the two main problems faced by the enterprises.

25. Only 6% of unincorporated non-agricultural enterprises had undertaken at least some work on contract basis. This percentage was higher for manufacturing enterprises (20%).

26. About 3% of unincorporated non-agricultural enterprises pursued mixed activities. Trading enterprises had pursued more mixed activities in comparison to manufacturing and 'other services' enterprises and OAEs had much more share than establishment for each of three broad activity categories.

27. 2% of unincorporated non-agricultural enterprises had reported receiving any assistance from government. About 1% of unincorporated nonagricultural enterprises received assistance from the government in the form of financial loans.

Economic Characteristics

1. At the All India level 26.4% female workers are engaged in un-incorporated nonagricultural enterprises. Among the major states, Andhra

Pradesh had the highest percentage (46.8%) of female workers.

2. Aggregated Annual Gross Value Added by the un-incorporated non-agricultural enterprises was estimated as Rs.628356 crores. This comes to nearly 10% of GDP during the period. This is also perhaps an under estimation since during 2010-11, the CSO-NAS estimate of the Gross Domestic Product of unorganized sector was Rs. 238870 (excluding Agriculture and Construction) which is nearly four times the survey estimate. All unorganized units are likely to be unincorporated units.

3. Manufacturing Sector contributed Rs. 154720 crores, Trading Sector contributed Rs. 243725 crores and enterprises engaged in other services contributed Rs. 229911 crores in 2010-11 CSO-NAS estimates for 2010-11 of the GDP share of unregistered [un-organised] manufacturing and trade were Rs.319969 crore and Rs.4854651 crore. This also indicates under estimation by the survey.

4. At the state level, contribution of Maharashtra was Rs. 76864 crores followed by Uttar Pradesh which was Rs. 65841 crores.

5. At the All India level, Annual Gross Value Added per enterprise in un-incorporated non-agricultural sector was Rs. 108951. The same for rural India was Rs. 64114 and for urban India was Rs. 160667.

6. At the All India level, the Annual Gross Value Added per worker in un-incorporated nonagricultural sector was Rs. 58193. For rural India, the same was Rs. 37241 and the corresponding estimate for urban areas was Rs. 78527.

7. At the all India level, the highest Annual Gross Value Added per worker for enterprise engaged in trading was estimated at Rs. 71412.

8. Annual emoluments per hired worker at the All India level was estimated at Rs. 47016.Annual emoluments per hired worker in rural areas was Rs. 36354 and the same in urban areas was Rs. 51602.

9. Value of own fixed assets per enterprise at All India level was Rs. 203364. Enterprises engaged in other services had recorded the value of own fixed asset per enterprise as Rs. 281590 which was higher than manufacturing (Rs. 144501) and Trading (Rs. 177872).

10. The survey revealed that the Annual Rent Payable per enterprise was Rs. 5821. For manufacturing, trading and other services enterprises, the Annual Rent Payable per enterprise were estimated at Rs. 5486, Rs. 3006 and Rs. 9078 respectively.

11. The survey revealed that outstanding loans and interest per enterprise at All India level during 2010-11 was Rs. 17681.

12. The Annual Value of operating expenses per enterprise at All India level was Rs. 379009. It has

been observed that principle expenses accounted for 94% of the total operating expenses.

13. The survey revealed that the Annual Value of Receipt per enterprise at All India level was Rs. 489755. Principal Receipt accounted for 91% of total Receipts.

14. There were 2.45 lakh non-profit institutions during the survey period employing 13.61 lakh workers at All India level.

The above mentioned NSSO survey gives us a clue regarding the importance of the unincorporated sector excluding construction in our economy. Significantly most of them are own account proprietorship enterprises with substantial ownership by SC/STs and OBCs. They receive practically no assistance from Government and the majority are not registered under any act.

III. Survey conducted by the Development Commissioner, MSME Sector

Also from the point of view of Micro, Small & Medium [MSME] enterprises we have an exhaustive survey by the Development Commissioner, MSME for 2006-2007 which was the fourth all India Census.

We present some salient findings from that survey [Fourth All India Census of Micro, Small & Medium Enterprises].

1. Total number of enterprises 15.64 lakh units out of which 7.07 lakh units are Rural and 2.15 lakh units are women owned enterprises.

2. Micro enterprises constitute 14.85 lakh units — 95% of the total and small constituted nearly 5 %.

3. Manufacturing constituted 10.49 lakhs [67%] followed by Repair& Maintenance units at 16% and Services 17%.

4. A significant number — 67% — use electricity and 24% use no power.

5. Proprietorship constituted 90% followed by partnership at 4%. Corporate forms are almost negligible.

6. ST/SC/OBC owned units constitute nearly 50% of the enterprises.

7. Micro enterprises provided 70% of the employment followed by small at 25%.

8. Numbers of exporting units were nearly 0.5 lakhs.

9. Total amount of export were Rs. 67914 crores.

10. More than 87% of the enterprises had no external finance and were self-financing and only 10% had finance through institutional sources.

Here again we find that the unincorporated form of organizations dominate the MSME sector.

To sum up, the share of the non-corporate sector in our national income is more than 45% and that of the private corporate sector is less than 18%. The remaining is shared by the government and private agriculture more or less equally. Within manufacturing, the share of the non-corporate sector is nearly 41%. Later in the volume, we will focus on service activities where the share of the non-corporate sector is more than 75% and that of the private corporate sector is miniscule.

Whenever we become ecstatic about India Inc., we need to exercise caution since India Inc. is a very small aspect of the economy. But ironically, in our context, gallons of ink and reams of paper are spent on the inconsequential or the trivia. Therein lies the clue to our distorted priorities, leading to debilitating policies.

CHAPTER 3

Significant Role in the Service Sector

We observe that the non-corporate sector dominates service activities, which, in turn, constitutes nearly two thirds of our economy. These are also the fastest growing activities. So justifiably, it is the non-corporate sector that should be termed 'the engine of our economic growth' and the Indian economy be called the partnership and proprietorship economy [P&P economy].

The growth of the economy in the nineties should be attributed to the partnership and proprietorship firms in service activities and not due to the reforms carried out by the government or the minuscule contribution of the corporate sector. But, ironically, this remarkable contribution of the P&P sector has not been adequately documented and appreciated.

Whenever the term 'service sector' is mentioned, the immediate recall is the IT sector and companies like

Infosys or Wipro. Factually, all software related activities come under business services, which is about 5% of our national income (Ministry of Statistics and Programme Implementation, Value Addition and Employment Generation in the Information and Communication technology [ICT] sector in India, April 2010; quoted in 'The Hindu'- May 31, 2010). The service sector covers a much larger canvas and this sector is the fastest growing sector in our economy, generating scope for large-scale employment. The activities, which constitute the service sector are mentioned below in Table — 3.1. We observe that this sector encompasses diverse activities carried on by large multinationals as well as roadside entrepreneurs.

Table — 3.1 — Activities Constituting the Services Sector

1.	Construction
2.	Trade
3.	Hotels and Restaurants
4.	Transport, including tourist assistance activities as well as activities of travel agencies and tour operators
5.	Storage and communication
6.	Banking and insurance
7.	Real estate and ownership of dwellings

8.	Business services including accounting, software development, data processing services, business and management consultancy, architectural, engineering and other technical consultancy, advertisement and other business services.
9.	Public administration and defence
10.	Other services including education, medical and health, religious and other community services, legal services, recreation and entertainment services
11.	Personal services and activities of extra-territorial organizations and bodies

Note: We have considered "Construction" as part of the service sector in our discussion even though sometimes, it is considered as part of the "Secondary sector". See "Report of the National Statistical Commission", [NSC] PP 186, Vol. II August 2001. Ministry of Statistics and Programme Implementation, New Delhi.

We find that nearly two thirds of our GDP comes under service sector activities [See Table-3.2 A&B]. During 2004-05 to 2011-12, the service sector has grown at 17% [at current prices] and 9.8%, [at constant 2004-05 prices] much higher than other sectors as seen from Table-3.2 A & B.

Table — 3.2 A — GDP shares and Growth Rates — 2004-05 to 2010-12 (current prices)

Sector	Sector Share	Sector Share	Growth Rate
	2004-05	2011-12	2004-05 to 2011-12
Agriculture & allied activities	19.0	17.5	14.6
Industry	20.2	18.5	14.5

Sector	Sector Share	Sector Share	Growth Rate
Services	60.8	64.0	16.8
Total	100	100	15.9

Note: Constructed from NAS-CSO data.

Source: St.10 at current prices NAS 2013, CSO New Delhi.

Table — 3.2B — GDP shares and Growth Rates — 2004-05 to 2011-12 (constant prices)

Sector	Sector Share Rs Crores	Sector Share Rs Crores	Growth Rate
	2004-05	2011-12	2004-05 to 2011-12
Agriculture & allied activities	565426 (19%)	739495 (14.1%)	3.9
Industry	600928 (20.2%)	1030086 (19.6%)	8.0
Services	1805110 (60.8%)	3474001 (66.3%)	9.8
Total	2971464 (100)	5243582 (100)	8.45

Source: St.10 and at constant 2004-05 prices NAS 2013, CSO New Delhi.

Note: Figures in brackets are percentages to column total

Between 1950-51 and 1990-91, the share of the services sector in GDP rose by only 13.07 %, which is an increase of about 0.33 percentage points per annum. However, between 1990-91and 1999-2000, the share increased by 7.29 %, which is an increase of 0.81 percentage points per annum. [NSC 2001 pg. 186]. Between 2004-05 to 2011-12 it has grown by 17 % per annum, i.e., 2.4 percentage points per annum. Clearly, the growth rate has been very significant in the last eight years.

It is generally accepted that the economic reforms were indeed initiated in the early nineties, but most of the policy changes brought about pertained to manufacturing and the financial sector related to government and corporate activities. The regulation and control pertaining to service activities were with the state governments and there were no reforms in these segments, as we will see later. **Hence, it is difficult to ascribe the growth of the service sector and that of the entire economy during the last two decades, to the reform measures initiated.**

The role of the non-corporate sector in **service activities** is very significant, listed in Table — 3.1, namely (1) construction (2) trade (3) hotels and restaurants (4) non-railway transport (5) storage (6) real estate ownership of dwellings and business services and (7) other services. These are excluding Railways, Communication, Banking, Public Administration and Defence. The excluded are predominantly government or under significantly organized sector (Banking). Table — 3.3 gives the share of these seven major service sectors in NDP for different years. We observe that the share of these seven service sectors in the NDP has consistently gone up from 34 % in 1990-91 to 53 % in 2011-12, showing an increase in the role of these activities in the economy during the period, but more particularly in the last two decades. [Table —3.3].

As pointed out by National Statistical Commission (NSC), although the service sector plays such a pivotal role in our economy, the database of this sector is highly disorganized. There is no well-organised mechanism for maintaining a regular and proper database for this sector. The services sector can be broadly classified into three segments, namely, the public sector, private corporate and the 'household' sector. The first two are considered as 'organized' and the rest consists of unincorporated enterprises including all kinds of proprietorship and partnerships run by individuals. The database for the organized sector is mainly the published accounts of the corporate and government entities.

The National Statistical Commission [NSC] points out that the estimates of Gross Value added per worker based on the follow-up enterprise Surveys of Economic Census [EC] periodically conducted by the Ministry of Statistics and Programme Implementation [MoS&PI], are often too low. Also, the estimates of the number of workers in different sub-sectors as per these surveys differ widely with those available from other sources like Employment-Unemployment surveys of the National Sample Survey Organisation [NSSO] and decennial population census.

Table — 3. 3 Share of Major Service Sectors in NDP at Current Prices (%)

Items	1990-91	2000-01	2004-05	2010-11	2011-12
Construction	6.4	6.6	8.2	8.7`	8.6
Trade, Hotels and Restaurants	14.1	15.6	17.5	18.6	19.5

Items	1990-91	2000-01	2004-05	2010-11	2011-12
Transport [Non-Railways] &storage	4	4.5	5.9	5.5	5.6
Real estate, Ownership of Dwellings &Business services	2.9	6	8.7	10.1	10.6
Other Services	6.3	8.7	8.4	8.2	8.2
Total of the above	33.7	41.4	48.7	51.1	52.5

Note: Computed by the author from NAS data; various issues CSO New Delhi

Source; pp32-33, NAS 1995, and pp22 NAS 2005, St.12 NAS-2013.

Table — 3.4 gives the share of the non-corporate sector in the activities like construction, wholesale and retail trade, hotels and restaurants, Road transportation and Storage, Real estate and business services such as medical, legal and so on. We find that the share of the unorganized sector, which is non-corporate in nature is nearly 75% in trade [wholesale and retail] hotels and restaurants. It is more than 80% in non-railway transport and nearly 65% in construction and more than 50% in storage and it is more than 60% in real estate and business services.

It is pertinent to point out that the estimates of the non-corporate sector in these activities need substantial improvements. As already noted, for instance the report of the National Statistical Commission [NSC 2001] points out that the estimates of the non-corporate service sector is based on data which suffers from an inadequacy in terms of sampling frame and sample size.

Table — 3. 4 Share of non-corporate sector in major service activities (NDP at current prices %)

Category	1980-81	1990-91	2000-01	2010-11	2011-12
Construction	48	55.5	59.1	62.3	64.6
Trade, Hotels and Restaurant	89.7	92.2	79.5	77.4	74.2
Transport [other than Railways]	65.9	77.7	78.8	80.6	81.4
Storage	67.5	49.4	48.3	48.9	51.6
Real estate, ownership of dwellings & business services.	99.5	99.0	77.3	62.2	60.8
Other Services	46.2	37.0	29.6	42.6	42.9
Total [Share in Service Activities]	74.4	73.5	65.3	66.5	65.8

Note: Share in current prices.

Source: NAS 1997,St 76.1- 2013, Central Statistical Organization, New Delhi.

Unlike the developed countries, the likes of Wal Mart, Sears, or Marks and Spencer in retail or Greyhound and Federal Express in transportation, or McDonalds, Burger King and Pizza Hut in restaurants, are not as yet the order of the day here. We will revert to the issue of entry on MNCs in these activities later in the book.

The size of the non-corporate sector in service activities and the phenomenal growth rates achieved in the last two decades needs recognition. **As said earlier, the Indian economy can be called the partnership and proprietorship or the unincorporated economy.** There is a witty saying in the army, that to move up the ranks what needs to be done is *"Salute all things moving and paint all things standing."* In the same vein, governments attempt to control and regulate an economic activity if it does not understand it and tax it if it is growing fast. This only brings out the ever-increasing needs of the government, which are mostly to meet the salary and pensions of its employees. But the gargantuan appetite of the government goes against the grain of our civilisational ethos and negates the entrepreneurship of the non-corporate sector of our economy.

Communists are arguing for de-toxification of our textbooks but what is needed more urgently is the de-toxification of our economy. It is required to calibrate the growth and development of the non-corporate sector, taking into account issues of credit delivery, labour markets, social security, savings and investments, globalization and the cohesion of civil society. In the forthcoming chapters, we explore each of these aspects of our non-corporate economy.

CHAPTER 4

Low Profile, Big Savers

The contribution of the Proprietorship and Partnership firms (unincorporated sector) to National Savings has not received the recognition it deserves. Once again, this aberration is largely, if not wholly, due to the terminology which labels the non-corporate sector as the 'household' sector, though many of them notch up turnover running into hundreds of crores. It is imperative to take a hard re-look at the antiquated nomenclature and terminology if this buoyant sector is to get its due.

We will now focus on the dominant share of unincorporated firms in the National Savings, a fact that has not been adequately recognized. These non-corporate sector firms are considered as households in the savings data prepared by the Government of India.

In the sixties, our savings rate used to be around 8% to 10% and the theory of the vicious cycle of poverty, namely, a low savings rate implies low investment, and hence, low income which, in turn, once again leads to a low savings rate etc., was made popular using India as an example. From the eighties, our savings rate has shown a significant increase and moved up to the region of around 20% to 24% and remained there throughout the nineties. In the last decade it grew to become more than 30%. The single largest contributors to our savings are the household sector. Partnership & Proprietorship firms [P&P] are treated as households in our savings data. In other words, when we talk of households, we need to remember that it contains both pure consuming or wage earning households, as well as mixed households having production activities. For instance, Nirma was a group of partnership firms, before it became a company. In the earlier period, the savings and investments made by them would have been shown as 'household savings' in our national income data.

Hence, whenever household savings are mentioned, we need to be alert to the fact that it contains P & P firms performing large manufacturing and service sector activities. There are many P & P firms having hundreds of crores of turnover, but still they would be classified as households in our system.

Table — 4.1 provides the savings of the different sectors of our economy, namely the government, the private corporate sector and households, for different years starting with the early nineties. We find that the savings rate of our economy has increased from the nineties to the recent years, from around 23% to around 34%. It has further increased to around 29% in 2003-2004. This phenomenal increase in savings has been achieved through the efforts of the household sector, which constitute more than 70% of the National Savings. This savings rate of the households is without taking into account investment in gold by this sector, since that is considered as consumption by our government economists. Actually, purchase of gold is considered an insurance and pension product by the lower classes and if we include that, our savings rate will be higher by another 2%.

Table — 4.1 — Savings Rate and Contributions by Different Sectors [%]

Items/Year	1990-91	2000-01	2004-05	2008-09	2009-10	2010-11	2011-12
GDS [as of per cent of GDP]	22.9	23.8	32.4	32.0	33.7	34.0	30.8
Govt.	1.8	-1.3	2.3	1.0	0.2	2.6	1.3
Pvt. Corporate	2.6	3.7	6.6	7.4	8.4	7.9	7.2
Household	18.5	21.4	23.6	23.6	25.2	23.5	22.3

Note: GDS: Gross Domestic Savings, GDP: Gross Domestic Product, GDP is at current Market prices.

Source Economic Survey, 2012-13, Table 1.6 pg A-10 . ,Ministry of Finance, Government of India

The substantial growth in the national income achieved in the last two decades is due to the increased savings rate in our economy, particularly the savings rate of the household sector.

Around 70-80% of savings in the country is due to the household sector that consists of pure consuming (wage earning) households as well as *non-corporate* (mixed income households). A portion of the savings is due to farm households, details of which are not separately available. We do not have category-wise income and tax details for recent years. The proportion of unorganized agriculture and other unorganized activities during 1999-2000 are 45% and 55%, respectively. Assuming that savings of the farm sector are similar to income proportions, 45% of household sector savings could be attributed to farm households. This may be an over-estimation, and, to that extent, it will only strengthen our thesis.

On this basis, savings from the non-agricultural households works out to be nearly 50% of the total [derived as non-agricultural share of 55% of the total household savings of 90% of that year]. The *non-corporate* share in this is not separately available from our national income statistics. It is important to separate and exclude the savings of the pure salary-earning households so that comparison with savings figures from the corporate and government sectors could be on a like-for-like basis.

This may be possible using available Income Tax statistics pertaining to salaried and non-salaried categories. It must be remembered that agricultural income in India is not taxed. The share of the salaried category in the returned income is around 20% of the non-corporate categories consisting of salaried and non-salaried individuals and partnership/Hindu Undivided Family form of activities.

[All India Income Tax Statistics, 1998-99, Directorate of Statistics, New Delhi]. (**This publication has not been brought out by the Income Tax Department in recent years.**)

If it is assumed that the proportion of the savings is similar to that of the proportions of returned income for these categories, then nearly 80% of the household (non-agricultural) savings are in a sense attributable to the non-corporate sector. That is, the household (non-agricultural) sector savings, can be disaggregated into their two constituent parts of pure (consuming) households and producing households, using the proportions of salary income and mixed income in the tax data. This could provide a rough indicator of the possible *non-corporate* share in the household savings.

On this basis, around 40% (80% of 50%) of the savings is attributable to the *non-corporate* sector, while the corporate sector share in savings is around 15% and government has minus 5% of the savings during that period. Therefore, the non-corporate sector (P & P firms) is a significant wealth creator in our economy and also a major engine of growth in our economy.

Table — 4.2 gives the savings made by the household sector and that of the foreign investment flows — both direct investment and portfolio investment. **In spite of the noise made about the importance of foreign investment in our economy, we find that their role is less than 10%.** FDI/FII in our economy is like pickles to curd rice and not the main dish. Still, so overpowering is our Anglophilia that it is made to appear that the entire Indian economy is dependent on foreign investment. Hence, even basic physical necessities like yawning or sneezing by Indians in public are frowned upon, since it could upset foreign investors. Why is that so?

The logic for the importance of foreign inflows in our economic growth can be summarized as follows. If India plans to grow at 10%, then it requires nearly 40% as the savings rate, since Incremental Capital Output Ratio [ICOR] is nearly 4. Our savings rate is around 32% and hence we need to strive to get foreign inflows to bridge the gap. That is, our own savings plus foreign inflows will be the investments in the economy sustaining 10% growth. These types of arguments have several assumptions. First and foremost is the assumption regarding the capital output ratio of 4. Is this mandated by God? Can we not take steps to reduce it since we are a capital starved nation? Second, the implied ICOR is mainly based on manufacturing activities. And that also on what are known as old economy industries. In new economy industries like the software sector, incremental output is more a function of adding more brain power rather than capital.

Table — 4. 2 Savings and Capital Formation
[Rs. Crore]

	1994 -95	2000-01	2004-05	2008-09	2009-10	2010-11	2011-12*
Gross domestic savings	251463	496272	1050703	1802620	2182338	2651934	2765290
Of which							
Household sector	199358 (79%)	446217 (89%)	763685 (73%)	1330873 (74%)	1630799 (75%)	1832901 (69%)	2003720 (72%)
Foreign Investment inflow	16133 (6.4%)	30224 (6%)	68259 (6.5%)	125600 (7%)	173200 (7.9%)	257500 (9.7%)	240600 (8.7%)
of Which							
A. Direct Investment	4126	18404	26947	190600	157800	118100	155000
B. Portfolio Investment	12007	11820	41312	-65000	15400	139400	85600

Note: * Revised Estimates

Source: Statement 18, NAS 2013 and Table 155 Hand Book of statistics on Indian Economy Sep 2012 RBI.

In the case of many service industries, incremental capacity or output is created based on the ingenuity of our non-corporate sector. For instance, anyone who has travelled by road in our country knows that many passengers travelling by bus are outside the bus (by hanging on to the window or door rails). In that sense, extra capacity/output is created. Many taxis in Bihar, UP and Bengal carry a couple of passengers to the right side of the driver, thereby creating a doubt regarding who is driving the vehicle. A barber in a saloon needs two more hands to shave an extra person rather than four more chairs. In other words, the concept of capacity is cosmic and is unlimited in our situation unlike western notions of limited capacity and the possibility of increasing output only by increasing capital.

We need to recognize the fact that the growth in the last two decades has come about due to the extraordinary savings generated by the non-corporate sector, which the leftists derisively call *petite bourgeoisie*. **There have been a thousand conferences where the role of foreign inflows [less than 10%] has been extolled, and our growth attributed to it, but the role of the household sector has rarely been talked about.** This is in spite of the fact that balancing the budget on a daily basis is an impossible task for housewives without access to the Nasik printing press. This is unlike the case of the Finance Minister, and these days, also private operators like the stamp scam accused, Telgi.

The next sections will elaborate on the pattern of household savings and the trigger for growth of the last two decades.

CHAPTER 5

Predatory State, Pauper Households

The absence of superannuation benefits in the household sector and a dramatic rise in educational and healthcare expenses has aggravated the sector's future uncertainties. Also the joint family system is declining. This gets particularly magnified when coupled with the predatory State's tax impositions intended at funding its profligacy, which it implements both through the direct tax as well as the service tax route.

Our focus now turns to the nature and structure of savings by the household sector and its changing composition. Although we have stated this earlier, for the sake of reinforcement and recall, it needs to be pointed out once again that in the government data pertaining to National Savings, partnership and proprietorship [P&P] firms i.e., the unincorporated sector are included under the household sector.

The savings rate of our economy, that is Gross Domestic Savings expressed as percentage of Gross Domestic Product at market prices has gone up from 12% in the sixties to nearly 34% recently. More than 70% of these savings are from the household sector consisting of consuming households and mixed income households, namely partnership and proprietorship activities. We estimated earlier the share of the non-corporate sector to be more than 40% of the gross domestic savings [GDS].

The household sector savings consists of physical savings and financial savings. Net additions to the physical assets of the households comprising investment in fixed assets of construction and machinery and equipment and change in stocks, is taken to constitute households' saving in physical assets. [NAS; Sources and Methods pp 226–2012].

Savings in the form of financial assets, are (1) currency, (2) bank deposits, (3) shares and debentures, (4) small savings represented as net claims on the government by households, (5) life insurance funds and (6) provident and pension funds.

We do not have any generalised social security system in our country. Actually, nearly 90% of our population is not covered by any social security system for their old age. This has been highlighted by the OASIS [Old Age Social and Income Security] Report of the Ministry of Social Justice and Empowerment in the year 2000. From this point of view, India is the only private market economy in the world, since the role of the state from the point of social security is negligible. Compare it to developed economies like USA, Germany, Japan, etc., where old age pension is provided by the state to all its citizens and, in fact, is currently being reformed through a noisy social and political debate.

In our context, individuals have to depend on their own savings and or joint family support in old age. Hence, there is a dire necessity for families to save in the context of increasing life expectancy and the decline in the joint family system. Not only that, the family has to save for the education of the children, which is very expensive. What is really important is that educational expenses are, in a perverse way, inversely related to the level of education, like kindergarten (KG) being more expensive than post-graduation (PG) in government institutions. Banks do not provide loans for school education but provide for IIT/IIM education. It is like giving loans for constructing the second and third floor of a building but not for the foundation. Indian women are obsessed with the education of their children and would like to put them in best private schools which means expensive ones. Every Indian woman wants her children to be better than her husband in life! Maybe she thinks husbands cannot be improved anymore and so takes it out on him by making his kids better than him!! Then, there are the expenses for their health care needs [which is more expensive than in UK], for their birth/marriage/death expenses which are part of the *samskaras* of an average Indian. Where do the savings of households go? The government appropriates a large portion of the savings of the households.

Table — 5. 1 Composition of House Hold Savings 2004-05 to 2011-12[%]

Item	2004-05	2005-06	2006-07	2007-08	2008-09	2009-10	2010-11	2011-12
GDS to GDP at factor cost	35	36	38	40	34	36	36	33
House hold Savings [HS] to GDS	73	70	67	61	74	75	69	72
Physical Savings [PS] to HS	57	50	51	48	55	53	56	64
Financial Savings [FS] to HS	43	50	49	52	45	48	44	36
Currency to FS	8	9	9	11	14	10	13	11
Net Deposits to FS	37	46	56	52	58	44	52	59
Shares and Bonds to FS	2	6	7	10	-1	5	0.5	-0.3
Net Claims on Govt. to FS	24	14	3	-4	-4	4	3	-3
Life Insurance to FS	16	15	16	22	23	24	19	19
PF and Pensions to FS	12	10	10	9	9	13	13	14
Total FS	100	100	100	100	100	100	100	100

Note: From currency onwards the percentages are to Gross Financial Savings of House holds GDS=Gross Domestic Savings; GDP=Gross Domestic Product;

FS=Financial savings ;Net claims on Govt= Small savings in Postal systems; Net deposits to FS= with banks

Source: St. 73, 10 & 18, National Accounts Statistics 2013; CSO New Delhi

Table — 5.1 provides the components of household savings from 2004-05 to 2011-12. We find that the physical savings, mainly houses etc. constitute more than 50% of the household savings. It also reveals that the capital formation in the household sector can easily be undertaken by the savings of that sector and that it provides a substantial amount of its savings to the government and the private corporate sector.

In the year 2011-12, deposits with banks (59%), life insurance (20%) and provident funds (14%) constituted the bulk of Finance Savings. Small savings in postal offices called Net claims on government has declined from around 25% in 2004-05 to -3% due to reduction in tax benefits. In spite of all the reports and discussions about the stock market being the barometer of the economy less than one per cent was invested through stocks and bonds in 2010-11 and it is negative in 2011-12.

To cap it all, the government has been a very inefficient user, which provides on the average a return, which is not capable of even covering the inflation rate. In other words, households are earning a negative or marginally positive rate of return which is supposed to help them in educating their children, taking care of health benefits, old age expenses etc. This grabbing of savings by households by the State is an old 'Socialist' paradigm which assumes that the State knows best, which, in our context, is laughable but for its tragic undertones.

For instance, if the household savings had been prudently used by community based local Parents' Associations, then we would have had better schools and more accountable teachers. The same is the case with hospitals. The uncertainties of the future faced by households, is aggravated by the predatory corrupt State, which furiously taxes the same hapless households both in the form of direct taxes, and recently, also through service taxes. For instance, of the aggregate income tax of Rs. 1,54,956 crore during 1998-99, the share of the household category was 55%, of which 40% was from the non-corporate sector [All India Income Tax Statistics — AIITS — p (iii), Directorate of Income Tax, New Delhi]. **(This annual report from the Income Tax Department is not available for later years.)** Actually, in the absence of any social security cover, the government should not be taxing the non-government, non-corporate employees/proprietors at all. It should also have given full tax credit for education and health expenses plus other ceremonies like birth/marriage and death since these are part of our cultural roots and civilizational ethos. But the cosmopolitan elite, which decide taxes and allocation of savings, may not even know about the *samskaras* or the cultural traditions of commoners. Other than the taxes by the State, the ever-present corruption also takes away a substantial portion of earnings of households. The community is alienated from the State and looks upon it as a nuisance factor that collects taxes and bribes.

The flow of funds accounts prepared by Reserve Bank of India [RBI, August 2000] in a time series fashion for 1951-1952 to 1995-1996 reveals that the household sector is a major source of funds for the activities of both the government and the private corporate sector in the last two decades. A large part of the savings also goes to the private corporate sector through the banking and insurance channels owned by the government.

Actually, the bank nationalization of the late sixties facilitated the process. Now, the private corporate sector wants to inflict a double whammy on households by trying to make them part of a 'consumerist culture'. The slogan of the Western economy is 'Shop till you drop' which is also the motto in the malls of Dubai or at the Changi airport of Singapore. The growth is stimulated by consumer spending and the off take by Wal-Mart shoppers is eagerly monitored in the USA as an indicator of growth. Buy and buy more is the slogan of the day, with 'shopaholics' being feted and dined.

The major equalizer in the Indian situation between the haves and the others is education, which has become very expensive in the last two decades. Education of two children and health care benefits for the family could take away nearly a quarter of the aggregate life earnings and *samskaras* take away another 25%. What is left is used for current consumption. We are talking of 90% of the households, namely those of the non-corporate sector, who are not part of the government or private corporate sector, and who have not heard exquisite words like 'perquisites and reimbursements'. All savings done by households for education is to enhance the 'equalizer' quotient on an inter-generational basis. It is based on the attitude of — *let my child be in a better profession/earn more than I do*. Hence, any attempt to lure people to 'Shop till you drop' will aggravate social tensions, and it is imperative we stress the traditional virtues of frugality and thrift to safeguard the social cohesion and welfare of families in the future. We need to urgently look beyond the hackneyed nineteenth century dogmas of 'socialism' and the 'market will solve all' mantra and evolve mechanisms to make our communities solve the problems of education and health using their own phenomenal savings.

This needs a closer examination of the tax system, capital formation, credit delivery mechanisms and the level playing field for the P &P sector, which we will attempt to do later in this book.

CHAPTER 6

India Uninc. and Capital Formation

Even though the government has been increasingly stepping up its rapacious appropriation of household savings, the fact is that its share in capital formation has fallen drastically. The appropriated funds that constitute the government's capital formation provide negative returns. Tax impositions — levied by the Centre to bail out the states — will go up as they usually do when governments go broke.

Analyzing the complex structure of the Indian economy poses major challenges, no matter what the perspective. However, the data on capital formation is the most formidable of these challenges that anyone analyzing the economy has necessarily to face. What is particularly problematic is that the data, to say the least, is far from reliable and is ridden with innumerable inconsistencies and adjustments.

For example, proprietorship and partnership [P&P]

firms are part of the household sector in the savings data and also in the data on domestic capital formation. In the savings data on the household sector, capital formation is presented as savings in physical assets by households. This includes consuming or wage earning households, agricultural households and partnership/proprietorship firms or mixed income households.

In the case of pure consuming or wage earning households, savings in the form of physical assets consists mainly of property or house construction. In the case of mixed households, it could be construction or acquisition of plant and equipment or other types of assets like transportation, properties etc. Table — 6.1 shows the share of the household sector, the private corporate sector and the government in the savings and capital formation in our economy for select periods from 1980 to 2012.

But, first a caveat to exemplify a point made earlier in this chapter. The estimates of total savings plus net capital inflow from abroad and the estimate of total domestic capital formation by type of assets do not tally. The latter is prepared using the measure of fixed capital formation in construction and machinery, and equipment and adding total estimated change in stocks across various industries.

The estimates of saving for the public and private corporate sectors are obtained using published information, and the financial saving of the household sector is obtained using information from banks, provident fund statistics, Life Insurance Corporation (LIC), etc. The saving in physical assets of the household sector is got as a residual after deducting (netting) the savings of public and private corporate sectors from total capital formation by type of assets.

National Accounts Statistics [NAS] of the Central Statistical Organization [CSO] treats the estimates of savings to be the more reliable of the two, and adjusts for the difference [called errors and omissions] in the estimates of gross domestic capital formation. In the adjusted series on investments, saving in the form of physical assets by the household sector is the same as that of unadjusted capital formation. This implies that the main burden of adjustment falls on the other two 'organized' segments, that is, the private corporate sector and the government sector.

A very significant fact is that NAS does not publish the adjusted GDCF series, sector wise. In other words, the savings and capital formation of the household sector, particularly P & P firms, might be understated. The upside of this is that to this extent our arguments will only be reinforced.

Table — 6.1 shows that the share of household savings in total savings has gone up from 70% in 1980 to more than 90% in 2000-01 and remains above 70% in 2012. The share of the private corporate sector has shown an increase from 9% to 24% and that of the government has declined from 18% to 4%. The private corporate sector has shown a consistently higher share in capital formation as compared to savings, indicating the flow of funds from the household sector through the intermediation of the banking and capital markets.

Table — 6. 1 Share of Different Sectors in Savings and Capital Formation 1980-2012 [%]

Year	1980-81	1990-91	2000-01	2004-05	2009-10	2011-12
Household Savings to GDS	73	84	92	73	75	72
Private corporate sector savings to GDS	9	11	18	20	24	24
Government Savings to GDS	18	5	-10	7	1	4
Total	100	100	100	100	100	100
Household share in GCA	42	44	43	41	35	40
Private Corporate share in GCA	13	17	26	32	35	30
Government Share in GCA	45	40	31	23	25	22
Valuables share in GCA	—	—	—	4	5	8
Total	100	100	100	100	100	100

Note: GDS: Gross Domestic Savings; GCA: Gross Capital formation by Assets, Valuables — Precious metals & stones that are not held for use as inputs into production processes;

Source: National Accounts Statistics (NAS) St.18 & St.19 CSO various issues

The share of the government in capital formation has declined from 45% to 22%, showing that it still appropriates a significant portion of household savings to carry on its capital formation activities, which mostly provide negative returns. In other words, the government has become a dis–saver during this period, rapaciously appropriating the savings of the household sector through compulsory savings like employees' provident fund (EPF) and intermediation like banking.

Table — 6.2 shows the share of households in savings and the mix of physical and financial savings. We find that the household savings was above 70% of the total savings in the economy in 2011-12. It was more than 90% during 2000-2001. The share of physical savings [capital formation] was of the order of 90% in the fifties and is now around 50%. In other words, a substantial portion of household savings is taken away by the government and the private corporate sector for their capital formation. Even then, more than 50% of the capital formation in our economy is due to the household sector.

Table — 6. 2 Components of House Hold Savings 1970 to 2012

Year	1970-71	1980-81	1990-91	2000-01	2010-2011	2011-12
Household Savings GDS	70	73	84	92	69	72
Physical Savings to HS	70	57	55	52	56	64
Financial Savings to HS	30	43	45	48	44	36

Source: St.18- National Accounts Statistics (NAS) CSO, –Various issues

Proprietorship and Partnership [P&P] firms constitute a large portion of the following eight activities, namely:

(1) Unregistered manufacturing

(2) Construction

(3) Trade, both wholesale and retail

(4) Hotels and restaurants

(5) Transport other than railways

(6) Storage

(7) Real estate ownership of dwellings and business services, and

(8) Other services

In other words, these activities can be identified with the non-corporate sector, which is the fastest growing sector in the last decade, acting as an engine of our growth. If we consider these eight sectors and then consider the share of capital formation to the share of the unorganized sector NDP in these activities, we get a clue regarding the capital formation of the P & P sector. It is to be noted that the national income data for the unorganized sector is available at current prices and hence we use the capital formation figures also at current prices to get the percentages. The capital formation by industry of use is 'adjusted' for errors and omissions to get the capital formation of these sectors.

Table — 6.3 contains the share of Gross Domestic Capital formation [GDCF] of these eight sectors to that of the unorganized sector NDP in these eight activities.

Table — 6. 3: GDCF of Unorganised sector to its NDP and share in total GDCF

Year	1993-94	1999-00	2000-01	2004-05	2010-11	2011-12
GDCF of the unorganized sector to total GDCF	35	33	39	47	41	46
Rate of GDCF of the unorganized sector	30	26	28	47	45	47
Rate of GDCF—whole economy	23	25	24	33	37	35

Note: Unincorporated sector consists of the unorganized part of the eight sectors mentioned in the text; un-organised is a subset of unincorporated sector. The rate of GDCF in the unorganized sector is computed using its GDCF to its share in NDP.

Source: St.20 and St 76.1 NAS, CSO various issues

It is to be remembered that only factor incomes, that is Net Domestic Products [NDP] at factor cost at current prices, are available for 'unorganized' activities. The rate of capital formation by the unincorporated sector is higher than the overall rate of capital formation in the economy. The un-organized sector constituting of non-corporate (Proprietorship & Partnership) has nearly 50 % of the GDCF in the economy. As we will see later, most of these eight activities [unorganized sector] have registered a compounded annual growth rate (CAGR) of nearly 8% between 2004-05 and 2011-12. This is one of the important reasons for the growth in the economy during the last decade. The government has become a dis-saver and its main role now is to feed its employees in the form of salary, wages and pensions. In other words, a vast army of government employees [Central, state and local government] of around 20 million are taken care by the remaining 380 million of the workforce, which also meets the extortionate and rent-seeking demands of the government employees. The private corporate sector depends on the government to facilitate appropriation of the savings of the household sector through the intermediation of the banking sector and capital markets.

The governments, both at the Centre and at state level, and more the latter, are broke and hence try to find newer ways to appropriate household savings. Central Government pension payments have gone up from Rs. 3300 crore in 1990 to Rs.22400 crore in 2000, showing a CAGR of nearly 21% which is much higher than the revenue growth. In the case of state governments, the share of pension payments to own revenue has increased from 3% in 1980 to 17% in 2001.[Report of the Group to Study the Pension Liabilities of the State Governments", pp95, Reserve Bank of India, October 2003]. To overcome this issue, Government of India and State governments moved to Defined Contribution — DC plans from Defined Benefit — DB plans in providing pension to its employees from January 2004. But newer freebie schemes like NREGA and proposed food security bill will more 'pauperize' the government further.

This would create an extraordinary situation, indications of which are already available, wherein the State will become much more predatory in trying to tax all 'human endeavours'. This is very typical, since when governments go broke they tend to become rapacious. Since the state governments have no political will to increase their income by taxes, the Centre steps in.

The idea of service tax arises out of such desperation, which only increases the dowry index for the male employees of indirect tax departments as compared to income tax employees. Such types of taxes will increase. In our tradition, this syndrome is ascribed to *Vinasha Kale Viparitha Buddhi* (Mental aberrations are common as one's end draws near,), assuming one associates *buddhi* with any government in the first place.

Given this scenario, what are the implications of the arrival of global corporations in sectors like retail trade, construction, restaurants and other services, where the P&P sector is currently dominant? This will be the focus of our later discussions.

Travails of the India Uninc.

Chapter 7	Growth drivers without benefit of reforms
Chapter 8	FDI in retail Trade: Fact and Fiction
Chapter 9	The Bias Against the Self-Employed
Chapter 10	The Sorry Saga of Contract Enforcement

Growth Drivers without benefit of reforms

In this chapter we question the rationale behind linking the growth of the last two decades to the Narasimha Rao government initiated reforms which were later sustained by other governments and gives concrete facts and figures to prove that the growth should be ascribed to the unincorporated sector's phenomenal contribution to savings and service sector activities. We highlight the fact that most of the regulations pertaining to this sector are under state governments and reforms have not taken place in those aspects.

All along, conventional wisdom has been that the accelerated economic growth in the last twenty years is due to the reform measures initiated in the early nineties by the Narasimha Rao government and continued later by various central governments. The period after 1992, particularly, is regarded as the 'Reform Era' when the current Prime Minister, Manmohan Singh was Finance Minister in the Narasimha Rao government. There is also another view held by some economists who claim that the growth rate has actually been increasing right from the eighties, and to some extent, the policies of Rajiv Gandhi [post 1984] were instrumental not only in opening up the economy, but also in triggering off the growth rate.

There is no doubt that the economy saw a larger growth rate in the nineties as compared to the sixties and seventies. This growth rate was essentially due to the growth in the service sector. But, there is a caveat here. Whenever the term 'service sector' is mentioned, it is generally linked to IT services and to companies like Wipro or Infosys. Factually speaking, all software related activities come under business services and Information and Communication Technology [ICT] and it may be around 5% of the national income. [The Hindu –31st May 2010]

Actually, the service sector encompasses a much larger canvas and it is also the fastest growing sector in the economy. More importantly, the growth in the economy during the last two decades was due to proprietorship and partnership firms in service activities like construction, trade [wholesale and retail], hotels and restaurants, non-railway transport, real estate, business and other services.

Table — 7.1 provides the share of national income of different sectors in 1993-94 and 2011-12. We observe from Table — 7.1 that the share of the service sector in the economy has grown from 49% to 66% during 1993-94 to 2011-12. In other words, a significant portion of our national income is due to service activities and this has increased substantially in the last twenty years.

Table — 7. 1 Share of National Income to NDP [%]

Category	1993-94	2004-05	2009-10	2010-11	2011-12
Agriculture and forestry, fishing	32.9	19.9	18.5	18.7	18.3
Mining, manufacturing, electricity	18.3	17.0	16.4	16.3	15.5
Services	48.8	63.1	66.1	65.0	66.2
Total	100	100	100	100	100

Note: We have included construction as part of services.

Source: St.12, National Accounts Statistics [NAS] — 2012, Central Statistical Organization [CSO]

Table — 7. 2 Share of Non-Corporate Sector in Service Activities — [NDP] [%]

Category	1993-94	2004-05	2010-11	2011-12
Construction	51.1	64.8	62.3	64.6
Trade, Hotels and Restaurant	88.8	77.8	77.4	74.2
Non-Railway Transport	68.9	77.9	80.6	81.4
Real estate, Business Services	94.2	70.3	62.2	60.8
Other Services	34.3	44.1	42.6	42.9

Note: At current prices

Source: St.76.1, National Accounts Statistics [NAS] — 2013, Central Statistical Organisation [CSO]

Table — 7.2 gives the share of the non-corporate sector [proprietorship and partnership firms] in service activities during 1993-94 and 2011-12. The share of the non-corporate sector in 2011-12 was more than 60% in most service activities. It was 80% in non-railway transport. We find that the service economy is essentially a non-corporate economy.

The real growth rate in the service activities dominated by the non-corporate is given in Table — 7.3 along with that of agriculture and organized sector manufacturing. We observe that the service activities dominated by the non-corporate sector have grown much faster than agriculture or organized sector manufacturing. Actually, the phenomenal growth in construction, trade, hotels and restaurants, non-railway transport and business services are the main reasons for the significant growth of the Indian economy in the nineties and later. We find that construction has grown by 9% CAGR, trade at 9% and non-railway transport at 8%.

Table — 7. 3 NDP and Growth Rate [at 2004-05 prices] in different activities 2004-05 to 2011-12 [Rs. Crore and %]

Category	2004-05	2011-12	Growth rate
Agriculture and Allied activities	527289	676703	3.6
Manufacturing	346495	608327	8.4
Of which			
Organized	205844	389667	9.5

Category	2004-05	2011-12	Growth rate
Unorganized [Non-Corporate]	140651	218660	6.5
Construction	218511	383118	8.4
Trade Hotels and Restaurant	464750	851370	9.0
Of which			
Trade	424594	785307	9.2
Hotels and Restaurant	40156	66062	7.4
Non-Railway Transport	154791	260766	7.7
Banking and Insurance	168112	455151	15.3
Real Estate, Ownership of dwellings and Business Services	229767	418977	9.0
Public admin. and Defence	149020	257803	8.1
Other Services	223791	343393	6.3
Total NDP [including other Activities]	2651573	4618809	8.3

Note: The NDP figures are at 2004-05 prices and the growth rate is the geometric average growth rate (CAGR) at constant 2004-05 prices during the period. It is computed from the NAS 2013.

Source: St.12 National Accounts Statistics [NAS] 2013, Central Statistical Organization [CSO], GOI, New Delhi.

It is important to take note of the service sector where non-corporate organizations are dominant and are regulated by rules and regulations of the state governments rather than those of the central governments. Except for direct and indirect taxes [income tax, service tax and central excise] all other tax impositions are in the hands of the state governments. Most of the regulations pertaining to the non-corporate sector are under the purview of state governments.

Some of these are listed below in Table —7.4:

Table — 7. 4 Regulations of Service Activities of the Non-Corporate Sector by State Governments

1.	Shops and Establishments Act
2.	Negotiable Instruments Act
3.	Road Transport Act
4.	Commercial Taxes Act
5.	Money Lending Regulations Act
6.	Urban Land Usage and Development Act
7.	Stamp Duty and other Registration Charges
8.	Acts for the Entertainment Industry
9.	Acts Pertaining to Educational /Medical/Religious Institutions etc

The instruments to generate taxes from the service activities of the non-corporate sector are also with the state governments. Some of these are included in Table — 7.5 below:

Table — 7. 5 Instruments of Taxation of the Service Activities by State Governments

Commercial Tax [one of the major revenue sources for state governments]
Road tax on passenger as well as on commercial vehicles
Tax on IMFL/licence fees on opium cultivation
Tax pertaining to *tendu* leaf/granite trade
Entertainment Tax
Professional Taxes
Cess on other activities

None of these Acts or Regulations or Instruments of taxation has undergone any major reforms or changes in the last twenty years. The reforms undertaken from the nineties by the Central Government have focused primarily on areas pertaining to the government itself, and large corporate sector and global companies in finance and other activities as seen in Table — 7.6.

Table — 7.6: Reforms in the Nineties by the Central Government

Abolition of Licensing in many Sectors
Abolition of Controller of Capital Issues [CCI]
Privatization/Sale of Equity of some Public Sector Companies
Granting licenses to Foreign Institutional Investors and Private Mutual Funds
Allowing Indian Companies to list abroad
Reforms in Direct and Indirect Tax Structures
Reforms in Import and Export duties /procedures
Reforms in Bank Capital/Investment Norms
VRS in Government Banks
Reforms in Government Pensions

Now, how do the reforms mentioned in Table — 7.6 affect the rules/regulations and heads of taxation given in Table — 7.4 and Table — 7.5, which are the most critical elements in the functioning of the proprietorship and partnership firms and the service economy? The reforms might have helped large corporates, global investors or multinational corporations (MNCs) but definitely not the non-corporate sector, which has been the engine of growth for the last twenty years. The fact of the matter is that the Savings Rate of the economy [Gross Domestic Savings (GDS) to Gross Domestic Product (GDP)] has grown significantly from a low of 23.3% in 1990-91 to 34% in 2010-11. What's more important is that 70% of this saving comes from the household sector, which includes proprietorships and partnership firms. The savings of the households have grown phenomenally from the seventies to the nineties and this has contributed to the significant growth in the economy. And this is not due to but in spite of the governments — both at the state level and at the Centre. A significant part of the savings has been appropriated by the governments [the Centre and states] through banks, postal schemes, provident fund, etc., for their unproductive expenditure. The balance has been used by the household sector in service activities where they dominate. It is ironical that experts do not want to acknowledge the extraordinary efforts and contribution of households in increasing the savings rate, to pull us out of the so-called 'vicious cycle' theory of poverty propounded in the sixties by many Western economists. This theory condemned countries like India to eternal deprivation since it postulated that low-income countries generate low savings and hence low investment, leading to low income, and once again in turn, to low investment.

But our household sector has proved the theory wrong. The customary wisdom of linking the reforms of the Central Government to the growth in the economy in the last twenty years may require a critical examination and perhaps a revision.

There is a Tamil proverb about a crow sitting on a palm tree and the fruit falling at that point of time and the onlookers ascribing the fall of the fruit to the crow. In ascribing the growth of the economy in the last twenty years to the reforms of the central government and not to the significant increase in the savings of the households, economists and other experts are perhaps making the same mistake.

CHAPTER 8

FDI in Retail Trade: Fact and Fiction

There is a clamour for Foreign Direct Investment [FDI] in retail trade, which is currently dominated by partnership and proprietorship [P&P] firms. Unfortunately, there is not much debate [let alone informed debate] among academics and other policy-makers about the far-reaching implications that the entry of global retailers would have on our economy. This is one area where the level playing field argument is not only meaningful but also significant.

Role of Trade in our Economy

The talk of current times is the retail revolution. It is a revolution which is applauded by planners, encouraged by the Government and eagerly talked about by experts. One group of experts feel that without FDI, the revolution may not come up to global standards. But not many seem to be worrying about the millions of small retail traders who will get marginalized in this era of so-called inclusive reforms.

Why Trade is the Cynosure of the Retail Revolutionaries

We find that Trade [Wholesale and Retail] constitutes one of the largest segments of our economy. It is next only to agriculture and has as much share as that of manufacturing.

Trade constitutes the second largest segment of our economy with a 16.6% share in GDP during 2011-12. In other words, in the aggregate Gross Domestic Product [GDP] of Rs. 83.5 lakh crore during that year, trade was of the order of Rs. 13.8 lakh crore. This is more than the 14% share of manufacturing in the same period. Agriculture constitutes nearly 17.5% of the share of GDP [National Accounts Statistics — CSO — New Delhi-2013].

We have provided in Table — 8.1 some salient aspects of trade which indicate its importance and phenomenal growth.

Table — 8. 1 Share of the Three Major Sectors in NDP and Growth Rates (At constant prices)

Categories	2004-05 (Rs Crores)	2011-12 (Rs Crores)	Growth Rate(%)
Agriculture and allied activities	527289 [19.9]	676703 [14.6]	3.6
Manufacturing	346495 [13.0]	608327 [13.2]	8.4
Trade	424594 [16.0]	785307 [17.0]	9.2
Total NDP [including other Activities]	2651573	4618809	8.3

Note: The NDP is at factor cost and at constant 2004-05 prices. Growth Rates are

Compounded Annual Growth Rates [CAGR}at constant 2004-05 prices during the period computed from NAS 2013.Figures in bracket represent the share of the category to total NDP.

Source: St.12 National Accounts Statistics [NAS] — Central Statistical Organization [CSO] New Delhi.

We find from Table — 8.1 that more than 17% is the share of trade in NDP during 2011-12 at constant prices [which is higher than manufacturing and even agriculture] and it is growing at more than 9%. Hence the interest of global players to enter retail trade.

Table — 8.2 provides the growth rate of different sectors during 2004-05 to 2011-2012 at 2004-05 prices. The growth rate in trade in real terms during 2004-05 to 2011-12 is at 9.2%, which is a significant growth rate. It is higher than that of agriculture or manufacturing sectors. We also find that the sectors like trade, non-railway transport, hotels and restaurants, and business services have been the drivers of economic growth in the last twenty years or so.

Trade is conducted by partnership/proprietorship organizations with active involvement from members of the family and community. The share in trade of these types of non-corporate organizations is more than 70% as was observed earlier [National Accounts Statistics — 2013]. The share of corporate organizations in trade is miniscule.

Table — 8. 2 NDP and Growth Rate in Different Service Activities 2004-05 to 2011-12 [Rs. Crore and %]

Category	2004-05	2011-12	Growth rate
Construction	218511	383118	8.4
Trade Hotels and Restaurant	464750	851370	9.0
Of which			
Trade	424594	785307	9.2
Hotels and Restaurant	40156	66062	7.4
Non-Railway Transport	154791	260766	7.7
Banking and Insurance	168112	455151	15.3
Real Estate, Ownership of dwellings and Business Services	229767	418977	9.0
Public admin and Defense	149020	257803	8.1
Other Services	223791	343393	6.3
Total NDP [including other Activities]	2651573	4618809	8.3

Note: The NDP figures are at 2004-05 prices and the growth rate is the compounded average growth (CAGR) rate at constant 2004-05 prices during the period. It is computed from the NAS 2013

Source: St.12 National Accounts Statistics [NAS] 2013,Central Statistical Organization [CSO], GOI, New Delhi.

At current prices the net value added of Trade was Rs.13.5 Lakh crores. Even assuming a conservative estimate of 15% margin on this value addition we get a figure of nearly Rs. 2 Lakh Crore which will make any global player salivate at the projected income statement.

Employment in Trade

Unfortunately we do not have exact numbers regarding

the number of families or individuals who are employed by our trade sector.

The figures provided [Table 8.3] by government in the Economic Survey is laughable since it mentions that 5.5 lakh persons were employed during 2011 in the private sector in the Wholesale trade and retail trade in the whole country. [Appendix Statistical Tables — Table 3.1 of the Economic Survey — 2012-2013]. With such an erroneous database that grossly understimates the numbers in this sector, it is no wonder that policy formulators and the business press are not concerned about the implications of FDI in the retail sector on employment.

Of course, this is only for the 'organized' part of the trade — mostly corporate. A 2003 State-wise survey by Ministry of Labour suggests that there are more than 45 lakh shops employing more than 30 lakh persons. Then there are nearly 9 lakh commercial establishments employing nearly 32 lakh persons. When restaurants are included, it suggests that there are nearly 70 lakhs persons in all earning their livelihood from these activities (Source: NSSO). It appears to be an underestimation since it does not fully cover all states and UTs and also owner-run establishments wherein the owner is also the employee.

The Census 2001 provides more elaborate data. It states that 2.69 crore people are main workers and 24 lakhs are marginal workers in wholesale and retail trade. This implies therefore that nearly 3 crore people (30 million) are dependent on it — 1.1 crore in urban areas and 1.9 crore in rural areas. Of the total, nearly 1.7 crore haven't finished their high school education.

Hence the livelihood of more than 30 million people are involved in the retail trade and going by dependents in the form of children and others, it will be safe to estimate that at least 120 million(12 crore) are going to be directly impacted due to the so-called retail revolution.

Table — 8. 3 Employment in Organised Private Sectors [Lakhs]

Category	1991	1995	2000	2005	2010	2011
Construction	0.73	0.53	0.57	0.49	0.91	1.02
Wholesale and Retail Trade	3.00	3.08	3.30	3.75	5.06	5.46
Transport Storage and Communication	0.53	0.58	0.70	0.85	1.66	1.89
Finance, Insurance and Real estate	2.54	2.93	3.58	5.23	15.52	17.18
Community Social and Personal Services	14.85	16.03	17.23	18.2	21.40	23.50
Total–including all activities	76.77	80.59	86.46	84.52	107.87	114.22

Note: Coverage in construction on private account is inadequate

Source: Ministry of Labor- quoted in the, Economic Survey 2012-13, Table 3.1 Employment in organized sectors-public and private; pp A-56,Min of Finance , GoI New Delhi

What is the Retail Revolution?

It has three major components. The real estate sharks will occupy prime land and in some cases evict the retailers and construct major malls. This will be a tremendous blow to small and medium retail shops. Many households are then likely to create retail shops inside their homes and store litres of colas and bundles of toilet paper. Moving the retail store into individual households will be the major retail revolution! The third aspect is the razzle–dazzle of shopping in comfortable surroundings.

The argument given is with respect to improvements in technology and introduction of software. As if to suggest that a computer generated unreadable bill is the panacea for all our problems when the local shop keeper can multiply and add in a jiffy.

It is also suggested that these new retail outlets will be open longer hours. This argument may be useful in the West where they close shops on Sundays and also close early. Here the local retailer keeps his shop open using his family labour for more than 16 hours per day on all days of the week. The *kirana* shops adjacent to most Indian homes open at 7 am and close at 10 pm every day for 365 days of the year. The shopkeeper is very efficient, has an efficient home delivery system and knows the tastes and price considerations of his customers. But he is labelled 'unorganized' by our experts and national income data and his contribution thereby diminished. The footfalls in his shop cannot be measured using Western models [since there is no place to keep anybody's foot inside his shop!] and so he is derided and abused. **It is like clubbing housewives along with prostitutes in our Census data to show them that they are involved in 'unproductive' activities. These are economic constructs imposed by the west on the** rest and it is a form of terminological terrorism which is mouthed *ad-nauseam* by our economists and policy planners without understanding their implications.

The Weak are Marginalized

The retail trade suffers from two major issues. One is the non-availability of credit at reasonable rates from institutions and another is the bribe given to extortionist Government *babus* and their minions.

Let us consider the case of a flower vendor based in an Indian city. Having been cheated several times of her savings by unscrupulous operators of chit funds and other such unregulated saving mechanisms, she made gentle attempts to open a bank account in the hope that it would enable her secure a loan at a later point in time. But the Core Banking Solutions [CBS] with its Central Server located at Davos or Basle did not 'recognize' the flower vendor. This system made the decision about accepting new customers under the 'Know Your Customer' [KYC] norms using the Multi-Factor Discriminate Model of Non-linear Credit Rating. The flower vendor was asked for photos, proof of address, PAN number, proof of date of birth, references and also given exotic choices of using debit card and net based banking.

Large corporates discuss prime lending rates or base rates. But the flower girl and the vegetable vendor get it at half per cent per day. [Returning half rupee for hundred rupees borrowed in the morning]. This works out to be more than 180% per annum. A local retailer of my acquaintance obtains his credit in an interesting way. He gets Rs. 45,000 [for a loan amount of Rs. 50,000] up front and pays Rs. 500 per day for 100 days to repay Rs. 50,000. It turns out to be more than 10% for three months. More than 70% of working capital requirements of retail trade in 2009-2010 have come from such non-bank sources.

The other perennial problem faced by the 'unorganized' retail trade is the 'organized' dacoity undertaken by the minions of the State. They need to bribe the cops, bribe the municipal authorities and other local goons who are the outsourced arms of the extortionist State. It can be as high as Rs.20 on an income of Rs. 200 or so per day. That is 10% of gross income. The same is true of the fruit seller, the street-side fast food joint, the local beauty parlour as well as the local chemist.

Instead of looking at these two important constraints imposed on the fast growing, productive, efficient and effective retail trade, our planners want to open it up to global sharks in the name of liberalization. It is interesting to observe that already large portions of the credit requirement of the retail trade are not met by banking channels. The credit requirement of this sector would be at least Rs. 8 lakh crore [60% of the gross value addition of Rs. 14 lakhs crore in 2011-12] since most capital in trade is working capital and not more than 30% comes from institutional credit.

A substantial portion of the retail trade is done by partnership/proprietorship firms or self-employed persons, all of which are categorized as households for savings and credit data in our economy. A major portion of the financing of this trade is done by non-institutional players like money lenders. We observe that the share of the house hold sector in outstanding bank credit has come down to 36% from 58% between 1990 and 2011 [See Table — 9.3] during which the household sector in trade, transport, construction, restaurants, and other business services has been growing at more than 8% CAGR. Here, households include agricultural households and to that extent, the fall is very significant. We find that 43% of the debt of rural households is from moneylenders and it is 25% in the case of urban households. [Computed from — Household Indebtedness in India; Statement 6; page 25; NSS, Ministry of Statistics and Programme Implementation–GOI — New Delhi; December 2005.] Hence the need to recognize the importance of the entire spectrum of the non-banking sector rather than look at this sector in a segmented fashion.

Planners should address this issue rather than wanting to invite major real estate agents to enter into the retail trade. The harassment from the various minions of the state machinery — as stated earlier — like the police, municipal authorities, check post officials, labour department, weights and measurements etc. [the list could extend to at least 50 agencies] and the bribe tax paid is mind boggling. At a conservative estimate of 5% of value addition, we find that at least Rs. 70,000 crore is the bribe received in 2011-12 by the various government extortionists called public servants. Street side vendors and hawkers have additional issue of zoning problems since the fact that they play a very important economic function and have substantial entrepreneurship is neither recognized nor appreciated by the metropolitan elite.

The pressure on the illiterate retail trader will be huge. He will borrow at much more atrocious rates to repay his past burden and in the absence of any social security net will resort to suicide. The Government including the PM has been talking of improving the living standards of SC/STs and OBCs and Muslims. It is pertinent to note that substantial portions of Muslims who are in business are in retail trade. In a sense, one part of Government does not seem to know what the other part is doing. The impact on the community will be phenomenal. Also, large numbers of retail traders are in their forties and fifties and their ability to get re-trained and move to other avocations will be impossible. It is interesting to note that significant players in the retail revolution are linked to the real estate business and it appears to have the makings of another mega scam, much larger than the SEZ scam!

The Gung-ho 'Go Global' Gospel

The 'Shop till you Drop Crowd' thinks that the panacea to all our ills is to encourage global chains in our retail markets. The argument is that the MNCs bring 'funds', 'efficiency' and 'cost effective' solutions. The consumer should therefore be happy!! But the fact is that MNCs do not normally bring funds from their home countries or any other external sources, since they can access funds in our domestic market by brandishing 'comfort letters' from their parent companies. There are many local financial institutions, both government and private, which would lend them below prime rates since they are 'global'! That the MNC will bring funds from abroad is a mirage and a belief, which should be taken with tons of salt. Remember Enron which was supposed to bring in Rs.10,000 crore. The final result is that our domestic government institutions today hold more than Rs. 6000 crore of worthless paper courtesy the money lent to Enron. Now the RBI is asking these banks to show it as bad debt. Rebecca Mark of Enron had claimed that millions were spent to 'educate' Indians as part of that project. We either refuse to get 'educated' in the true sense or perhaps have to be more 'educated' in the Rebeccian sense since not only do we never learn, we dream the same wrong Technicolor dreams aided by pink paper.

The other aspect is regarding the 'technology' or 'knowledge base' that they bring with them. What technology? Do we want to 'dumb down India' as Wal-Mart has done to the US? Should we replace the street corner shopkeeper who can add fifty items without a calculator with a counter girl [no sexist bias] who cannot add five numbers without a machine?

Another issue is in terms of reduced cost. Has anyone done a proper study of the 'aggregate cost' of these global retail chains? Most American homes have enough stock to fill a small Indian retail store in their basement. They have at least a month's stock of cola and six months stock of toilet paper since Sam & Co. decided that mom and pop stores (*kirana* stores) needed to be shifted to individual households by offering great discounts. The refrigerator of every house is also a mini retail shop and basements are go downs. In other words, individual households have become retail outlets on the basis of their credit cards. In the US, it was an issue of shortage of labour, but India has surplus labour, which is part of the large self-employed group. For the economic expert, goods held by households are consumption but those held by mom and pop stores is inventory. Hence, inventory reduction has been achieved in the economy!! There is not much space available in Indian houses to convert them into such 'retail stores'.

One more aspect is the fuel cost of thousands, driving miles to go to that super market situated away from the main city centre and spending thousands of man or woman-hours doing nothing between the aisles. Do we want such a model here?

Should millions of small shopkeepers become unemployed to suit some 'efficient' model that in reality is not so 'efficient'? Are we intrinsically against self-employed groups? Another issue is the enthusiasm shown by real estate developers in the retail sector and it speaks volumes about the type of interest among different groups. Unfortunately, such issues are not even debated. Of course, experts have not bothered much since it is the *petite bourgeoisie* who will suffer. And the *petite bourgeoisie* are not the vanguard of the revolution, unlike government employees!!

International Practices

The global chains like Walmart have not succeeded in Germany or Japan but in Mexico since the former two countries have well developed regulations and local competition to protect community based local shops. In developing countries with weak ownership records the real estate sharks will lead the retail revolution.

Experts and policy makers want Indians to emulate the Japanese, the French, the Germans and at least the South Koreans in every respect. All petroleum services and products, rice, tobacco, salt, alcoholic beverages and fresh food traded at public markets are excluded in Japan from any 'distributional aspect' by companies from other countries. Australia, Japan and South Korea do not allow whole trade services in petroleum, petroleum products, rice, tobacco, salt, milk, fertilizers, etc., by foreign companies.

The French using their Loi Royer regulation restrict any development of hypermarkets to protect what they call the 'Centres of French towns and villages and the living of small shopkeepers'. Germany has legislative constraints on outlets above 1200 sq. metres in size no dissimilar to France's Loi Royer. This is in spite of the fact that trade constitutes a relatively smaller portion of their economy, both in terms of employment and value addition, as compared to India.

Laws are Meant for the Weak and the Meek

The controversy regarding FDI in retail trade has other dimensions. It was suggested that global giants like Metro could enter wholesale and not retail, since by law they cannot carry on retail trade activities. Ministers remonstrated that the law needed to be amended. After all, Indian laws have been amended thousands of times and doing it once more to facilitate the grand entry of global malls and hypermarkets is child's play! Then there were reports that these retail giants would procure directly from farmers in the agricultural marketing yards. At this juncture, it was pointed out that they couldn't trade in agricultural commodities. The whole issue is a riddle packed in an enigma, wrapped in a puzzle and delivered in mystery. The transparency in some of these areas, to say the least, leaves much to be desired.

The policy of the Government of India at the Cancun summit for the purpose of discussing trade and services was not to even discuss certain areas of services like law, accountancy and distribution services consisting of wholesale trade and retail. But in practice, the present FDI allows 100% in single brand retail like IKEA and up to 50% in multi-brand retail. But pressure is mounting to ease this also to 100% with no debate or discussion. Also there was a move to make global retail giants like Wal-Mart source atleast 30% of their wares locally. But that has also been silently given up. Over and above all of these, there are allegations of bribery and corruption against

Wal-Mart with reference to entering Indian markets and investigations are currently on. The three monkeys of the Mahatma have become the national motto with respect to FDI in the service sector.

The argument so far cited in not to be construed as an argument against globalization or against foreign companies in Indian trade.It seeks to draw attention to the fact that the process is not transparent. It is *ad hoc*, haphazard, and full of discretions and improvisations on the way. But national policy formulations affecting millions of livelihoods is not akin to enacting amateur *tamasha, theru koothu* or *jatra* where you improvise as you go along. A national policy based on improvisation is a sure recipe for disaster. One gets worried if our trade policy is available for trade. Unfortunately, our system in the government will sell it to the lowest bidder!!

We should not start with the premise that the *paan* chewing, dhoti clad, English-ignorant retail trader is 'inefficient' and 'cost ineffective' and should be bleached by globally accepted detergents for cleansing. What he needs is a level playing field in the full sense of the term with access to affordable credit and the abolition of the inspector raj, namely, harassment by minions in the bureaucracy.

What is to be done?
Government should enhance credit availability through institutional channels by fixing targets if needed. It should facilitate modernization of spot markets like APMC and

encourage linking up retail using technology to get power of large purchases. The zoning system should be introduced to facilitate the livelihood of hawkers and other petty traders. A percentage of bribe tax should be impounded or Government employees in identifiable areas should be levied a cess to create Social Security for retail traders. A ministry to exclusively develop and take care of domestic trade should be formed.

Last but not the least, let the reformers many of whom are beneficiaries of pension from global institutions understand that the retail trader in his fifties who is illiterate and who has borrowed at exorbitant rates and who has to bribe on a daily basis does not have future with this revolution. His need for credit and protection from harassment ought to be considered seriously as we are still a savings based, family oriented economy.

In a well-attended seminar, a retail expert stated that the progress of India will be measured by the footfalls in malls. There was applause. It shows that we have sold our civilisational soul for the cause of the well-heeled soles. Tomorrow's headlines are going to be regarding suicide by retail traders.

The sooner we strengthen and facilitate our small business, the better for employment and society.

CHAPTER 9

The Bias against the Self-Employed

Our government's policies are likely to displace the self-employed and render them unemployable. When people are left to fend for themselves without being imparted any alternative skill or training which could help in rehabilitation, one is forced to conclude that if this isn't a blatant bias against them, then what is?

There is a major debate going on regarding the National Rural Employment Guarantee Act [NREGA] and the usual suspects are mouthing the usual slogans like kick starting the economy, increasing the savings rate, reducing the tax rate, bringing down the fiscal deficit etc. The NREGA is expected to reduce unemployment, create enduring assets, augment rural income, provide an antidote to inflation and channelise community efforts. But the largest segment of labour are the self-employed and the policies formulated by the government appear to be targeted at pauperizing them.

Large Role in National Income

Table — 9.1 provides the share of different groups in the national income pie. We find that the so called non-corporate sector consisting of proprietorship and partnership firms[P&P sector] constitutes nearly 40% of our national income, while that of corporate groups is hardly 23% and that of the government is 20%. As previously discussed, it is actually 45% for Uninc. and 18% for Corporate sector. The P&P sector is dominant in service sectors like construction, trade, non-railway transport, hotels and restaurants and other services. These are the fastest growing sectors in the economy.

Since private sector executives, editors of English language newspapers and bureaucrats — all belonging to 'Employee Groups' — are primarily the ones who are opinion makers and policy formulators, the travails of the self-employed are neither fully comprehended nor debated.

Table — 9. 1 Share of Different Sectors in National Income

Category	1980-81	1990-91	2000-01	2004-05	2010-11	2011-12
Organized						
Government	17.50	23.90	22.7	21.6	20.0	19.8
Private sector	12.50	12.30	18.7	19.5	22.6	22.9
Un-Organized						
Agriculture	38.08	31.46	25.1	18.9	17.8	17.3

Category	1980-81	1990-91	2000-01	2004-05	2010-11	2011-12
Other activities	31.92	32.34	33.5	40.0	39.6	40.0
Total	100	100	100	100	100	100

Note: 1. Agriculture does not include Government and Corporate Agriculture. They are included under respective shares as part of organized. These are based on NDP at factor cost and current prices.

Source: St 24, St 76.1 National Accounts Statistics [NAS], 1997 & 2013 Central Statistical Organization [CSO] — New Delhi.

Declining Share in Credit from Banks

The share of the self-employed in savings is significant. In India, the self-employed sector is included as part of the household sector. We observe from Table — 9.2 that more than 70% of National Savings has come from households, and of this, at least 70% has come from non-salary groups, namely self-employed categories.

Table — 9.2 Share in Savings

Items/Year	1990-91	2000-01	2004-05	2008-09	2009-10	2010-11	2011-12*
GDS [as of per cent of GDP]	22.9	23.8	32.4	32.0	33.7	34.0	30.8
Govt.	1.8	-1.3	2.3	1.0	0.2	2.6	1.3
Pvt. Corporate	2.6	3.7	6.6	7.4	8.4	7.9	7.2
Household	18.5	21.4	23.6	23.6	25.2	23.5	22.3

Note: GDS: Gross Domestic Savings, GDP: Gross Domestic Product, GDP is at current Market prices. *- Revised Estimates

Source: Ministry of Finance, Government of India And Economic Survey, 2012-13, Table 1.6 pg A-10.

Table — 9.3 reflects the share of different sectors in credit off-take from banks. In spite of the significant share of households in savings and national income, their share in credit off-take has declined from 58% in 1990 to 36% in 2011. In other words, the commercial banks have turned away from self-employed groups.

Table — 9.3 Distribution of Outstanding Bank Credit by Categories [%]

Category	March 1990	March 1996	March 2005	March 2008	March 2009	March 2010	March 2011
Household Sector (1)	58.3	51.1	37.9	36.8	33.0	32.8	36.2
Private Corporate sector (2)	31.3	38.6	46.6	46.5	48.0	48.6	44.1
Public sector (3)	10.2	10.3	15.5	16.7	19.0	18.6	19.7
Total	100.0	100.0	100.0	100.0	100.0	100.0	100.0

Note: (1) Household sector includes Partnership, Proprietorship concerns, joint families, associations, clubs, societies, trusts, groups and individuals for all account.

(2) Private Corporate sector includes private Sector and cooperative sector excluding those mentioned in (1).

(3) Public Sector, that is all Government activities, includes joint sector undertakings.

Source: Extracted from table — 1.15;Outstanding Credit of Scheduled Commercial Banks according to Organizations; Basic statistical returns ; Various years; RBI

Largest Category in Employment

From the point of view of employment, we find from Table — 9.4 that the self-employed constitute more than half of workforce in India in 2001.

Table — 9. 4 Share of different Categories of the Work-force 2001 [Million]

Category	Number in Mn.
Total number of workers	402
Cultivators	128
Agriculture labourers	107
Organized sector — Govt. — Private —	28 19 09
Household sector	16
Other workers	123

Source: Economic Census 2001 and Table 3.1Economic survey 2002-03, Census data for 2011 with detailed break-up is not yet available

This is in contrast to the US scenario where only 7% are in this category during the similar period as seen in Table — 9.5.

Table 9. 5 Share of Different Categories of Workers in USA in 2000[%]

Class of workers	Per cent
Private Wage and Salary Workers	78.5
Government Workers	14.6
Self-employed: Own unincorporated business	6.6
Unpaid Family workers	0.3
Total	100

Source: US Bureau of Census

Hence many policies pertaining to labour, which are

appropriate in the Western context, may not be appropriate in our situation. We have given in Table — 9.6 the salient social aspects of the self-employed category in India based on an NSS survey.

Social Segments of Self-employed

We have the exhaustive Economic Census 2005, conducted by the Central Statistical Organization [CSO] which covers 41.83 million enterprises engaged in different economic activities other than crop production and plantation. It deals with own account enterprises as well as establishments, an enterprise run by employing at least one hired worker. It covers private profit and non-profit institutions, co-operatives, and all economic activity-linked institutions including *dharamshalas* and temples.

Table — 9.6 gives the salient findings pertaining to **ownership** of the enterprises, both own account enterprises and establishments employing labour. This reveals that more than half of the 42 million enterprises are owned by individuals from the SC/ST/OBC groups.

Table 9. 6: Social Group of Owners of the Enterprises [%]- 2005

Item	Rural	Urban	Combined average
SC	10.00	6.97	8.82
ST	4.60	2.13	3.64

Item	Rural	Urban	Combined average
OBC	40.57	34.19	38.08
Total of the Above	55.17	43.29	50.54

Source: Economic Census -2005, Table 2.5; All India report — CSO

This encompasses manufacturing, construction, trade, hotels, restaurant, transport, finance and business and other services.

Economic Census reveals that out of the total of 41.83 million enterprises in the country, 37.63 million [90%] were found to be self-financing. This speaks volumes about our credit delivery systems to these self-employed groups, particularly those belonging to the vulnerable sections. Instead of fostering credit delivery at affordable cost and enhancing self-employment, our policy planners are keen to create a huge body of unemployable persons by their policies.

Creating Unemployable Persons

There was a brief news item some time ago, unnoticed by many, regarding the Supreme Court nod for 'smart licence plates'. An estimated 80 million vehicles in India will have electronic number plates fixed to them by RTOs to prevent car thefts and facilitate monitoring. Each electronic plate would cost around Rs. 800 to Rs. 1000 [depending on the vehicle], totalling up to a neat Rs. 4000 to Rs. 8000 crore. Four major companies — only four — namely Shimnit Utsch, Real MazonIndia, Promuk Hoffman, and Tonnjes Eastern Security Technologies, are set to make huge income from this business This is only for the existing stock of vehicles. As far as future business is concerned, it would grow in alignment with the growth in the automobile sector.

Millions of persons who were earlier painting and/or engraving these licence plates will become redundant. About 240 to 400 million-man hours of work will be made redundant [assuming that it takes 3 to 5 hours per plate] in the next few years, since these are re-done at least once in four years. There has not been any attempt to re-train or impart newer skills to the affected persons currently engaged in these activities to face the challenges of the reforms demanded by the metropolitan elites. In the fifties, kitchens used to have mainly brass and copper vessels. Now modern kitchens have vessels made of hydro-carbons which implies millions of metal vessel makers have become unemployed. It is interesting that there is no debate, no discussion and even the usual Left experts have not conducted seminars on this vital issue which is going to result in huge loss of employment. No seminars by Federation of Indian Chamber of Commerce and Industry [FICCI] or Round Table by Confederation of Indian Industry [CII]. There is total silence. Two opposite groups, namely the crusaders of globalization and leftist intellectuals interestingly appear to support the slow death of the self-employed groups. The Globalizer would like the entire country to be a giant corporation owned and funded by FDI where everyone is a wage or salary earner. For the Leftist thinkers, it is a historical and an inevitable process wherein the *petite bourgeoisie* are destined to become proletariat. And jobs in sick companies in the public sector are more important than the livelihood of millions of street corner painters of signs.

Due to faulty policies supported by the metropolitan elites and Marxist intellectuals, we may end up having a huge populace of unemployable persons who are currently self-employed. The policies to be adopted in the service sector in retail trade, restaurants [*dhabas*], construction, road transport, etc. is going to require massive employment guarantee schemes even in urban areas, which will make the State wither away.

The poverty of this philosophy pertaining to removal of poverty is that the government will end up converting all self-employed people unemployable and then go about starting the NREGS. Added to that is the new act on Food Security which will guarantee food to more than two-thirds of the population. It will convert proud Indians who work/earn/eat into entitlement based state dependent citizens. It is a case of nationalising families to pauperize society.

CHAPTER 10

The Sorry Saga of Contract Enforcement

The labyrinthine course our legal processes take makes enforcing contracts impossible. Particularly hard hit by our protracted court procedures which totally ignore the time value of money concept is our non-corporate sector with its limited financial flexibility. It is high time that the legal system is innovatively revamped.

The risk premium on investment is a function of the type of instrument, interest rate, forex fluctuations, inflation, etc. In our context, there is an unstated but important risk — namely, risk associated with enforcing any contract.

The contract could be one between a landlord and tenant, a contract for services like house construction, contract for purchase of vehicle in the second hand market, contract between lender and borrower in the financial market, contract for services to be obtained like that of plumbing, electrical, cooking for functions, etc., contract for travel to long distances [arranged tours], contract for undergoing major operations, contract with lawyers to enforce these contracts — in all these cases we find that there is a phenomenal amount of time and cost involved in trying to enforce any of these.

Significant portions of transactions are 'relationship based' and not 'contract based'. Particularly in the case of the initiation of the deal, it is based only on referral, trust and 'relationship'. There may be a written contract, but neither party takes it seriously.

If there is no problem in the informal arrangement, then things move in the right direction. But if the arrangement fails, then the contract has to be invoked to settle the dispute. Therein lies the tragedy. We then invariably find that the so-called contract is not worth the paper it is written on. It could take ages to go through the labyrinthine steps of the judicial procedure. Using a simple cost of capital model one can derive an optimal solution in terms of using extra-legal processes to settle contracts. Hence, one of the major areas of concern in our economic system is the capability to enforce contracts in a timely fashion.

We have provided in Table — 10.1 the situation prevailing in 2011 and we find the numbers are mind-boggling. Of course, the proportion of civil cases varies across states, but it is on an average, around 30% to 50%.

Table — 10. 1 — Cases Pending Age-Wise

Court type	Total	More than one year
Supreme Court	58,519	37,385 [64%]
High courts	41,30,732	N. A
District and subordinate Courts	2,68,51,766	N.A

Note: 1. For SC as on 31-12-2011
2. For High courts the data is as on 30-09-2011
3. For District and other subordinate courts the data as on end 31-03-2012
4. Refers to both civil and criminal.
5. N.A — Not Available

Source: Indiastat.com

The legal system fails to fully comprehend the concept of Time Value of Money, which is the basis of all activities in the market system. Over four million cases are pending in 18 High Courts alone and more than 58,000 cases are pending in the Supreme Court for admission, interim relief or final hearing. This is not the full story, since a million more cases are pending at the lower courts. We also find that a significant portion of the cases have been pending for over five years in the Supreme Court. Since Indians believe in re-birth, we can rest assured that the accused in this birth may become a judge in the next, etc. and finally justice will be met over a karmic cycle.

The most protracted lawsuit ever recorded was in India (which has the dubious distinction of entering the Guinness Book of Records). A 'Mahant' who is a keeper of a temple, filed a suit in Pune in 1205 A.D and the case was decided in 1966 — a full 761 years later. However, we can take consolation that this is not the average time taken by the Indian courts for deciding cases. It is estimated that on an average between seven to fifteen years are taken for a case to be decided in an Indian court.

If we take the fairly recent example of Nick Leeson of the Barings Bank caught for misdemeanour at the Tokyo Stock Market (he operated from Singapore), we get the real picture. His saga started in 1995. Not only has he been punished, he has also come out of jail after undergoing punishment.

The last one heard of him, was that a book written by him is being made into a movie. In the case of the Harshad Mehta scam [year 1992], we find that the complete disposal of all the cases has not taken place till date in 2013. Mehta himself is no more.

It is difficult, nay impossible, for a tenant to be evicted by the landlord after the end of tenancy in a house property, for a creditor to collect his debts, for a lessor to repossess his leased assets from the lessee if there is a default, for a depositor to collect his principal and interest from the borrowing entity, for a bond holder to redeem his investments from corporates, using the legal system. The system in practice does not accept asset ownership as natural, and due to the socialistic propaganda of more than fifty years, considers default/illegal possession/occupation etc. as a natural right of the 'underdogs'.

The right of the lessor to repossess the leased asset in the event of a default committed by the lessee was not very clear until the Bombay High court clearly ruled that the "lessor has a right" to repossess the leased asset in the event of default by the lessee. (Twentieth Century Finance Corporation vs. SLM Maneklal Industries Ltd). This 'right' was later upheld by the Supreme Court.

In such a situation, the proprietorship and partnership [P&P] sector, with relatively lower financial flexibility, suffers the most. It is not in a position to use the legal route and hence, resorts to arm twisting to assert its 'rights'.

'Collection agents', 'Re-possession agents' and other types of assorted strong-arm tactics are becoming rampant in enforcing contracts. Press reports suggest that the infamous Romesh Sharma of Delhi (who was arrested in 1998 for committing various crimes), was one of those whose services was used by many to enforce tenancy contracts by forcible eviction of residential and business premises.

A report from Kochi talked about the police having initiated a detailed inquiry into the operations of the 'repossession teams' employed by finance and hire purchase firms for recovering loans. This follows the arrest of two senior officials of a finance company and seven members of a 'repossession gang'' for their alleged role in violence perpetrated against a borrower, which led to the death of two individuals. Official sources said that repossession teams are used even by hire purchase firms selling household appliances.

This points towards an ominous trend developing in the system, wherein the affected parties take law into their hands for enforcement of property rights. This gives rise to the issue of police at the local level becoming active in the unorganized credit markets. Even well-established multinational banks are engaging 'Re-possession agents' and recently, even the local police or their proxies as collection agents. This has far reaching implications for the financial system. The reforms should have addressed this issue, since the maximum impact is felt by the P&P sector. Unlike large corporates or the government, their financial flexibility is lower and hence the waiting time factor is crucial for their survival.

It is extremely important to recognize the social capital we have accumulated in the form of community and family linkages and we need to think afresh instead of getting boxed into the Anglo-Saxon jurisprudence system. We need to remember that we have less than ten thousand police stations in our country but more than two million temples, i.e., places of worship. In other words, by and large, contract compliance is more due to the fear of God than of legal processes. One of the alternatives, which should be seriously considered, would be to encourage community-based arbitration recognized by law as binding on both the parties. This type of system is prevalent for instance in the stock exchanges, wherein disputes pertaining to member brokers are settled through arbitration which are binding on members.

The reforms of the legal system, including introducing innovative ones, particularly at the lower levels of judiciary, have not been addressed as a basic issue since the government itself is one of the largest litigants. As far as the government is concerned, the concept of Time or Value of Money itself does not exist, let alone the Time Value of Money.

Credit Delivery to India Uninc.

Chapter 11	Bank Lending and Non-corporate Sector
Chapter 12	Critical Role of the Non-Bank Financial Sector [NBFS]

Bank Lending and Non-corporate Sector

The credit available from banking sector is not adequate for India Uninc. Banks are more focussed on the corporate sector and investing in gilts. The role of the Non-Banking Financial sector should be acknowledged and integrated with mainstream financial markets.

The growth in the service sectors in the last decade has been much higher than that of manufacturing and agriculture. There is no doubt that the economy saw a larger growth rate in the last twenty years as compared to the sixties and seventies. This growth rate is essentially due to the growth in the service sector.

But, there is a caveat here. Whenever the term 'service sector' is mentioned, it is generally linked to IT services and to companies like Wipro or Infosys. Factually speaking, all software related activities come under business services and ICT [Information and Communication Technology] services may be around 5% of the national income.

But the service sector encompasses a much larger canvas and it is also the fastest growing sector in the economy. More importantly, the growth in the economy during the last two decades was due to proprietorship and partnership firms in service activities like construction, trade [wholesale and retail], hotels and restaurants, non-railway transport, real estate, business and other services.

Table — 11.1 provides the share of national income of different sectors in 1993-94 and 2011-12. We observe from Table — 11.1 that the share of the service sector in the economy has grown from 49% to 66% from 1993-94 to 2011-12. In other words, a significant portion of our national income is due to service activities and this has increased substantially in the last twenty years.

Table — 11. 1 Share of National Income to NDP [Percentage Share]

Category	1993-94	2004-05	2009-10	2010-11	2011-12
Agriculture and forestry, fishing	32.9	19.9	18.5	18.7	18.3
Mining, manufacturing, electricity	18.3	17.0	16.4	16.3	15.5
Services	48.8	63.1	66.1	65.0	66.2
Total	100	100	100	100	100

Note: We have included construction as part of services.

Source: Stt.12, National Accounts Statistics [NAS] — 2013,Central Statistical Organization [CSO],

We have already seen in Table — 3.4 that the share of the non-corporate sector in 2011-12 was more than 60% in most of the service activities. It is to be noted that unorganized is a sub-set of non-corporate and in that context these are underestimates since NAS data is collated for unorganized .We observed from Table — 7.3 that the service activities dominated by the non-corporate sector have grown much faster than agriculture or organized sector manufacturing. Actually, the phenomenal growth in construction, trade, hotels and restaurants, non-railway transport and business services are the main reasons for the significant growth of the Indian economy in the nineties and later. We find that construction has grown by 9% CAGR, trade at 9% and non-railway transport at 8%.

Credit Delivery Mechanism

The credit availed by the P&P sector comes in the form of payables/receivables from bank sources or the Non-Banking Financial Sector [NBFS].

The financing of activities in areas like trade (wholesale and retail), hotels and restaurants is mainly from the Unincorporated businesses [UIBs], that is money lenders — where the rates of interest are much higher, at least twice that of a government bank. These are 'Cash Flow Based' lending rather than 'Asset Based' lending. The organized non-banking sector is more into 'Asset Based' borrowing for items like equipments, trucks [new and second hand] etc. The levels of risk undertaken by the NBFS is significant, since they lend with the least paper work. This is one of the major reasons for the large margins seen in trade, both wholesale and retail. For many of the fast moving consumer goods (FMCG), we find the difference between company balance sheet figures and the street price figures to be more than 35% and one factor in this is the 'Open Market' interest paid by the trade channels. In the case of cash crops and vegetables, the gap between producer prices and consumer prices can be as high as 70% to 80%. Here again, financing costs plays a major role, both for holding and transport.

On the other hand, we find that the banking sector has been investing, to the extent of 45% to 50% of its resources, in government securities in the last few years. This is what is called 'Lazy Banking' by Dr. Rakesh Mohan, formerly Deputy Governor of the Reserve Bank of India [RBI]. The lending pattern of banks reveals an interesting picture, wherein the share of the P&P sector has come down even though the non-corporate sector [predominantly in services] is the fastest growing sector in the economy. In Table —11.2 one can observe the share of the non-corporate sector along with the private corporate and government sectors in the credit outstanding of scheduled commercial banks.

Table — 11.2 Distribution of Outstanding Bank Credit by categories [%]

Category	March 1990	March 1996	March 2005	March 2008	March 2009	March 2010	March 2011
Household Sector (1)	58.3	51.1	37.9	36.8	33.0	32.8	36.2
Private Corporate sector (2)	31.3	38.6	46.6	46.5	48.0	48.6	44.1
Public sector (3)	10.2	10.3	15.5	16.7	19.0	18.6	19.7
Total	100.0	100.0	100.0	100.0	100.0	100.0	100.0

Note: (1) Household sector includes Partnership, Proprietorship concerns, joint families, associations, clubs, societies, trusts, groups and individuals for all account.
(2) Private Corporate sector includes private Sector and cooperative sector excluding those mentioned in (1).
(3) Public Sector, that is all Government activities, includes joint sector undertakings.

Source: Extracted from table — 1.15; Outstanding Credit of Scheduled Commercial Banks according to Organizations; Basic statistical returns ; Various years; RBI

Distortions in the Banking System

We find from Table — 11.2 that the share of the Uninc. sector has come down to 36% from 58% in the last twenty years, during which time the role of the Uninc. sector in trade, transport, construction, restaurants, and other business services has been growing at more than an 8% compounded annual growth rate (CAGR) (see table 7.3). Here, households include agricultural households, and to that extent, the fall is very significant. Hence, the growth rate of the economy in the nineties is neither related to economic reforms of the central government, nor to the credit mechanisms of the banking sector.

Table — 11. 3 Outstanding Credit of SCBs — Size of loan up to Rs 25 crores:

(In Lakhs)	Mar-00		Mar-05		Mar-10		Mar-11	
	No. of accounts	Amount outstanding	No. of accounts	Amount outstanding	No. of accounts	Amount outstanding	No. of accounts	Amount outstanding
upto 10 lakhs	54,085,209 (99.40)	14589937 (31.70)	76,379,233 (99.00)	38074692 (33.00)	116,252,358 (98.0)	78037871 (23.40)	1,179,255,950 (97.70)	86168756 (21.20)
upto 50 lakhs	5 4,284,893 (99.80)	18349586 (39.90)	76,991,817 (99.80)	48054547 (41.60)	118,257,220 (99.60)	108533162 (32.60)	1,202,612,880 (99.2)	122518825 (30.10)
upto 1 crore	54,320,824 (99.90)	20515002 (44.60)	77,056,223 (99.90)	51672603 (44.70)	118,424,427 (99.70)	117954649 (35.40)	1,204,550,270 (99.60)	133598874 (32.80)
upto 10 crores	5 4,365,164 (100.00)	31126396 (67.70)	77,135,212 (100)	69991776 (60.60)	118,591,634 (99.80)	160657063 (48.10)	1,206,679,290 (99.70)	183218936 (45.00)
upto 25 crores	5 4,368,748 —	35465898 (77.10)	77,144,439 —	80288674 (69.50)	118,614,765 (99.90)	188310864 (56.40)	1,206,958,610 (99.90)	214664310 (52.70)
Above 25 crores	54,370,397 —	46008070 (100.00)	77,150,794 —	115246794 (99.80)	118,636,305 (100.00)	334516933 (100.00)	1,207,240,950 (100.00)	407564699 (100.00)

Note: Figures in brackets are percentages to total.

Source: Extracted from table 1.12"Scheduled commercial banks in India from various issues of RBI. Figures in brackets are percentages to total Figures in brackets are percentages to total.

This form of banking is not only lazy banking but also banking with significant structural distortions. The share of the private corporate sector in national income is around 18% but it takes away nearly 45% of the credit provided by the banking sector. The fastest growing Uninc. sector gets lesser share of bank credit, which reveals that the non-banking financial sector is playing an increasingly important role in the credit delivery mechanisms in the economy.

This is in spite of the fact that the household preference for bank deposits as a saving medium, has been continuing uninterrupted. Bank deposits as a percentage of household financial savings have risen from 37 per cent in 2004-05 to 59% in 2011-2012 (see table 5.1).

Of course, Finance Ministers often meet bankers and 'impress upon' them the need to step up credit to the 'unorganized' sector. There is an implicit belief, among planners, that post-nationalization, banks will meet what are called their 'social obligations' through directed lending. Table — 11.3 shows the outstanding credit of loan accounts from scheduled commercial banks [SCBs] for a select period.

We observe from Table — 11.3 that the number of accounts for smaller customer has shown significant increase in the last ten years but the share has come down. For instance, up to Rs. 10 lakhs category, this amount outstanding to total SCB outstanding has come down from 32% to 21%. Same is the case for up to Rs. 1 crore borrowers — from 45% to 33%. Even for up to Rs. 10 crore borrowers the proportion has come down from 68% to 45%. We find that there is something that is really problematic in our banking sector, particularly in providing credit to the sections, which not only require them the most, but are also those which are the fastest growing sectors.

Asset Based versus Income Based Lending

It is to be noted that the market knowledge and information regarding these activities are not fully available with commercial bankers on an updated basis. The typical bank manager of a public sector bank has a two to three year tenure in a particular branch and is also shifted across activities like foreign exchange, administration, agricultural finance, personal banking, training, industrial lending, etc. By and large, the public sector banks have been geared to 'Asset Based Lending' rather than lending based on cash flows that are forecast. Even in asset based lending, they are more tuned to lend based on Paper Financial Ratios. But activities like trade, transport, hotels and restaurants, construction, etc., where there are significant fluctuations in the cash flows on a daily basis, require a totally different mindset and approach. In other words, to say the least, risk assessment capabilities of commercial bankers are inadequate, in the context of these activities. Also, funds need to be available to these players without much paperwork and based on personal assessment and at odd times. The traditional public sector banker is not geared for such risk management. He is not promoted or given extra incentives for taking risks. Rather, his promotion is a result of a number of years of 'unblemished' service.

Hence, these activities are mostly financed by the Non-Banking Finance Sector [NBFS]. Large segments of disparate activities are clubbed together under a single banner called NBFS. It ranges from unincorporated entities like moneylenders to large companies dealing in thousands of crores of rupees in the leasing businesses. It also includes share trading companies and truck financiers. There has not been any significant attempt to focus on the distinct activities of these constituents by the planners.

To sum up, the growth in the economy during the last decade has been facilitated by the NBFS and this has not been adequately recognized or appreciated. The saga of excellent credit delivery mechanisms with reliable credit assessment systems and collection mechanisms of the NBFS sector, tuned to our ethos and cultural roots, has not been written about since the metropolitan elite are allergic to indigenous institutions and the communists are stuck in their nineteenth century rhetoric of revolution through nationalized banks. But we must focus on the NBFS and suggest ways to alter the existing cult of 'Lazy Banking' that they are steeped in, for the purpose of sustainable growth in the economy. The issue of integrating the financial markets by leveraging on the strengths of the NBFS is critical for the economy.

CHAPTER 12

The Critical Role of the Non-Banking Financial Sector [NBFS]

The non-banking financial services organizations have emerged as highly resourceful credit delivery channels, especially for the unorganized sector. Given their extensive network, their penchant for quality credit appraisal and their level of acceptability among their customers, they are far from receiving their due recognition. Hence, there is a need to have their role recognized better and integrated with the mainstream financial sector, if the objectives of the reforms are to be achieved.

The growth in the economy in the last two decades has been propelled by the growth rate in the service sector. The real growth rate [at 2004-05 prices] of service sector activities between 2004-05 and 2011-12 is 9.8% which is higher than the GDP growth rate of 8.45% as seen earlier [table 3.2 B]. Hotels and restaurants has grown by 7.4%, trade has grown at 9.2% and non-railway transport at 7.7% [see Table — 7.3].

A substantial portion of the financing of service sector activities which are engines of growth of our economy is undertaken by the NBFS.

For instance, the share of trade in 2011-12 at factor cost at current prices in national income was 18% at Rs. 13.5 lakh crore [out of Rs. 75 lakh crore]. Of this, the share of non-corporate sector was nearly 75% [National Accounts Statistics — 2012], or approximately Rs. 10.1 lakh crore. If 75% needs to be financed [which could be an underestimation since we are looking at value addition and not sale] by the institutions, then Rs. 7.6 lakh crore is the credit need of the trade sector. We find that the financing of trade (non-food credit plus food credit) by the banking sector is Rs. 209,304 crore in 2011 [Rs.128, 000 + Rs. 81,304], which is about 28% of the credit availed by the sector. [Annual Report RBI — 2012] In other words, more than 70% of the financial requirement of the non-corporate sector in trade is met by non-banking sources. This is an underestimation, since a substantial amount of the food credit given by banks goes to government organizations like Food Corporation of India.

A similar type of analysis suggests to us that in un-registered manufacturing, the net value addition is Rs. 312, 477 crore in 2011-12. We find nearly 85% of operating expenses is raw material. Using the estimate of 90% from Annual Survey of Industry [ASI] data, the share of short-term borrowing (working capital purposes) would be

Rs. 281,229 crore. Again, we find that the bank credit to small-scale industries is Rs. 259,200 crore in 2011-12 [of which at least 70% can be estimated to belong to the registered category] based on share in value addition. This means out of Rs. 259,200 crore of bank credit to small scale sector, Rs. 181,440 crores goes to registered and the remaining Rs.77,760 crores goes to unregistered. This means more than 70% of the borrowing requirement of unregistered manufacturing is met by non-bank sources.

The share of the construction industry in gross value addition in 2010-11 is Rs. 595,454 crore. We find that the lending by commercial banks for construction activities in 2011 is Rs. 336,156 crore, which is around 55% [assuming working capital equivalent to gross value addition] of the aggregate borrowing needed. Hence, nearly 45% of private construction activity is financed by the non-banking sector. The non-corporate sector has a large presence, more than 60% of this industry.

Let us remember that truck financing activity in our country is the most innovative and efficient symbol of the non-banking sector which has revolutionized trade, commerce, industry and agriculture in our country. The second hand truck financing mechanism has created a strong backbone for the transport industry by focussing on the *aam aadmi* and this has been one of the major contributions of this sector to the economy.

The Non-Banking Finance Sector (NBFS) is much larger than Non-Bank Finance Companies (NBFCs) since the former includes many non-company forms of organizations like chits, moneylenders [Unincorporated Bodies — UIB's] etc.

NBFCs are classified in terms of activities into Asset Finance Companies (AFC), Investment Companies (IC), Loan Companies (LC), Infrastructure Finance Companies (IFC), Core Investment Companies (CIC), Infrastructure Debt Fund — Non-Banking Financial Companies (IDF-NBFC), Non-Banking Financial Company — Micro Finance Institutions (NBFC-MFI) and NBFC — Factors. During 2011-12, two new categories of NBFCs, viz., Infrastructure Debt Funds — NBFC (NBFC-IDF) and Micro Finance Institutions (NBFC-MFI) — were created and brought under separate regulatory frameworks. In addition, a new category of NBFC — Factors was introduced in September 2012. Earlier in April 2010, a regulatory framework for Non-deposit taking Systemically Important Core Investment Companies (CIC ND-SI) was created for companies with an asset size of Rs.1 billion and above, whose business is investment for the sole purpose of holding stakes in group concerns, are not trading in these securities and are accepting public funds. Prudential requirements in the form of Adjusted Net Worth and leverage were also prescribed for CIC-ND-SIs as they were given exemption from (NOF) Net Owned Funds, capital adequacy and exposure norms.

Table — 12.1 Number of NBFCs Registered with the Reserve Bank

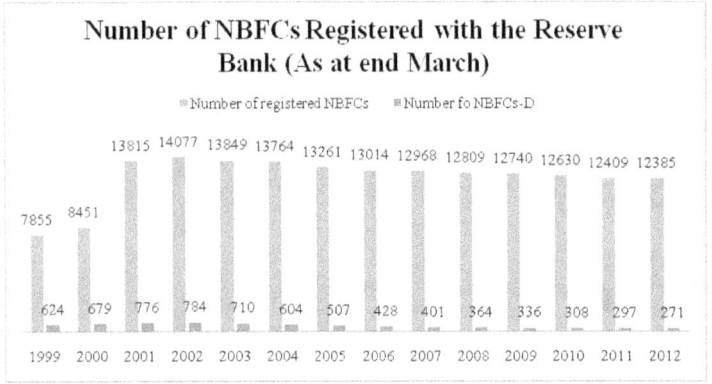

Number of NBFCs Registered with the Reserve Bank (As at end March)

Note: NBFCs –D — Deposit taking NBFCs

Source: pp nb 127 chart 6-1; Report on Trend and Progress of Banking in India 2011-12

The number of NBFCs registered with RBI at the end of March 2012 is 12385 and of that, deposit taking NBFCs are 271 in number which has declined from 679 in 2000. During 2011-12, there was a significant increase in the gross NPAs to total advances of NBFCs-D, which is a deviation from recent trends. Net NPAs which remained negative till 2011 from 2008, with provisions exceeding NPAs registered an increase of 0.5% of total net advances as on March 31, 2012.

Table — 12. 2 NPA Ratios of NBFCs-D

As at end March	Gross NPAs to Total Advances	Net NPAs to Net Advances
2002	10.6	3.9
2005	5.7	2.5
2009	2	#
2010	1.3	#
2011	0.7	#
2012 P	2.1	0.5

Note: P — Provisional, # -Provision exceeds NPA

Source: Table VI-.27 pp132; Report on Trend and Progress of Banking in India RBI;2011-12

In end-March 2012, of 190 reporting NBFCs, 187 had Capital to Risk (Weighted) Assets Ratio (CRAR) of more than 15% (see Table — 12.3) This could be an indication that the NBFC sector is undergoing a consolidation process in the past few years, wherein weaker NBFCs are gradually exiting and paving the way for stronger ones. The ratio of public deposits to Net Owned Funds (NOF) of NBFCs taken together has more or less remained same as at end-March 2012. There was a significant increase in NOF and public deposits of NBFCs-D during 2011-12. The increase in NOF was mainly concentrated in the category of Rs. 500 crore and above.

Table — 12. 3 Capital Adequacy Ratio of NBFCs-D

CRAR Range AFC		2010-11			2011-12P		
		LC	Total	AFC	LC	Total	
1)	Less than 12%	1	1	2	1	1	2
	a) Less than 9%	1	1	2	1	1	2
	b) more than 9% and upto 12%	0	0	0	0	0	0
2)	More than 12% and up to 15%	1	2	3	1	0	1
3)	More than 15% and upto 20%	5	3	8	8	3	11
4)	More than 20% and up to 30%	19	3	22	16	2	18
5)	Above 30%	142	27	169	131	27	158
	Total	168	36	204	157	33	190

Note: AFC — Asset Finance Companies, LC — Loan Companies P: Provisional

Source: Table VI-30; pp 135; Report on Trend and progress of Banking in India; RBI; 2011-12

Table — 12. 4 NPA Ratios of NBFCs-ND-SI Sector

				per cent
			As at end	
	Item	Mar-11	Mar-12	June-12
i)	Gross NPAs to Gross Advances	1.72	2.08	2.26
ii)	Net NPAs to Net Advances	0.69	1.25	1.37
iii)	Gross NPAs to Total Assets	1.28	1.48	1.61
iv)	Net NPAs to Total Assets	0.51	0.88	0.97

Note: ND-SI:Non Deposit taking systematically important

Source: Table VI-39; pp138; Report on Trend and progress of Banking in India;RBI; 2011-12

The financial performance of the NBFCs-ND-SI sector deteriorated marginally as reflected in the decline in net profit during 2011-12. Both Gross and Net NPAs to total asset of the NBFCs-ND-SI sector increased during the year (Table 12.4). The same trend continued as on June 2012.

In conclusion, one can say that the role of the non-banking sector in the credit delivery system in both manufacturing and service sectors like trade, construction, hotels and restaurants, transport, etc., are significant and they play a more dominant role as compared to the commercial banks.

But unfortunately, the planners, instead of nurturing and enhancing their credit delivery mechanisms, are focusing more on control and regulations .The past failures of some Non- Banking Finance Companies has shifted the focus to the liability side of them whereas the asset, or lending side is more important in an emerging market like India.

Under the current RBI Regulations [Section 45-S of the RBI Act], a butcher or barber or baker can borrow money but not a moneylender[UIB] A moneylender can lend but not borrow except from relatives. In the context of safeguarding the interest of the depositors, we have gone to the other extreme, which has an impact on the credit markets, particularly pertaining to retail trade and restaurants, which are dependent on the unincorporated money lender for their business activities. It is also possible that the deposit taking activity has gone behind the 'veil' of unincorporated activities and it is much more difficult to 'unveil' a situation in the unincorporated sector than that in the organized sector.

The Economic Survey mentions that *"Internationally, acceptance of public deposits is restricted to banks alone and non-banks including NBFCs can raise resources from institutional sources or by accessing the capital market only. The RBI is planning to hold discussion with the NBFCs in regard to their plan of action for voluntarily phasing out acceptance of deposits in line with international practices."* [Economic Survey 2004-2005 pp.73 Ministry of Finance, Government of India — February 2005]

This does not fully reflect the situation, since there are thrift institutions and financial companies in the USA and partnership firms, building societies and credit unions in the UK, which are similar to our NBFCs, and they play a large role in taking deposits as well as in lending. They meet the requirements of what are called the mid-market households and small businesses. Also, we have to remember that the structure of our economy is non-corporate [having a share of more than 45%] compared to that of USA or UK where more than 70% of the economy can be traced to the corporate sector's activities, whereas in our case it is around 15%.

It is noteworthy that the number of NBFCs has declined drastically in the last few years due to regulatory steps undertaken by the RBI in terms of registration and rating, etc.

As at the end of March 2012, the total number

of NBFCs registered with Reserve Bank were 271 (NBFC-D), and 12,385 were the non–deposit taking NBFCs (see table 12.1). The total public deposits with NBFCs were of the order of Rs. 5841crores. As on March 31, 2012, 80% of the NBFC-D maintained the Capital Risk Weighted Asset Ratio [CRAR] above 30% (see table12.3). The net NPAs to total assets of NBFCs — ND have shown a substantial an increase from 0.51 as on March 2011 to 0.97 in June 2012.

Chit Funds

One of the components of NBFS (Non-Banking Financial Sector) is chit funds which are beneficial to ordinary people and are investment and consumption vehicles. Recently in West Bengal, a multi-level marketing firm 'Saradha Group' failed and it was blamed on chit funds.

This would be hilarious but for its ominous implications for the chits industry. Saradha had more than 160 entities/activities and not even one of them was registered under the chit fund category.

The mainstream media which thrives on abysmal ignorance in matters of finance repeatedly refers to Saradha as a chit fund and sometimes as a 'cheat fund' scam. It is obnoxious since the scam has nothing to do with chit fund activity. There are reports that some members of the Parliamentary Committee on finance headed by Yashwant Sinha — former Finance Minister — are discussing the possibility of abolishing all chit funds in the light of the Saradha scam when Saradha group did not have any activity linked to chit funds. This is like amputating the left leg when there is gangrene in the right leg.

In this connection, let us examine what a 'Chit Fund' is:

1. Chit Funds are defined under Sec. 45 I(c) of the RBI Act. RBI Notification No.DNBC.39/DG(H)-77 dated June 20, 1977 categorises it as a miscellaneous non-banking company (MNBC).

2. Since the subject is in the concurrent list (entry 7 of List III) of the Constitution, administration of the rules is with the respective State Governments. The company should be registered with the Registrar of Chit Funds of the State of their operation.

3. Chit fund company means a company managing, conducting or supervising, as foremen, agent or in any other capacity, chits as defined in Section 2 (b) of 'The Chit Funds Act, 1982'.

4. Any company carrying out the operation of 'Chit Fund' should have the words 'Chit', 'Chitty' or 'Kuri' as part of their company name.

5. Chit fund companies are not allowed to accept deposits from the public, trade in stock, equity or other cash management.

6. Chit funds, as of now, are not allowed to carry on other businesses without the permission of the Registrar/State Governments.

A chit scheme generally has a predetermined value and duration. Each scheme admits a particular number of members (generally equal to the duration of the scheme), who contribute a certain sum of money every month (or everyday) to the 'pot'. The 'pot' is then auctioned out every month. The highest bidder (also known as the prized subscriber) wins the 'pot' for that month. The bid amount is also called the 'discount' and the prized subscriber wins the sum of money equal to the chit value less the discount and the fixed fee to the foreman. The discount money is then distributed among the rest of the members (or the non-prized subscribers) as 'dividend' and in the subsequent month, the required contribution is brought down by the amount of dividend.

Now given these characteristics and parameters, it is very clear that Saradha never was a chit company and nor did it intend to be one. There are many multi-level marketing outfits which collect funds from gullible public and utilise the funds in the unorganised credit market or in real estate etc. In this case, the Saradha Group seems to have invested substantially in smaller print and visual media ventures also.

It would not be easier for such entities to operate without the cooperation of police and other political leaders and Ministers. There was a similar case in Bangalore sometime before and in that case the receipts were given as 'donations' to temples. There is a huge appetite for use of funds and also a large number of gullible people invest in such offers due to ignorance or greed or both.

On the contrary, there are many chits companies in the southern part of India which are thriving for the last many decades, some for even over hundred years. Capitalising on the social networking and community participation, this institution has survived over several decades, even after the influx of several other organised financial institutions and the increased complexity of financial markets. Under this model, money is circulated to the entire cross section of our society; be it housewives, salaried class, businessmen, Government servants, club members under different names namely: *kitties*, *bisies*, *kuries* and Chit funds.

Benefits from Chits

The uniqueness of the chit fund industry over other financial intermediaries is its ability to evaluate the intrinsic strengths of potential clients, mainly on the faith of the subscribers' ability to repay, providing succour to lower/middle income groups, helping finance small businesspeople who are often wedged between the exorbitant costs of moneylenders and the stringent procedures of banks. The chit is seen not merely as an investment but a drop-by-drop plan to get lumpsum financing for marriages, education, housing, business, etc. at a future date. Chit funds are self-liquidating in nature and similar in character to mutual benefit funds.

To illustrate the above, let us consider an example of a chit scheme with the following characteristics. Chit value: Rs. 5 lakh Duration: 50 months; Members: 50.

The membership contributions in this case would initially be, say, Rs. 10,000 a month. In the first month, the collections would, therefore, be Rs. 10,000 multiplied by the number of members — Rs. 5 lakh in all. This amount is called the 'pot' which is auctioned out at the end of the month. Now, let us assume that the highest bid in the first month's auction is (20%) Rs. 1,00,000. This is called the 'discount'. The highest bidder now gets an amount equal to the chit value, less the discount — i.e. Rs. 4 lakh. The discount amount, less 5% commission to the foreman, is then divided among the 50 members equally.

For the subsequent month, therefore, the contributions of these members reduce by the amount of the dividend (i.e. the contribution in the second month for the members would be Rs. 8,100.) This process gets repeated for all months till the end of the scheme. The contributions are the same for each member, but the total amount taken out or bid by each member varies.

In case of default or delayed payment, the chit fund organiser/foreman has to bear the deficit on behalf of the defaulting and delaying members.

Hence the primary use of Chit Funds include:

- To address consumption needs such as, marriage, education, property purchase and so on.
- To pay off costlier loans from outside sources like loan from money lenders.
- To address working capital, business expansion or start-up capital needs of small businesses, besides providing bridge loans.
- For an emergency or simply as savings for future needs.

In the context of reduced availability of bank financing many small and tiny business people use chits for their credit requirements. It is important that in our knee-jerk reaction to scams we do not throw the baby out with the *'balti'*. As a first step, mainstream media [MSM] must stop calling Saradha type scams a chit fund scam. It is a multi-level marketing scam assisted by political leaders.

Be that as it may, it is important that genuine chits numbering thousands and facilitating consumption and investment requirements of a large number of middle-class people should not be strangulated in the name of 'cleaning' the sector.

It is very unfortunate that the debate on the Saradha multi-level marketing scam is again and again being discussed as a chit fund gone bad. The solutions being bandied about call for banning all chit fund activities in the country. Though there is no denying that what happened with the Saradha Group and other multi-level marketing/ Ponzi companies has robbed millions of people of their savings, putting the blame on chit funds is like rubbing salt in the wounds. A ban on all chit funds would cause havoc since there are millions invested in safe chit funds. Any general ban will cause harm on such a scale that even our nationalised banks will feel the heat.

The fact is Ponzi (multi-level marketing) schemes such as Saradha have nothing to do with chit funds. In the case of the Saradha group, they had around 160 companies in areas such as realty, agro, media, exports, etc., but not one of them was a chit fund.

In fact, the white-collar crimes executed by Saradha-type companies are the most unsavoury aspects of globalisation and a growing economy. Fraudulent multi-level marketers reach victims via all modes of communication — postal services, telephone, email, internet sites, television, radio, and even in person. Viable mass-marketing fraud groups require a variety of resources to operate, including the means to target and communicate with prospective victims, obtain and launder illicit proceeds, and evade detection by law enforcement and investigative agencies.

Thus they also include legitimate business services, communication tools, payment processors, fraudulent identification documents, and even counterfeit financial instruments. As a whole, nowadays, fraudulent mass marketing operations are increasingly interconnected and fluid, with groups shifting alliances according to the particular needs of a scheme. In Bangalore, one recent scheme by Vini-Vic, which cheated a large number of people, gave 'receipts' to customers which clearly indicated that they were providing donations to a temple!

So why not address the real issue instead of trying to find a scapegoat in chit funds?

In many parts of India, chit funds address gaps left by the traditional banking sector. They mobilise huge amounts of small savings, and in return allow members to have access to lumpsum amounts that they would often not be able to get from traditional banks. Easy accessibility and flexibility are important aspects of this form of financing. Compared to banks, chit funds require less documentation, are more flexible about collateral, and allow members to determine their own interest rate (within the constraints of a given chit scheme).

Furthermore, there is no need to determine upfront whether funds are used for saving or borrowing. This is a salient feature of chit funds as it not only puts in place a disciplined savings mechanism, but also allows access to cash when needed. In addition, as chit funds use the funds of participants, there is much lower capital requirement for the institution (unlike banks).

It is estimated that the value of chit turnover in states such as Kerala, Tamil Nadu and Andhra is almost Rs. 10,000 crore each per annum. Though no authentic figures are available, the size of the unregistered chit fund industry as estimated by the Association of Chit Funds is almost 100 times that of registered ones. As the growth of this unregistered sector is not in the national interest, there is an urgent need to ascertain the exact volume and take remedial measures to contain the same.

The average value of each chit registered with the office of the registrar in rural areas is around Rs. 1 lakh — whereas in urban and metro cities the average value goes up to a maximum of Rs. 10 lakh and Rs. 50 lakh respectively. The presence of more than 30,000 registered chit operators generating several lakhs of employment opportunities, either directly or indirectly, especially in rural areas, without taking any subsidy from the government speaks volumes about its contribution to the national economy.

In the case of chit funds, the Finance Ministry constituted a Key Advisory Group in 2011 to

(1) Review the existing legal/regulatory/institutional framework for chit funds/*nidhi* companies and their efficacy;

(2) Prepare an action plan, including policy initiatives, for orderly growth of the sector;

(3) Recommend legal/institutional/regulatory initiatives and related measures for the orderly growth of the same.

Though the group has submitted its report in May 2013, it is yet to be formalised due to lack of co-ordination between the central and state governments. It is also ironical that while the government, seeing the potential of this industry, took the trouble to study this sector and has in principle agreed with most of the recommendations of the group in order to improve financial inclusion, the perception is still negative.

In a large country like India, with substantial growth seen in service activities where the share of proprietorship and partnership firms are significant, it is important that we recognize the role played by non-bank entities in the credit market. They have an extensive network and substantial credibility among their constituents, comprising both borrowers and lenders. Their ability to tap the public for deposits is the linking point for meeting the requirements of the customers on both sides, since the base is the unincorporated sector in both the situations. It is necessary for banks to treat them as channel partners and provide credit to them. But at the same time, they should have the flexibility to access deposits from the public like any other financial institution. Being a lender without being a borrower from the public is like asking a teacher to only teach [this is the output] and not study [this is the input].

Financial systems are fascinating learning tools where the input/throughput/output mechanism in terms of borrowing, processing and lending enhances and enriches the institutions. If any one node is missing, they do not learn and then, they mostly fail. In a developing country like ours, we need multiple institutions catering to different segments and capable of accessing funds from the public, from the market and from the institutions. Unless an institution accesses funds using an extensive network, it will not understand the magic of the lending market. A prudential lender is one who borrows efficiently. It is actually two sides of a coin.

Making institutions lend without allowing them to borrow from the public will weaken the learning curve and goes against the canon of the 'Triple Nodes' of a financial intermediary, namely, borrow, analyze/process and lend. Not the least, it may create moral hazards — if institutions only lend without borrowing from the public — in a country like ours. Let us have prudential regulation by all means, but not by throwing the baby out with the bathwater.

We suggest that we integrate our financial market by creating a new financial architecture of a Concentric Circle of financing institutions.

Concentric Circle of Banking Institutions

There is a need to integrate domestic financial markets by making the NBFS channel partners of large banks. The reforms have focused only on the liability side of the NBFS and its failures, but the asset side is equally important in terms of credit delivery to large segments of our economy. The focus is more on the failure of some institutions. There are two types of failures. One is the malfeasance on the part of promoters in terms of running these institutions, which has resulted in loss to the depositors. This is related to the operational and supervisory mechanism. The other type of failure is related to the riskiness of the underlying assets invested in by these entities and that is part of the business risk phenomenon. There is a need to understand the risk-return paradigm of any financial operation. Now, these entities are into cash flow based lending for activities like trade, hotels, construction etc. They do not have the benefit of the sovereign guarantee provided to public sector banks, nor do have they have any insurance facility as in the case of bank deposits through the Deposit Insurance and Credit Guarantee Corporation (DICGC). They also do not have the 'comfort letters' provided to MNC bankers in India by their parents abroad.

In such a situation, some failures are to be expected when we are dealing with thousands of institutions. In the case of failure of commercial banks, particularly public sector banks, it is described as a systemic failure and the government pumps in more funds for re-capitalizing these institutions. Protecting depositor interest should go hand in hand with enhancing credit delivery to the largest sections of our economy, which are not currently bank-dependent for their activities.

In a sense, the non-banking finance sector is the best route to finance these activities in the service sectors. This is due to the fact that in their area they are market savvy and have the ability to rate the partnership/proprietorship groups and monitor them and recover the money lent to them.

Already, we find that in truck financing, the large domestic and foreign banks are utilising the NBFCs as channel partners. Hence, the public sector banks could finance the non-bank financial institutions on a wholesale basis, and they, in turn, could fund the requirements of the non-corporate sectors in a chain of retailing credit and recovery functions. If the banks finance the NBFCs after rating them even at 4% to 5% above the Prime Lending Rate (PLR) or base rate, then these institutions could fund the non-corporate sector at perhaps 8-10% and above the PLR. This would still be lower than the open market rates of two and half to three times the PLR at which this sector, in many of these activities, is getting financed.

The financing to the non-bank organizations (both corporate and unincorporated) by the commercial banks should be treated on par with priority sector lending as long as the end use is for these sectors.

The commercial banks could be given the powers to licence these entities and provide credit to them to reach the larger market. It can also be specified that only licensed non-corporate bodies will be permitted to operate in the credit market in terms of collecting deposits and also availing of loans from the banking institutions. This would provide opportunities to banks to enlarge their scope of operations and also provide the Unincorporated bodies (UIBs) to carry on their business with loans from the banking system. It will also introduce orderliness in terms of banks rating these entities for licensing them and reviewing it annually. The depositors are also protected to some extent because of the assessment made by the commercial banks for licensing them.

This concentric circle of banking will bring to an end the current inverse relationship between size of borrowings and the cost of borrowings without much cognizance being taken of the credit rating of the borrower. It would also facilitate the creation of a proper database in these activities for credit rating of these entities.

Integrating Financial Markets

There are efforts by the government, both at the central and state level, to allow global companies into activities like retail trade, transportation, construction and restaurants. If the competition from the international giants have to be effectively met by our local institutions, then it is an imperative to put in place a cost effective and efficient credit delivery mechanism to cater to the needs of the current players.

Globalizing our financial sector without domestic

integration of the financial markets may lead to a situation of cherry picking by the global players and/or linkages created only at the 'creamy layer' level without adequate strengthening of the base of the system. The paradigm of taking the UIBs as channel partners by the commercial banks on a large scale would facilitate the players in these fast growing sectors to compete effectively with global players in the emerging scenario.

Hence we suggest steps, which will facilitate

- Reduction in interest cost, and hence, benefits to the ultimate consumer.
- Enhancement of credit delivery mechanisms
- Introduction of rating processes at the retail level
- Creation of a level playing field when global players enter the retail sector
- Reversal of the inverse relationship between the size of borrowing and the cost of borrowing
- Strengthening the professionalism of the NBFS sector through education and training
- Integration of the financial markets

We need to recast the financial architecture of the Indian financial system if it has to ensure growth of the economy along with adequate availability of credit to the fastest growing sectors of the economy. The aggregate monetary policy of the central banker can be achieved if and only if the role of non-banking financial institutions, including the UIBs, are recognized, encouraged and integrated into our financial system.

Taxation and Bribery

Chapter 13	Taxation: Coverage Issues
Chapter 14	Bribery and Corruption

Taxation: Coverage Issues

The perception that India is an under-taxed economy is a myth, if one takes into account the endemic issue of under-coverage as well as corruption in the system.

There is a view among some experts that India is an under-taxed economy. Finance Ministers are convinced about this most often and exhort people to pay their dues. Advertisements are issued to induce people to pay taxes and novel schemes are suggested before every Budget to augment government revenue through taxes. One of the common arguments is based on the share of taxes to Gross Domestic Product (GDP), and it is suggested that it could be much more. Another is in terms of the composition of the taxes, namely direct and indirect, and it is suggested that indirect taxes, which are regressive, are a larger share of the pool.

Table —13.1 gives the share of taxes to GDP for select

years from 1991. We find that the share of taxes — both direct and indirect taxes — have been around 15% of GDP from 1990-91 till 2009. It was 17% in 2012. The share of indirect taxes was of the order of 11% and that of direct taxes was 6%. Based on this data of direct taxes to GDP of nearly 17%, many experts, particularly of the Left line of persuasion, argue that we are an under-taxed nation from the point of view of direct taxes. But as we will show, they do not take into account the payment [called bribe, rent seeking, speed money, lubrication money, etc.] to be made to government employees for carrying on any activity, and to that extent, total taxes can be said to be much higher than reflected.

Table — 13. 1 Level and Composition of Taxes — Centre and States [as % of GDP]

Year	1990-91	1995-96	2000-01	2005-06	2009-10	2011-12(E)
Direct Taxes	2.09	2.92	3.31	4.54	5.84	5.99
Indirect Taxes	12.87	11.37	10.77	11.37	9.66	10.65
Total Tax	14.96	14.29	14.08	15.91	15.50	16.64

Source: Table 1.8 Tax to GDP Ratios, Indian Public Finance statistics, 2011-12. GOI

Note: E -Estimate

Table — 13.2 gives the level and composition of taxes of the Central government from 1990-91 to 2011-12. We find that there is a major shift in the proportion of direct taxes from 1990-1991 to 2011-12. It has gone up from

19% of total taxes to nearly 55% during this period and the proportion of indirect taxes has come down from 78% to 44% during the same period. A substantial fall is seen in customs duties due to our international commitments. Excise duties have shown a decline from 43% to 16% during 1991 to 2012. The share of personal income tax showed an increase from 9% to 19%. It is to be noted that personal income taxes and excise duties are shared with state governments.

Table — 13. 2 Level and Composition of Taxes — Centre [%]

Year	1990-91	1995-96	2000-01	2005-06	2010-11	2011-12(P)
Corporation Tax	9.3	14.0	16.8	17.4	37.7	36.3
Personal Income Tax	9.3	14.8	18.9	27.7	17.5	18.6
Direct Taxes	19.1	30.2	36.2	45.1	55.3	54.9
Customs	35.9	32.1	25.2	17.8	17.1	16.8
Excise	42.6	36.1	36.3	30.4	17.4	16.3
Service tax	—	0.8	1.4	6.3	9.0	11.0
Indirect Taxes	78.4	69.1	62.9	54.4	43.4	44.0
Others	0.5	0.7	0.9	0.5	1.3	1.09
Total tax	100.0	100.0	100.0	100.0	100.0	100.0

Note: Direct taxes also includes taxes pertaining to expenditure, interest, wealth ,gift and estate duty. And "Others" includes taxes of Union Territories & other taxes. P- Provisional

Source: http://indiabudget.nic.in, table 3.4, Sources of tax revenue. Economic survey 2000-01,2006-07,2012-13

The aggregate taxes do not reveal the full picture of evasion and coverage. In Table — 13.3 the number of returns filed by different categories of assesses during 2008-09 to 2010-11 has been provided. We find that there are nearly 3.1 crore individual assesses. **Till 2000 All India Income Tax Statistics (AIITS) used to provide detailed category wise statistics. This publication has been discontinued. In other words, the Finance Ministry has become shy of providing details of tax assessed etc.**

Let us consider the figures in Table 13.4. It says that there were no salaried persons in the country with an income of more than Rs.1 crore and, in all, there were around 250 persons above the Rs. 25-lakh annual income level — for 2000. In the case of the self-employed, the number is around 900, with none in the Rs. 50 to Rs. 100 lakh category.

Table — 13. 3 Category — wise Number of Income Tax Assesses in India (2008-2009 to 2010-2011)

Year	Company	Individual	HUF	Firms	Trusts	Others	Total
2008-09	327674	30101260	768845	1310849	71145	70854	32650627
2009-10	367884	31384084	806236	1354330	76898	95994	34085426
2010-11	496872	31035394	761911	1229722	119378	95487	33739124

Source: Indiastat.com, Lok Sabha Unstarred Question no. 2062, dated on 02.12.2011

Table — 13. 4 Number of Returns Individuals — Salaried & Non-Salaried Persons[2000]

Range of Income Rs. Lakh	Salaried Number of Returns	Non-Salaried Number of Returns
25-50	103	672
50-100	155	NIL
100+	NIL	258

Source: All India Income Tax Statistics [AIITS] — Directorate Of Income Tax — New Delhi–2001

When one looks at Table —13.4, one feels that a relief fund should be created for all our top film stars, cricket players, surgeons, lawyers, chartered accountants, architects, tax consultants and other self-employed persons. They all seem to be in distress!

In Table — 13.5, the number of returns from some categories of services as published by the IT Department in 1998 have been provided. The numbers speak volumes about the coverage and also about the nature of underlying collections.

Table — 13.5 Number of Returns from Some Service Activities [1998]

Nature of Business	Number of returns of Non-Company Organizations — All India
Utensil shops	10,539
Crockery and Glassware	3158
Furniture Shops	5477
Medical Shops	45847

Source: All India Income Tax Statistics [AIITS] — Directorate Of Income Tax — New Delhi—2001

We find that in the whole country there were only 10,539 utensil shops and 5477 furniture shops, which were in the taxable category in 1998. You may be able to identify as many such entities in your town itself. In the recent (2013) budget speech, the Finance minister mentioned that 42,800 people are assessed to tax for income of more than Rs. 1 crore. This is out of 3.10 crore assesses.

The argument by many experts is to strengthen, enhance, improve and network the IT department. The issue is not that. It is much more serious and cancerous. When one visits the Postal Department Officers' quarters in, say Mumbai, one finds mostly cycles and scooters. But the lifestyle and possessions of some tax officials are totally different. That should provide clues to the issues facing us.

At the same time, we find the income of government employees increasing more in proportion to inflation in the last forty years. We have provided in Table —13.6 the increase in salaries of public sector employees in relation to inflation. We find that the emoluments have increased by 12260 per cent during 1971-72 to 2011-12, during which period, the consumer price index has gone up only 2216 per cent. This implies that the Government employees are net gainers, with real income protected during this entire period. Hence, decline in real income cannot be a reason in this case, if at all it is ever a justifiable reason, for rent-seeking from ordinary citizens.

Table — 13. 6 Per capita Emoluments of Public Sector employees *in relation to increase in average* All India consumer Price index [1960=100]

Year	Number of Employees (in lakhs) *	Per Capita Emolument [Rs]	Increase over 1971-72 [%]	Consumer Price index [1960-100]	Increase over 1971-72 [%]
1971-72	7.01	5920	—	192	—
1980-81	18.39	14239	140.52	401	108.85
1990-91	22.19	49179	730.73	951	395.31
2000-01	17.40	219672	3610.67	2190	1440.62
2010-11	14.40	703718	11787.13	4103	2036.98
2011-12	13.98	731995	12264.78	4447	2216.15

Source: pp A-57;Table 3.2; Economic Survey –2012-13, Ministry of Finance, GoI New Delhi.

Note:*Excluding casual and daily rated workers

We also notice that the pension benefits of government employees are one of the best in the world since it is defined benefit till 2004 and post January 2004 it is defined contribution, commutable, inflation indexed and family security — inclusive. If you were employed in World Bank /IMF or in the UN, the pension in US dollars is not taxed. Hence, lack of social security at the time of retirement cannot be a complaint for government employees.

Another related issue is the numbers of hours of 'Effective Work' put in by government employees, particularly at the lower levels. It is surmised that on any given day in many government offices, just two hours is spent on real work, effectively speaking. It implies that the emoluments are for 10 hours of work per week, which is much lower than even the European standards of 30 to 35 hours of work per week. A large number of employees who are seen playing cards during office hours, on the lawns of various Bhavans of New Delhi during winter, maintain that they provide 'outside' support to the government!

The important issue is the 'Own Account' collection by government employees [which is variously referred to as bribes, corruption, speed money, grease, rent seeking, etc.] and collection on 'Client Account', namely the government. It is to be noted that only employees in revenue departments like sales tax, excise, customs, and income tax, etc., can collect money from citizens on 'Client Account' and 'Own Account', whereas employees in practically all other Departments starting from birth certificate issuance to burial ground in charge [that is womb to tomb!] can collect payments only on 'Own account'.

This 'Own Account' collection, coupled with client account collection [regular taxes] constitute a large percentage of our national income, and from that perspective, we are a highly taxed nation. We will explore later the estimate of 'Own Account' collections in the Uninc. context and their implications.

CHAPTER 14

Bribery and Corruption

Government taxes are just the tip of the iceberg; collections on 'Own Account' are as large as those on the 'Government's Account,' and the only antidote to this evil is shrinking the size of government officialdom by recognizing that Government is a problem instead of being a solution.

Government employees collect taxes on **'Client Account,'** that is, for the government, and on 'Own Account,' that is to increase their incomes. It is not just supplementing the income, as we will see, it is more, sometime much more than the core income. The collection on **'Client Account'** can be done only by employees in tax-related departments [like direct and indirect taxes], but collections on **'Own Account,'** can be mobilized by any employee or his agent for any human endeavour of any citizen for inaction or speed by inducement, lure, threat or intimidation. It is to be noted that Own Accounts cannot exist without political patronage.

Government employees collect 'Own Account' taxes from citizens in this country on many counts, some of which are presented in Table — 14.1. We find from the table that this Own Account tax collection is related to our *Samskaras* (culture) from birth to death and the important point to note is that it is not considered as improper anymore. We conducted an informal survey during 2001-2002 in different locations in one city to get an idea of the type of Own Account transactions and to make an estimate regarding the amount.

This, coupled with various news reports about graft cases/Lokayukta reports published in newspapers, etc., were used to arrive at the following estimates. This mainly deals with non-corporate [proprietorship/ partnership] users and individual citizens. Large volumes of Own Account transactions on major/minor projects by ministers, both at the state level and at the central level etc. were not covered by this survey.

Also, it should be noted that every 'Own Account' tax does not have a corresponding 'Client Account' [government account] taxes. As already noted, only employees in the tax collection/revenue departments can collect 'Client Account' taxes with receipts. Equally, they can also collect 'Own Account' taxes and reduce the flow to the government.

Table — 14. 1 Activities for which taxes are levied by government employees [Own Account]

Activities for Own Account Taxes	Details
Acquiring Assets	Land, Houses, Cars, Scooters, — Paid directly or as 'Service Charges' through the society, dealer etc., Any Asset Acquired by a citizen entails own account taxes if it is to be recognised by registration.
Carrying on trade/ business	Smaller the business larger the percentage. Retail pushcart dealers/ street vendors estimatedly pay police or their agents Rs. 20 to Rs. 30 per day from their earnings of Rs. Rs.100 to 500. Fast food restaurants pay Rs. 500 to 1000 per week to the health inspectors of the local municipality.
Identity establishment	Birth certificates/death certificates/ Ration Card/Passport/Caste certificates. The amount varies from Rs. 100 to Rs. 1000, depending on the bargaining power and urgency. The minimum is Rs. 100.
Acquiring Contracts	For roads, water pipes, cables, houses for low income groups, stadium, parks etc. varies from 1 to 3% of the amount
Availing 'Free' services	Government hospitals, schools, Electricity Board, water works, RTO. It varies from Rs. 10 for a bedpan service at a government hospital to Rs.10,000 for vehicle fitness inspection certificate.

Activities for Own Account Taxes	Details
Closing the Eye — Services	Traffic Police, building set-off, wrong construction, basement parking as shops, illegal electric/water/phone connection, violating labor laws. Bringing in foreign goods not allowed above specified limit. Keeping cattle in city, felling public trees etc. The amount is negotiable with a minimum of Rs.100. At a very low level it is paying half the fare in public buses to travel without a ticket.
Provision of Government Gratis	Old age pension, free credit through some Govt. schemes, land compensation, fire compensation, riot compensation. It is again anything between 2 to 50 per cent of the amount. In many situations the 'fee' is after delivery like American plaintiff lawyers who collect a percentage as fees [contingent claims] after winning the case
Reducing Waiting Time	All activities of Government. The percentage varies from 2 to 20 per cent with a minimum of Rs. 100 to Rs.200

During the course of our study in one locality in the city, we found that there were nearly 1000 street vendors who had set up temporary shops and roadside vendors who were operating on the streets. Each of them was paying 'agents' sums ranging from Rs. 10 to Rs. 50 per day [depending on their size] either in cash or kind.

This would not be possible without the knowledge and connivance of local political leaders and police. It falls under the second category in the table given above. This comes to an average of Rs. 20,000 to Rs. 40,000 per day. There are nearly fifty small and big locations like that in the city. It adds up to nearly Rs. 10 to 20 lakh per day. We estimate that for all categories, the revenue generated in one city on 'Own Account' could be around Rs. 100 lakh per day. The city where our survey was conducted was not even one of the metros. And, this is only for those nodal points, which are not directly involved in collecting 'Client Account' [government] taxes. Based on an average of 250 days of government activities, we can surmise that the annual amount in one city alone will be around Rs. 250 crore. This is an underestimation, since 'Own Account' collections under category two [carrying on trade business] can be even for 300 days since roadside vendors do not have holidays. On a national level of say, 100 cities/towns it would be Rs. 25,000 crore.

According to the Economic Survey, the combined tax receipts of the Central and State governments in 2001-2002 was Rs. 313,974 crore [Economic Survey 2003-2004, page 41 Table-2.11]. If we use the thumb rule and conclude that there was an under-collection of taxes to the extent of 30%, then the actual taxes should have been Rs. 448, 534 crore. The difference of Rs. 134, 560 crore arises out of 'Own Account' reasons. Of this, even if 25% is collected as 'Own Account' [the tax saved by the payer is 75% of this] then the amount is Rs. 33,640 crore. Putting these two together, we get an estimate of Rs. 58,640 crore or say Rs. 60,000 crore as the consolidated 'Own Account' collection.

According to National Accounts Statistics, the total GDP was Rs. 21 lakh crore in 2001-2002, and this amount of Rs. 60,000 crore constitutes around 3% of the total GDP. The aggregate taxes were of the order of 15% of the GDP, as seen earlier. This implies that 'Own Account' taxes constitute at least one-fifth of 'Client Taxes,' namely, those received by the government. This is without taking into account huge corporate transactions on contracts worth billions of rupees on airports, expressways, power plants, IT parks, purchase of weapons etc. If we add them, then the 'Own Account' collections could be at least 6%-8% of the GDP constituting significant portion of the taxes received by the client, which, in this case, is the government. At 2011-12 GDP of nearly Rs. 84 Lakh crore [assuming similar 6 to 8% of bribery levels] we get an amount of Rs. 5 to 7 lakh crore of bribe money generated due to interactions with Government organs. Other than this it is to be recognised that black money is generated in private sector also.This combined with estimated black money held abroad as of 2006 — at 500 Billion USD to 1.5 Trillion USD [Rs. 25 Lakh crore to Rs. 75 Lakhs crore] makes a huge amount of domestic and global black money of India [R.Vaidyanathan — Eternal India — April 2009– New Delhi]. Also significant amount of gold ornaments and other valuables are kept in the lockers of foreign banks abroad.

But our focus here is bribe aspects of the Government functions.

This is one reason why a large number of posts in various government departments, particularly at the state level, are auctioned and conferred upon the highest bidder. It is no secret that in the Police Department in many states, 'critical' location postings require substantial payments, and so is the case in Sales Tax, Land Registration, etc. Needless to add, these 'Own Account' collections are done with the connivance and/or encouragement of political leaders who get a large share of this. The nature of sharing and the estimation of that would be an interesting exercise.

The important issue is regarding the usage to which this 'Own Account' taxes are put. It appears that a substantial portion of the unorganized credit market is serviced by Own Account taxes and police persons are emerging as major credit providers/collectors in the unorganized markets. It has far reaching implications for our civil society and credit markets.

More important at the current juncture is the clamour for the National Rural Employment Guarantee Act [NREGA] and the enthusiasm shown by Leftist economists and intellectuals regarding the large government outlay on this score. It could be as low as Rs. 10,000 crore or as high as Rs. 1 lakh crore depending upon the final amount to be provided. But the important issue, not addressed by Left economists, is the issue of 'Own Account' taxes such a scheme will generate. The survey that I refer to was more than a decade ago, but even today (2012-13), one can surmise that the percentages have not changed. So officially nearly 6% to 8% of GDP is present as bribery amount to government officials. The proposed food security act will increase the nature of 'leakages'. It will only enlarge the taxes levied by government employees and that will create larger social issues. **In tackling poverty and unemployment, we should remember that the government is not the solution — rather, it is the problem**. Hence, the government should drastically reduce or remove taxes and regulations and encourage philanthropy for productive purposes. As the recent tsunami disaster relief reveals, the initiative could be left to social service organizations like Ramakrishna Mission or AIM for SEVA who identify the target group much better. The 'Social Capital' in the form of community and family efforts could go a long way in ameliorating problems related to unemployment rather than the government taxing its citizens and spending on it, since, on both counts, there will be a huge 'Own Account' collection by its employees. Entitlement based economy creates only bribe entitlement for the babus and much better to think in terms of creating productive employment. The best way the government can generate more employment is by shrinking itself and encouraging private initiative and allowing the pushcart vendor and the self-employed trader to live in peace and with honour and dignity.

Social Security for the
Self Employed and the Role of Gold

Chapter 15	Foolish Government and Smart Women — Role of Gold in our economy
Chapter 16	Demography is Destiny
Chapter 17	Reverse Mortgage as Old Age Security
Chapter 18	Savings or Consumption Driven Society

Foolish Governments and Smart Women — Role of Gold in our economy

The total absence of old age social security in India makes it imperative for certain categories of people like women and self-employed groups to look at gold, which is a highly liquid, transferable and low cost asset to acquire, for safeguarding their future. The government, on its part, has to change its stance, acknowledge the role of gold, and regard it as an investment and not merely a consumption item.

In any seminar on the Indian economy, the discussion invariably turns to savings in the economy. The savings rate, which is a percentage of savings to national income, was around 30% to 32% in the last decade. Compare this to a savings rate of less than 10% during the sixties. Typically, such increases are immediately taken note of, and then the experts [coincidentally most of them are from Delhi!] bombastically conclude that the savings rate should be further increased to boost the economy some more. Then follows the routine criticism from these quarters about unproductive investments undertaken by households in buying gold, which is already substantial, and, if anything, increasing over the years.

India is one of the largest buyers of gold in the world. More than 90% of this is for the purposes of jewellery. Table — 15.1 documents the purchase of gold for jewellery–making in different countries, with data taken from World Gold Council [WGC]. We find that during the past, demand in India was more than 25% of global consumption. In recent times, the attraction of smuggling has come down due to the liberalized import policy. Incidentally, the domestic production of gold is very negligible, running into barely a few tonnes per annum.

Purchases made in Middle East are also mostly by people of Indian origin and, to that extent, the demand from 'Indians' is much larger. What is being bought in the Gulf States this year by non-resident Indians (NRIs) will reach India maybe in a year or so. At an average price of say Rs. 25000 for ten grams, we can estimate that more than Rs. 215,000 crore has been spent in buying gold in 2012 by Indian households, which is much larger than the aggregate capital raised from the stock markets. The purchase of gold by households is not treated as savings in our statistics. It is treated as consumption by households, which is curious since households treat purchase of gold as 'investments,' whatever the economists in the government may think. Recently, a small part has been considered in Gross Domestic Capital Formation as 'investments' but not explicitly in 'savings' data. Hence, this seems to be part of 'adjustments' in GDCF. 'Experts' are more or less unanimous in their opinion that households, and particularly women in India, are making 'unproductive' investments in gold jewellery. They would rather have it that households invest in government bonds, which can be used to pay salaries to government employees! The increase in current account deficit (CAD) in recent times (2013) has been due to major import items like petroleum products, gold, edible oil, other consumer items etc. But gold has been identified as the main culprit and steps have been taken by the RBI and the Finance Ministry to reduce import by increasing import duty restricting banks from lending against gold etc. The import of 'capital goods' mostly from China is a major reason for CAD, but that has not been adequately focussed on.

Table — 15. 1 Gold: Jewellery Demand
1995-2012: India Leads (tonnes)

Countries	1995	2000	2005	2009	2010	2011	2012
India	477	855	722	579	1006	986	864
Greater China	427	329	293	472	667	821	817
Japan	272	98	74	-9	-19	-30	7.6
Indonesia	119	107	81	35	48	55	52
Vietnam	36	60	61	73	81	101	77
Middle East	365	498	388	246	234	188	178
Turkey	139	207	248	107	111	143	119
USA	315	396	377	265	235	200	162
Italy	110	78	71*	41	35	28	24
U.K	46	65	59*	32	27	23	21
Total—Including others	2864.5	3287.9	3091.9	2503.1	3217	3487	3163
Gold price ($/oz)	384.1	279.1	444.5	972.3	1224.5	1571.5	1669.0

Note: 1 Tonne=32,151 troy oz of fine gold, *

Source: World Gold Council [WCG] — Gold Demand Trends various issues.

But why do households invest in gold? It is not for the return but for security. All discussions on return on gold is infructuous, since households do not buy gold to sell or make gains.

Gold is the major social security for a large number of Indian households, which do not have any social security at all. The OASIS [Dave Committee] report indicates that nearly 90% of India's workforce, particularly the self-employed, are not covered by any retirement scheme that enables them to save for economic security during their old age [OASIS report page 6].

The problem is more acute for the wives of these self-employed, since they do not have any independent access to income or savings. Even if they are employed, it is used for current consumption. Amongst the poorer segments of society, a good portion of the income of the man would be used for drinking, gambling, etc., and hence not much would be left over by way of old age security. The joint family system is breaking down and so traditional support models are getting weakened. Under the circumstances, it is natural that the Indian woman would like to own some assets, which are useful after the death of the husband. Real estate is relatively costly, not divisible and not portable. As against that, gold ornaments are portable and divisible. A chain can be converted into two bangles. One can have small pieces of jewellery like a small nose ring or ear stud, unlike land, which has to be bought in the form of large plots or constructed dwelling places, both of which are expensive to acquire.

Transfer of ownership is also very easy in the case of gold. In the case of gold ornaments, one can say that possession is ownership. In other words, if the mother-in-law removes her chain and gives it to her daughter-in-law, then it belongs to the daughter-in-law by tradition. That imply bequeathing is easier without Government interference. Also, one can get loans against gold by pledging it with a moneylender any time of the day or night, seven days of the week. The millions of moneylenders are actually the All Time Money [ATM] of our country, since they act as ATM machines with a personal touch.

In other words, gold represents the most liquid form of assets in India. One can also say that gold is the most politically correct metal, which can be owned. In traditional Indian families, sometimes, shares or fixed deposits are disposed of without the knowledge of the housewife. But gold is always sold with the consent of the housewife. Of course, if it is a case of jewellery that she is wearing, then it cannot be disposed of without her knowledge!

The so-called superstition that mandates a woman not to remove the *mangalsutra* around her neck till the death of the husband is an insurance protection to the woman against rapacious relatives and children. It is assumed that the gold ornaments will work as social security for her in case of any major emergency or after the death of the head of the household. Bollywood blockbusters of earlier times typically had scenes wherein the heroine removed her bangles or chain to be pledged for the benefit of her ailing husband to the accompaniment of mournful background music. Although a tearjerker, it did reflect the ground reality better than the views of experts!

It is important to note that gold ornaments are used as collateral in the credit markets by the Unincorporated sector. Hence gold is a highly liquid asset, portable and easy to transfer, which acts as social security and insurance for the middle and lower class woman as well as collateral for trade.

The total stock of gold is estimated between 12,000 to 15,000 tonnes [WGC], which may be an underestimation. Actually since the vaults of Sri Anantha Padmanabhaswamy temple at Trivandrum were opened to value the gold, diamonds etc., nobody talks of estimates of stock of gold in India anymore!

At this juncture, it is useful to understand some recent developments, which have important implications for Indian households. Many of the central governments in Europe are unloading their stock in the market. Gold is not treated as a unit of measure of safety or as a hedging instrument. The era of gold standard has come to an end and with the development of the derivative markets. It has lost its earlier attraction for hedging.

As the largest buyer of this metal in the world, we should play an active role in the international markets and leverage our position to shape policies pertaining to gold. Any large buyer of a commodity, say oil or coffee or zinc or maize wants to and does have a say in the accelerated disposal of that commodity in the world market. What does India do? Nothing, since our government is not concerned about the welfare of the people of India, but only about some ideological shibboleths.

Why is that so? It is because there is a substantial disconnect between the government and the middle class in our country. Planners and policy makers are either Socialists or globalizing Metropolitan Elites who are also mostly rootless wonders. Socialist experts feel that the middle class or petite bourgeoisie are naive to invest in unproductive assets instead of joining the working class in the struggle to get social security for all. Even the proletariat have opted to buy gold since our government, no matter of which shade or hue, cannot be relied upon to provide any security at old age and to be truthful.

Globalizing Metropolitan Elites feel that the middle class is foolish in investing in gold since 'experts like them' have defined it to be unproductive. They are concerned about reforming the government pension system, which is under severe strain, since both Central and state governments are broke. Their prime objective is to increase the pensions of the executives of India Inc., with more tax concessions!

Under such a situation, the most entrepreneurial and hard-working, self-employed groups of the Uninc. sector in India are facing a huge challenge to protect their future. Their position is that of a nut caught in the nutcracker with the Socialists and Globalizers acting as the two arms. It is necessary for the self-employed to mount pressure on the government to understand the role of gold. It is not the Indian woman who is naive or foolish, but the government, which is insensitive and ignorant to the emerging old age security crisis. Actually Indian women are generally smarter and frugal than the Government in terms of financial planning and budgeting.

In the context of 'Digital Cash' becoming more active, the number of transactions may increase to trillions and the number of trans-border entities issuing them will also increase. This would be more so with increased outsourcing activities. Since 'Digi-Cash' does not have any sovereign guarantee, the role of gold as a medium of exchange and as an underlying standard will increase. As the monetary transactions in the net-based world increase, the concern for the underlying lack of 'Sovereign Guarantee' should be highlighted. In the context of a possible decline of the US Dollar, this may not be very difficult to visualize. Along with this, a campaign should be launched by India to confer the status of Standard of Security on gold [if not as an exchange] and this may enormously help the billions of self-employed in India who own this asset and who have to take care of themselves in the coming decades.

CHAPTER 16

Demography is Destiny

The ageing population in developed countries, coupled with the proclivity of workers there to work for fewer hours is triggering off a boom in outsourcing. The elderly population is also slowly increasing in our context. What implications will this outsourcing boom have for cultural and employment trends in India?

It is often said that demography is destiny. There has been a debate about demographic trends in India as revealed by the 2001 and 2011 census. Equally interesting developments are taking place in the demography of developed countries, which will have far reaching implications for us, especially for the proprietorship and partnership [P & P] sector and households.

The Hexagon and the Pyramid

The age bomb is ticking in the West. It will significantly

affect their 'white collar work force'. In the next few decades, there is going to be a huge explosion in out sourcing or off-shore work, since onshore work creates what is politely called 'social costs' — which means brown sweat in the midst of white scent. And that is not very desirable.

Let us look at the possible demographic profile of Europe and US in the next few decades as taken from UN population projections. The average total fertility rates in the year 2000 in developed countries was 1.57 and in developing countries, it was 3.05. The rate for Europe is 1.4 and for Japan is 1.3. USA is just 2.1, India 3.1 and China 1.72. It is felt that a rate of 2.1 is an appropriate replacement rate, taking into account some amount of infant mortality. Over the next decade, the situation could worsen. Estimates suggest that in the next 50 years, USA will grow by 100 million in terms of population numbers and Europe will be less by 100 million. For instance, in another forty years, the German population would decrease by nearly 30%. One third of the population will be more than 65 and they will outnumber children by two to one. Italy's rate is 1.2, and in that Catholic country in another forty years, more than 40% of the population will be above 65 years of age. In Russia, two out of three pregnancies are terminated before birth and Russian women average 2.5 to four abortions each and the death rate is 70% more than the birth rate. Putin warns that in 15 years there will be 22 million less Russians, that is, a seventh of its current population. Japan is already facing the age crisis.

In addition, the Whites in England do not have enough children, with London readying itself for a non-white majority in a decade. One could go on in this vein.

The ageing of the developed countries coupled with a desire of the labour class, including white-collar workers, to work for lesser hours, is creating a catastrophe.

The following diagram [Exhibit 1] is a diagrammatic representation of the age structure — that is, number of people in different age groups. The horizontal axis shows different age groups and vertical axis shows percentage of people in those age groups.

Exhibit 1
Developed Countries

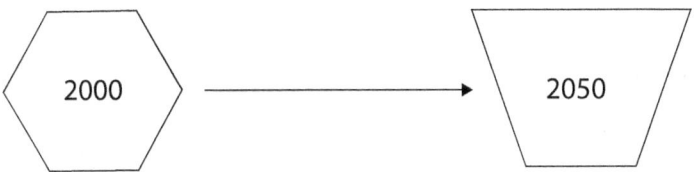

The developed countries with a hexagonal age structure are slowly moving into trapezoid or inverted pyramid-shaped structures.

Developing Countries

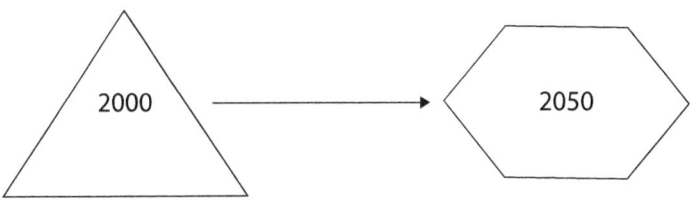

In the case of developing countries, they will move from a pyramid age structure to perhaps the hexagonal structure.

This is the nature of the crisis. There will be an acute scarcity of labour in the developed world, and whatever is available will come at a steep price. The elderly will also demand better protection, and the State will spend all its money to become the new caring 'parent' (or, 'offspring') for these old people. Since societal norms [in terms of caring for the elderly by offspring etc.] do not exist anymore, the aged are the responsibility of the State and this implies more taxes and a lesser amount available for other activities of the State. Hence, there is a massive crisis in Social Security funds in Europe and the US.

It is the Pool and not the Rate

It is not only an issue of low wages; it is the pool of talent which is available in a country like India. The role of this demographic pattern has some interesting results [Exhibit 2]. Again, there are several layers of this pool and so, over pricing worries do not exist. Indian youngsters in this IT world are enthusiastic and willing to put in 70 to 80 hours including on Saturdays and Sundays. That is a story which is yet to be written. The story of sacrifice, the story of work culture, and simply, the 'enthu' to get things done.

Exhibit 2

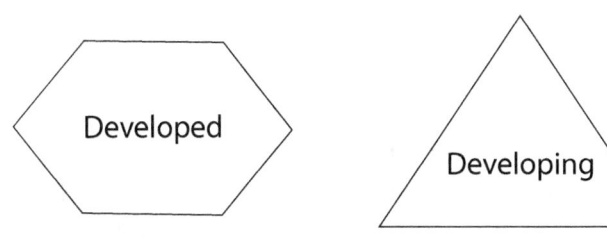

Wealth:60 per cent of the World's GDP	Labour Force: 80 per cent of world's work force
Controlled by mature adults	Dominated by young adults
Looking for higher returns	Willing To work for low pay

Another issue is related to the increasing content of the 'outsourceable' portion in many activities. In service sectors like banking it is more than 60%, including software/voice/ audio, etc. In some manufacturing activities, the software content is more than 30%. This would induce large firms to go in for more and more outsourcing.

Already we find that the remittances by the labour of India at more than 70 billion USD is higher than the net private capital flows from outside at 26 billion USD. This is primarily the flow, from blue collar workers from the Middle East, USA and Europe, etc., to India. This will undergo an interesting shift, since, by the process of outsourcing, labour will not move, only work will move. It could be medical transcription, record keeping for social security, call centres, back office work for banks, insurance companies, mutual funds, pension funds or maintenance of IT infrastructure — the possibilities are infinite. Most human endeavors can be off shored. As of now, only 'brown collar' work, like garbage removal, road cleaning or grape picking cannot be moved off shore.

Impact on local Employment Needs

Offshore centres are slowly shifting to smaller towns since not only does that bring down wages, they also get the additional benefit of accessing a larger pool of youngsters to replenish this ever depleting pool which is characterized by a very high attrition rate. The Uninc. sector will be tremendously impacted in the coming decades because of this tectonic shift taking place in the employment scenario of young persons. Regular manufacturing companies in the domestic sector are already finding it difficult to get capable youngsters because they flock to the IT and ITES sectors in the thousands. It will substantially increase the cost of domestic labour in these activities to 'dollar' levels. Also, consider the impact on infrastructure. There is a tremendous need for Indian society to calibrate this explosion in the coming decades.

The Aged Empire will Act

As of mid-2013 Spain's jobless rate for people ages 16 to 24 is approaching 50% Greece's is 48% and Portugal's and Italy's, 30%. For Britain, the rate is 22.3%, the highest since such data began being collected in 1992. (The comparable rate for Americans is 18%.) Most of them do not have skills.

Now, the issue is the reaction of the 'Aged Empire' to these developments. Hence, this would make nation states in the West unhappy with the global corporations as already seen in the Kerry campaign (in 2004) and legislation to 'control' outsourcing in many states of USA. In the year 2011, USA imported USD 803 billion more than they exported [USD 2283 billion of import against USD 1480 of export]. The share of China in some segments of the US markets [like toys, sports goods, camping gear, household items, etc.] is more than 60%.

So, the process of globalization has created a severe twist in the Western tail. And when there is a twist in the tail of a monkey, it becomes active and may even become angry! This gives rise to the following possibilities. One possibility is to encourage a large inflow of such skilled professionals into these countries from India, but the events following 9/11 are proving that it is not going to be a solution that either USA or Europe would adopt. Hence, there would be lot of noise about 'Security Issues' in outsourcing and there may be a demand that Indian labour be screened by US Security before they are employed by BPOs. This would create a pool of RNIs [Resident Non-Indians] who live in India but hold US green cards of the 'Security Cleared Category'. One need not be surprised if in a few years there is a huge pool of young men and women who are 'US Security Cleared' [USC] but living in India. This will create a large 'Sub-Divide' within the Digital Divide.

Angry Farmers

Large tracts of land are needed to create these off shore centres and already farmers in the outskirts of Bangalore have held agitations for a fair price for their land. There is the possibility that their land be treated as an equity investment and long term benefits provided to them in the form of share in profits. Since most farmers do not possess interchangeable skills to be fruitfully employed elsewhere, social cohesion will be established. The time has come for agencies like NASSCOM to ponder over these issues.

Will it be on our terms?

The other issue is regarding the culture, language, eating habits, sexual attitudes and family values of this mass of men and women. Already there are several reports to suggest that fast food is the norm and casual attitude to sex and family is seeping into the system of these youngsters. The accent is modified to suit the requirements of the old ladies of Hull in England or Peoria in USA and the work timings of off-shore centres are such that they suit doctors in New York or advocates in Amsterdam! Plus, the billion dollars earned are again kept in treasury bills of the US and European governments. That is work hard to be a lender to the master.

Of course, there are arguments about India moving up the value chain in all these cyber activities. That could take place, but in this business where 'knowledge' is the capital, it is always easy for large corporations to buy people at an attractive rate. Hence, our efforts may not bear fruit in the 'traditional' sense. Remember even Hotmail was bought up in the end. Civil society needs to debate these issues and calibrate change since Indian society has always dealt with challenges in a spirit of tolerance and evolution and sometimes lost out. Hence we need to be proactive and let the world stew in its old age juice! For at least forty years the global cycle is ours, simply because no one else, including China, has the numbers, the language proficiency and the skills. And of course the other neighbour, Pakistan is more known for the export of the other IT, namely International Terrorism!

Let the holiday, attitude, language, manners, culture and work issues be dictated by us, namely the global back office. Thomas Babington Macaulay in his now infamous 'Minutes' talks of creating men with Indian Bodies and British Souls, but in the emerging scenario, unless we are alert and active, we may end up with men with no soul and only obese Western bodies built up through the consumption of untimely fast food.

CHAPTER 17

Reverse Mortgage as Old Age Security

The government must not only recognize the need for taxing the self-employed but also pay attention to the healthcare and old age needs of this sector. It should also provide some funds for this segment to be meaningfully utilized in social security schemes. Given the total absence of old age annuities in the unorganized sector, the versatile yellow metal should be used for the purpose of structuring reverse mortgages which can translate into annuities for this sector.

Just before the Budget, the Finance Minister is inundated with hundreds of tax-related suggestions. It is not that all of these — even the most legitimate ones — are accepted. A very major lacuna that still exists, if we look at the structure of taxes meant for different categories, is that the self-employed do not have Medicare or pension facilities, particularly in old age which is when they need them the most. It is high time that we re-look at the income tax aspects of the self-employed, modify income tax and introduce innovative instruments to make their surplus available to the community at large.

There has been an important development in the savings rate of our economy, which has not been adequately appreciated by the business media and economists. The self-employed category has contributed significantly to the economy through its savings, particularly in the context of the low interest rate regime in the last few years.

We have referred to the growth in the savings rate from 8% in the sixties to more than 32% now. We have also established that the single largest contributor to our savings is the household sector. Proprietorship & partnership firms [P & P Sector], namely the entire self-employed category are treated as households in our savings data. In other words, when we talk of households, we need to remember that it contains both pure consuming or wage earning households as well as mixed households having production activities. Hence, whenever household savings are mentioned, we need to be alert to the fact that it also contains P & P firms performing manufacturing and service activities.

Gross Domestic Product and Savings

Gross Domestic Product (GDP) at factor cost at constant (2004-05) prices in 2011-12 is estimated at Rs. 52,43,582 crore as against Rs. 49,37,006 crore in 2010-11, registering a growth of 6.2% during the year as against the growth rate of 9.3% during the previous year [Central Statistical Organisation — NAS 2013]. At current prices, GDP in 2011-12 is estimated at Rs. 83,53,495 crore as against Rs. 72,66,966 crore in 2010-11, showing an increase of 15% during the year. The growth rate of 6.4% at the constant prices in the GDP during 2011-12 has been achieved due to lower growth in agriculture (3.65%), trade, hotels & restaurants (6.2%), financing, insurance, real estate & business services (11.7%).

Gross Domestic Saving (GDS) at current prices in 2011-12 is estimated at Rs. 2765290 crore as against Rs. 2651934 crore in 2010-11, constituting 30% of GDP at market prices as against 34% in the previous year. The rise in GDS compared to the nineties has been contributed to by all sectors. In respect of the household sector, the saving in the form of financial and physical assets has gone up from Rs. 1832901 crore [69% of the National Savings] in 2010-11 to Rs. 2300720 crore [72% of the National Savings] in 2011-12. As we have seen in Table 5.1, a substantial part of the savings of the household goes to the banking sector.

Table — 17. 1 Category wise number of Income tax assesses in India

Category	2008-09	2009-10	2010-11
Company	327,674	367,884	496,872
Individual	30,101,260	31,384,084	31,035,394

Category	2008-09	2009-10	2010-11
HUF	768,845	806,236	761,911
Firm	1,310,849	1,354,330	1,229,722
Trusts	71,145	76,898	119,378
Others	70,854	95,994	95,847
Total	32,650,627	34,085,426	33,739,124

Source: Indiastat.com

Table — 17. 2 Tax collected under Corporate Income tax and Personal Income Tax in India (In Rs. Crore)

Year	Corporate Income Tax	Personal Income Tax
2008-09	213,395	61,433*
2009-10	244,725	133,338
2010-11	298,688	148,247
2011-12	323,224	171,575

Note: * Figure are April to October # Provisional

Table 17.1 depicts the different category of income tax assesses in India. We find during 2010-11, there were 3.1 crore individual assesses. Table 17.2 provides the information that personal income tax collections have gone up from around Rs. 62000 crores to Rs. 171575 crores from 2008-09 to 2011-12.

We have data for 1998-99 and 1999-2000 about different sections of tax payers from All India Income Tax Statistics which for reasons best known to the finance ministry has been discontinued now.

We find that nearly 45% of the tax burden falls on the

self-employed, consisting of P& P segments including non-salary groups. Actually, the burden is much more now for these groups since a substantial portion of service tax is also borne by them. The self-employed are active in (1) Unorganized manufacturing activities (2) Construction (3) Wholesale trade and retail trade (4) Hotels and restaurants (5) Non-railway transport (6) Real estate, (7) Ownership of dwellings and Business services, and (8) Other services. In these activities, the share of the self-employed or non-corporate sector varies from 50% to 80% and on a weighted basis it is around 70%.

Table — 17. 3 Share of Self-employed in GDP and Income Tax [Rs. Crore]

Column	Category	1993-1994	1998-1999
1	GDP	781,345	1598,127
2	Share of Self Employed in GDP	237,018	473,152
3	Income Tax total	17,192	18,360
4	Income tax of Self employed	7,844	8,244
5	3 to 1	2.2%	1.2%
6	4 to 2	3.3%	1.7%
7	2 to 1	30%	30%
8	4 to 3	46%	45%

Source: Computed by author from data of AIITS & NAS various issue

We have provided in Table — 17.3 the share of the self-employed groups in Gross Domestic Product and also in taxes, and find that they pay significantly higher taxes in relation to their share in the income. We find that the self-employed sector accounts for 30% of the share in GDP but has more than 45% of the share in income tax. Their share of income tax to their GDP is 3.3% in the earlier period of 1993-94 [100 basis points more] compared to 2.2% for all other categories of taxpayers. In the latter period of 1998-1999, it is still higher by 50 basis points.

But, we know that substantial numbers of self-employed professionals like doctors, advocates, architects etc., are not adequately covered by income tax. It is impossible under the existing structure to enhance the coverage and any attempt will only lead to larger corruption. The idea should be to make available some share of the surplus of these groups to society at large. At the same time, the self-employed have a grouse that they neither have medical insurance nor any pension schemes to fall back upon in old age.

Pension Coverage

Government employees are covered by defined benefit, non-contributory, commutable, inflation indexed, pension plans. They also have family pension benefits. After fifteen years of retirement, the commuted portion is reverted to the retiree in computing pensions. Other than that, they have gratuity, general provident fund, leave encashment, leave travel facilities, etc. **The government has introduced a contributory pension plan for those who joined service after January 2004.**

Those who are employed in the organized sector also have the benefit of EPF or other pension programmes. In the case of the self-employed, they need to take care of themselves during their old age. This is particularly problematic in the context of the decline in the joint family system and the low interest rate regime. Unfortunately, even contribution to a pension scheme by a partner is not recognized as allowable expense of a firm, unlike executive benefits provided by a company in this regard.

One possibility will be to encourage the self-employed to go in for pension products offered by the Life Insurance Corporation of India (LIC) or under National Pension System [NPS] of Pension Fund Regulatory and Development Authority of India, and increase the threshold limit to Rs. 500,000 and tax them at the time of maturity in the form of tax deducted at source (TDS) but at a low rate like 10%. This would be easier, operationally, than trying to tax the estimated current income. This would also provide social security to large groups of self-employed people. Similarly, the contribution made by the self-employed to the construction and maintenance of old age homes can be exempt from taxes to the extent of say Rs. 1 lakh per annum. This will help in directly using their surplus for the cause of the socially handicapped. The old age homes can offer discounts or free service to the current donors when they grow old. This will increase the pool of facilities available for elderly people.

Medical Insurance Benefits

In the case of government and organized sector employees, we find that health care facilities are available or reimbursements are made. In the case of the self-employed, they need to take care of their requirements out of current income and savings. This is all the more difficult during old age, given the fact that there is very little support from the joint family system. Here again, the government can think of allowing large health care expenses and premiums exemptions up to Rs. 1 lakh for tax purposes. The contributions/donations made by the self-employed to clinics and hospitals can be exempt, up to, say, Rs.1 lakh. This will increase the availability of funds in the healthcare sector. Clinics and hospitals could evolve schemes to offer discounts/free treatments to such donors in future.

Incidentally, a similar provision can be made for contributions to the free meal schemes of temples or of educational institutions.

Enlarging Social Benefit

It is important for the government to recognize the limitations of taxing the self-employed in a country like India where issues of corruption abound. It is imperative that the State recognizes that community efforts and social surplus are desirable goals. In other words, taxation is not the only instrumentality to benefit society at large or achieve the highest social goals. We need to find innovative ways to facilitate social security and healthcare needs of the self-employed, particularly in their old age, and at the same time achieve desirable social goals of extracting some surplus from the well-off segments of the self-employed. We require old age homes, clinics and hospitals, and good schools, and hence, efforts are required to enhance the development of this infrastructure using the surplus of the self-employed rather than using only the instrumentality of income tax.

Ageing India

Three important aspects of our emerging demographic profile require a close look and appraisal. One is that the longevity of people, particularly those who come from the middle class, is increasing. The joint family system is on the decline and there is no universally applicable social security system. Combined with this is the issue of changing lifestyles of the elderly in terms of travel, entertainment etc. which are expensive. The number of elderly people is increasing and expected to reach around 11 of the population within the next eight years.

Table — 17.4 projects the elderly population profile in the coming decade. It shows that the current level (nearly 8%) of the population is expected to move up to constitute 12.5% of the population in another fifteen years. In terms of actual numbers it runs to more than 100 million in the present situation itself.

Table — 17. 4 Percentage distribution of Projected Population by Age and Sex (1996-2026)

Age-Group	1996	2001	2006	2011	2016	2021	2026
60-69	4.2	4.3	4.5	5.0	5.4	6.3	7.3
70-79	1.8	2.1	2.3	2.4	2.8	3.2	3.8
80+	0.8	0.6	0.7	0.8	1.0	1.2	1.4
Total of 60+	6.8	7.0	7.5	8.2	9.2	10.7	12.5

Source: Population Projections for India and States 1996-2026, Registrar General, Ministry of Home Affairs, Govt. of India. India Stat.com

The ability of the State to provide any generalized social security is non-existent since it is not in a position to meet the pension obligation of its own employees. The savings of most of the middle class is inadequate to provide for their old age, particularly in the case of widows after the death of their husbands.

In such a context, it is imperative that we think of innovative solutions taking into account our own ethos and cultural uniqueness. We find that housing and gold are two major assets, which are owned by the middle class. Even the poor own gold at least in small quantities, in the form of ornaments.

Gold is a Large Saving Instrument

India has been one of the largest buyers of gold in the world markets from ancient times. The desire for gold arises from the point of view of possessing attractive jewellery as well as security in times of difficulties. Also, gold is divisible, unlike real estate. It is also highly liquid.

It is easy to bequeath and less cumbersome in terms of transferability.

We have discussed earlier about the demand for gold in the last few years by the Indian households and know that around 30% of the global demand is from India.

However, the scenario is slowly changing. Nowadays, we find that the younger generation is not too inclined towards gold ornaments. Whatever is given or acquired is stowed away in bank lockers in the case of a substantial number of middle class families. If the son or daughter migrates abroad, the parents actually pay rent on an annual basis to keep the gold in bank lockers. Also there is increasing demand for gold coins and bars from younger generation rather than Jewelry.

Given the demographic shift and social security requirements during old age and the stock of gold ornaments, we can think of using Reverse Mortgage instruments to utilize gold and provide pension annuities to individuals and survivors.

Reverse Mortgage for House Owners

To a typical house owner, a mortgage looks like the opposite of a bond. A future homeowner will usually sell a home mortgage to generate immediate cash to pay for a home, obliging him to make periodic payments to the mortgage holder. The standard mortgage is structured so that equal monthly payments are made throughout the term. This is in contrast to most bonds, which have a final payment, equal to the face value at maturity. Most standard mortgages allow for early repayment of the balance. Mortgages are not usually thought of as securities, since they are written as contracts between two parties, for example a homeowner and a home finance bank. However, mortgages are typically 'bundled' into large packages and traded among financial institutions. These mortgage–backed securities are quite liquid.

In the US, **Reverse Annuity Mortgages** are gaining popularity among elderly homeowners. In the US, a Reverse Annuity Mortgage typically involves an elderly person entering into an agreement with a financial institution, such as a bank. The individual receives a lifetime, fixed monthly income in return for phased surrender of the ownership of, say, his home, which is substantially debt free. The financial institution gains title to the property, at the owner's death, which it can sell for a profit. Recently, an interesting variant has emerged. The homeowner obtains a loan on the security of his or her home. A portion or all of the loan proceeds is used to purchase an immediate life annuity. When the elderly person's home is sold because of death or otherwise, the loan is repaid from the sale proceeds and the individual would have enjoyed a lifetime income from the annuity in the interim. The heirs of the elderly may decide to pay back the debt and keep ownership of the house, if they so decide.

In other words, a Reverse Mortgage effectively allows a person to annuitise his house. He decides to receive a fixed monthly payment for the rest of his life. It is tax-free because it comes in the form of a loan. It falls due upon the death of the surviving spouse and is settled with the sale of the property. During the time of the mortgage, the house is owned and used by the person. The monthly payment received is computed, using standard annuity methods that take into account the age of the person and life expectancy. In addition, the current and projected future value of the property and the amount of equity on the house a person wishes to assign to the loan company are considered.

For example, a person may choose to take the loan [annuities] against only 50% of the equity stake in his house. This would obviously cause a reduction in the size of the monthly cheque he receives. A person may want to maintain some equity in his property, so that he can bequeath a portion of it to his heirs. If property prices decline after one takes out the loan, it will not affect the remainder of the estate. Under such circumstances, the lending company bears the loss. This is similar to the traditional annuity in which the insurance company bears the loss of continuing annuity payments in the event of the person living beyond the 'actuarially' estimated lifetime.

A loan mortgage is a non-recourse loan. This means that there is no personal liability to the person or his heirs. No matter what, the lender can only look to the property for repayment. Repayment is due after all homeowners permanently vacate the home [that is, they either die, sell, or permanently move out]. That payment comes out of the equity in the home, or by other means agreed upon.

If there is excess equity, then it goes to the person or the heir. Typically, the property is sold and the loan is repaid. Or if the heir so wishes, he can repay the loan and keep the property. The money received can be used by the person to pay off debts, deal with financial emergencies, travel, increase monthly income, pay for home improvements, help children or grand-children or establish a cash reserve for future emergencies. It is available for those who are above 62 years in the US context, particularly for being eligible for Housing and Urban Development [HUD] Reverse Mortgage schemes.

Using Gold for Reverse Mortgage

We can introduce such a scheme using gold ornaments as the underlying asset and this can be offered by the mutual funds, banks, proposed pension fund providers and life insurance companies.

It can be used not only as an annuity for pension purposes; it can even be used for credit delivery purposes if appropriate mechanisms/regulations and instruments are evolved. It would go a long way in enhancing the usage of gold stock available with households in our country. It would also facilitate the credit requirements of proprietorship and partnership firms and also help in providing pension annuities to the self-employed, which are not covered by any retirement benefit schemes.

Several legal and other issues should be sorted out before introducing reverse mortgage on gold ornaments. There will be common turf issues. For instance, life insurance companies may claim the domain on the plea that since the lenders need to pay installments over the lifetime of the property owner, the transaction is governed by the Insurance Act. But if the transaction is viewed as an investment activity, since the acquisition price is paid in several installments over the life time of the property owner, then any financial institution can deal in Reverse Mortgage.

Banks, mutual funds, life insurance companies and pension funds should compete on a level playing field in the Reverse Mortgage market. Institutions belonging to the Non-Banking Financial Sector [NBFS] are also suitable for entering such Reverse Mortgage deals since they have market knowledge, particularly regarding households and their gold holdings. NBFS monitoring mechanisms are praiseworthy as seen from their expertise in transport vehicle and consumer goods lending markets. They would be able to assay the gold and also assess the issues of ownership and the equity component.

But, before anything concrete can happen, many in-depth studies have to be undertaken by the Reserve Bank of India (RBI) and the Pension Fund Regulatory and Development Authority [PFDRA] before the introduction of the Reverse Mortgage scheme using Gold to understand the nature of amendments needed in existing laws like the Public Property Act, Income Tax Act, Insurance Act, Stamp Duty and Registration Act, Money Lenders Act, etc. Centre-state co-operation is required in bringing in the changes. It is appropriate that the Ministry of Finance takes up this important and innovative task as a major test case in enhancing retirement benefits for the self-employed without spending from the exchequer and at the same time bring the stock of gold available with households into productive usage.

CHAPTER 18

Savings or Consumption Driven Society

We need to revert to our traditional virtues of thrift and savings before we create an impression of blindly aping the Western consumerist cult.

As stated earlier, our savings rate in the sixties used to be around 8% to 10% and the theory of the vicious cycle of poverty, namely, a low savings rate leading to low investment and hence low incomes, which, in turn, gave rise to a low savings rate, etc., was popularised using India as an example. In a sense, that theory suggested that countries like India are doomed to failure due to the low savings rate. From the eighties, our savings rate has shown a significant increase and it was around 20% to 24% throughout the nineties. Recent statistics suggest that it is of the order of 32% of our national income. More than 70% of our National Savings is due to household savings.

As stated earlier, partnership & proprietorship firms [the P & P sector] are treated as households in our savings data.

The savings rate in the developed economies, particularly in Europe and USA, has declined significantly in the last decade. Also, the household savings as a percentage of household disposable income has declined drastically, and this has caused alarm bells to ring among economists who used to argue for consumption driven growth.

Table — 18.1 gives the household savings rate as a percentage of disposable household income for different developed countries as provided by OECD. We find from Table — 18.1 that the household savings have significantly declined in the case of most of the developed countries, particularly in the nineties. It is negative in the case of Denmark [that is, they are dis-savers] and is around 4% in the USA.

This has come about due to the emergence of the consumption driven economy propagated by the experts in the eighties and nineties. It was felt that the consumption of households will create enough demand-pull, which in turn would generate productive activities, and the important thing to monitor is the retail off take in the departmental stores. Actually, monitoring retail sales has become the biggest obsession among economists, in many Western countries. It has become a credit card driven economy, with each household accumulating goods in their basements. What has happened in the process is that most middle class American households have a large retail shop inside their home. The interest on loans was kept low so that borrowing led consumption could be accelerated. Of course, countries like India, China and many other East Asian and Arab countries are financing the US economy by investing in their treasury bills for rates lower than 4%. It has become an economic axiom that US consumption is the key to global growth.

Table — 18. 1 Household Saving Rate

Country	1995	2000	2005	2010	2011	2012
Australia	5.3	1.8	1.9	8.9	9.9	8.9
Canada	9.3	4.4	1.7	4.8	3.5	3.5
Denmark	0.2	-4.0	-4.2	-1.0	-0.6	-0.6
Germany	11.2	9.4	10.7	10.9	10.4	10.1
Japan	12.2	7.3	1.4	2.1	2.9	1.9
Korea	18.5	9.3	7.2	4.3	3.1	2.8
USA	5.2	2.9	1.5	5.1	4.2	3.7
France	15.7	14.3	14.8	15.9	16.2	16.2
UK	9.4	4.2	2.8	6.6	6.0	5.3

Note: Net saving as a percentage of disposable household income. In the case of the UK it is gross saving.

Source: Household savings — OECD fact book. [http://www.oecd.org/dataoecd/5/48/2483858.xls]

The lack of savings by households has an impact not only on the current situation but also on distribution of wealth over time. We can use a thumb rule to conclude that whenever the savings rate of a society is less than 10% of its disposable income [with stable taxation and inflation] then the society is bound to get into difficulties. Many households begin to rely more and more on social security and this liability, in some countries, is either not funded, or, inadequately funded. This, in turn creates substantial issues of solvency of the government and the ability of the government to take care of the old age security of its citizens.

This, coupled with the declining population growth rate and longevity of the current generation, creates an explosive situation of a bankrupt state exchequer and lower accretion to the social security fund.

The decline, and in many cases, the extinction of the joint family system in these countries adds to the agony of the elderly in terms of their old age security and health and emotional care. The increasing number of children born out of wedlock to younger girls and single mothers creates additional dependency numbers for the State. The consumption driven society turns out to be a 'Responsibility Denial' society. A couple of years ago, hundreds of aged people died in France from the heat due to lack of care by their family and the State. Younger family members had all gone on vacation in the summer leaving the old to the vagaries of nature. And the State is blamed for not taking care of the old! The slogan of 'Shop till you drop' is slowly changing to 'Shop and get dropped'. Consumers are feted and savers are frowned upon. But the wheel is slowly but surely turning. Suddenly the good old virtues of saving and thrift are becoming the fashion from Alberta to Auckland. The limits to consumption led growth have at last dawned upon people. On a global scale, the consumption led growth of some countries like the USA is supported by saver countries in the developing world. But how long can these anomalies continue?

Table — 18.2 shows the savings of the different sectors of our economy, namely, the government, private corporate sector and households for the different decades starting from the fifties. We find that the savings rate of our economy has increased four times from the fifties to 2010-11, from around 9% to around 34%. This phenomenal increase in savings has been achieved through the efforts of the household sector, which constitute nearly 90% of the National Savings in the earlier periods. This savings rate of the households is without considering investment in gold by households, since our government economists consider that as consumption. Actually, purchase of gold is an insurance and a pension product for the lower classes, and if we include that, our savings rate will be higher by another 2%.

In our context, partnership and proprietorship enterprises involved in business are also included as households. If we consider only the disposable income of households, then the savings rate as a percentage of that will be more than 40%. We are becoming a saving society, which is the main driver of our economy. The dependence on Foreign Direct Investment (FDI) and Foreign Institutional Investors (FIIs) is significantly lower because we are a saving society. The growth in our economy is not driven by FDI/FII but by our own savings.

Table — 18. 2 Savings Rate and Contributions by Different Sectors [%]

Willing To work for low pay	1950-51	1990-91	2000-01	2004-05	2010-11	2011-12
GDS [as of % GDP]	8.9	22.9	23.8	32.4	34.0	30.8
Govt.	1.8	1.8	-1.3	2.3	2.6	1.3
Pvt. Corporate	0.9	2.6	3.7	6.6	7.9	7.2
Household	6.2	18.5	21.4	23.6	23.5	22.3
HS to GDS	69	84	92	73	69	71

Note: HS: Household Savings GDS: Gross Domestic Savings, GDP: Gross Domestic Product, GDP is at current Market prices.

Source: Table 1.5, ppS-8, Economic Survey 2011-12, Ministry of Finance, Government of India

It is at this juncture that we find experts and corporates in India suggesting that the middle class should consume more. Shopping is made a virtue and life style. Indian women are encouraged to go out and buy and buy till their hands bleed. The hidden persuaders [kings of advertising] are in the open. Plastic credit cards are offered for the asking [many times without even asking!] and consumption is now the modern mantra. What we may not realize is that today's mantra 'Consume or perish' will soon become 'Consume and perish'! The government is discouraging savings by keeping many borrowing rates low and removing tax breaks for saving.

But, the Indian middle class needs to save much more than citizens of any other country in the world. We do not have universal medical care, and hence, during old age, the cost of health care has to be borne by the middle class.

We do not have universal social security. Out of more than 400 million of the work force in our country, nearly 20 million government employees [Central plus state and local governments] and around 40 million private employees [who are covered by the Employees' Provident Funds [EPF] Schemes] have only retirement benefits.

A large number of the middle class and poorer segments are not covered by any social security schemes. Also education is a major reason for savings by households. Nursery to high school education is getting expensive and for school education, banks do not provide loans. For college education, banks do give loans. Good education for their children is an obsession among women in India. As it is light heartedly mentioned women would like their children to do better than their husbands. They get actively involved in choosing and monitoring the progress of their children. Expenses on education at school level makes more demand on savings.

The fourth point is about *samskaras* or what are known as family obligations to birth/marriage/death etc. of relatives and expenses thereon. Actually poorer segments spend more on these. **So old age security, old age health needs, school education of children, *samskaras* are the four major reasons for saving by households.** None of these is likely to change in the near future and so savings rate will continue to be high. Table — 18.3 provides the age composition of the elderly as estimated by the Census office for different decades. As can be seen, nearly 7% of the population is above 60 years of age as of 2001 census.

Table — 18. 3 Number and Proportion of Elderly in different Age Groups

Age	Number (Mn)					% Of elderly				
	1961	1971	1981	1991	2001	1961	1971	1981	1991	2001
60+	24.7	32.7	43.2	56.7	79.36	5.63	5.97	6.49	6.76	7.71
70+	8.6	11.3	15.5	21.1	32.01	1.96	2.07	2.33	2.51	3.11
80+	2.5	3.2	4.1	6.4	10.76	0.57	0.58	0.62	0.76	1.04
90+	0.5	0.7	0.7	1.2	2.73	0.12	0.13	0.11	0.15	0.27
100+	0.1	0.1	0.1	0.1	—	0.02	0.02	0.02	0.02	—

Source: Census India — Various Issues: Note: 90+ in 2001 include age group 100+.

Table — 18.4 outlines the projections given by India's Census Division. It says that the population above 60 years is around 7.5% by 2006 reaching 9% by 2016 and 12.5% by 2026. This indicates that a substantial portion of the elderly need to be taken care of.

Table — 18. 4 Percentage distribution of Projected Population by Age and Sex (1996-2026)

Age-Group	1996	2001	2006	2011	2016	2021	2026
60-69	4.2	4.3	4.5	5.0	5.4	6.3	7.3
70-79	1.8	2.1	2.3	2.4	2.8	3.2	3.8
80+	0.8	0.6	0.7	0.8	1.0	1.2	1.4
Total of 60+	6.8	7.0	7.5	8.2	9.2	10.7	12.5

Source: Population Projections for India and States 1996-2026, Registrar General, Ministry of Home Affairs, Govt. of India. India Stat.com

As per Census-2011, we find that there was around 405 million-strong total workforce consisting of 311 million rural and 92 million urban workers.

The social security coverage of most of the agricultural and non-industrial workers is inadequate. This is one area where the policy planners and society need to focus on rather than on consumerism. Only their savings can protect them. Western economics starts with the premise that "Wants are unlimited and resources are limited". Our civilization's ethos is based on 'limited wants' in the context of conserving for the future and conserving nature. It has the cross-sectional advantage of nurturing nature and inter-temporal benefit of taking care of the elderly and planning for social security in old age. The greed-based market economy may not offer solutions to the problems of the multitude if we focus only on a consumption-driven society. Fear-based totalitarian systems like communism have also failed. We need to evolve a third way which is environment friendly and take into account intergenerational equity not by the fiat of the State but by the suasion of social norms. It is perhaps time to move away from consumption-driven economy to a savings-nurturing society. Otherwise, we will prove that the only lesson we learnt from the economic history of the plastic card addicted debt ridden Western society is our refusal to learn any lessons at all.

Stock Markets: Role in our Economy

Chapter 19	Stock Markets: Are they Barometers?
Chapter 20	Indian Financial Markets — *A cul de sac*

Stock Markets: Are they Barometers?

There are a number of hyperbolic myths and incorrect assumptions surrounding the Indian stock markets. This has led to the stock markets being unjustifiably regarded as the barometer of our economy.

January and February are those months of the year when pre-Budget suggestions keep flowing into the Finance Minister's office. These suggestions inevitably relate to reforms or modification of Budget reforms. While the suggestions are diverse, many of them are aimed at boosting the stock market, and through that, the economy. But what is really strange is that many assume that the stock markets represent the state of the economy.

For most experts on the Indian Economy, what applies to the New York Stock Exchange [NYSE] or Chicago Board of Trade [CBOT] in relation to the US economy automatically applies to our economy in relation to our stock markets. It would be simply an amusing or a laughable matter, but for the fact that Finance Ministry mandarins are also caught in this web of confusion.

That is the main issue with this distorted obsession with the markets, and it is based on several factually incorrect assumptions about the role of the markets.

Stock Markets: Whom do they represent?

Let us look at some of the assumptions regarding our market and check how true they really are.

Proposition 1: The listed corporate sector is critical to the economy and has a dominant role in it.

The National Accounts Statistics (NAS) bifurcates sectors into organised and unorganised. All things labelled 'unorganised' are non-corporate organisations even while a large part of what is called organised comprises proprietorship and partnership firms. The corporate sector is a small part of what is called organised.

As stated previously, in fact, it is the non-corporate sector, comprising partnership and proprietorship firms, which has the largest share in our national income (nearly 45%), followed by agriculture (17%) and government (20%). Incidentally, in activities like trade (wholesale and retail), transport (other than railways), construction, and hotels and restaurants, the share of the non-corporate sector is more than 70%. [See Table — 19.1]

Table — 19. 1 Share of Non-Corporate sector in the Economy

Category	1980-81	1990-91	2000-01	2004-05	2010-11	2011-12
Government	17.5	23.9	22.7	21.6	20.0	19.8
Private organized	12.5	12.3	18.7	19.5	22.6	22.9
Non-Corporate of which	73.0	63.8	58.6	58.9	57.4	57.3
Agriculture	38.1	31.5	25.1	18.9	17.8	17.3
Others	34.9	32.3	33.5	40.0	39.6	40.0
Total	100.0	100.0	100.0	100.0	100.0	100

Note: (1) Agriculture does not include Government and corporate Agriculture. They are included under respective shares as part of organized. These are based on NDP at factor cost and current prices.

Source: National Accounts Statistics [NAS], 1997, 2002, 2004,2013 Central Statistical Organization [CSO] –New Delhi

Private organised includes the non-corporate sector also. Hence the share of the corporate sector is less than that of the organized sector by at least 5%–namely 18%. The share of Uninc. is around 45% as seen earlier.

The major characteristic of corporate India is that it accounts around 18% of our national income. The service sector is currently the main driver of our economic growth. In the last decade, the average annual growth rate of the service sector was more than 8%, and they are the engines of our growth.

The share of the corporate sector in our domestic savings is less than 10%. In contrast, in the developed countries it is more than 50%.

The largest component of our savings (more than 70%) comes from the household sector, which includes all partnership/proprietorship firms even if they are in manufacturing or trade, transport, construction or hotels. Hence the proposition that the corporate sector is critical to our economy and has a dominant role in it is not borne out by facts. But it is repeated *ad nauseum*, since such is the case in the UK and the US and one begins to think that this is so for all countries. For instance, the share of Corporate business in USA is more than 75% of its GDP.

So Proposition 1 is neither true nor valid.

Table — 19. 2 Share of Corporate Business in the GDP at current prices in the USA Bn. USD

Category	2005	2009	2010	2011	2012
Corporate Business *	9921.6 [76]	10596.7 [74]	11054.8 [74]	11559.5 [74]	12195.4 [75]
Non Corporate Business	1599.5 [12]	1913.6 [13]	1927.5 [13]	1971.9 [13]	2025.4 [12]
Government	1574.3 [12]	1907.6 [13]	1975.9 [13]	2002.4 [13]	2023.7 [13]
Total GDP	13095.4 [100]	14417.9 [100]	14958.3 [100]	15533.8 [100]	16244.6 [100]

Note: * farm and non farm business, Figures in brackets are percentages to total.

Source: Table 1.3.5 Bureau of Economic Analysis — US Department of Commerce

Proposition 2: The stock market is a barometer for assessing the performance (past and future) of the corporate sector

We have nearly 7.2 lakh companies incorporated under

the Companies Act (as of 2011) and more than 9,000 scrips (shares and bonds) of 5,000-and-odd companies are listed on the stock exchanges. Of these, only 3,000 or so are traded at least once a year; and only 100 or so can be considered as active shares. Some 50 shares constitute nearly 65% of the market.

Though market players and exchanges brag about India having the largest number of listed scrips (like having the largest cattle population in the world), only about 100 are active. More than 70% of trading, even in these scrips, is not for delivery. It is for trading and squaring-off purposes. In other words, market participants do not ever own these scrips — they merely use them for speculation.

So even Proposition 2 is invalid: the stock market is no barometer of the Indian corporate sector, leave alone the Indian economy.

Proposition 3: The stock market helps channel savings in our economy.

This is the most amusing assumption of the lot. At best of times, the primary market has garnered some savings from the public through initial public offerings, but more often than not, the money ends up in stocks linked to the Oswals, the Bhansalis, the Mehras, the Deepaks, the Ruias and Mallyas — not to speak of hundreds of other entrepreneurs who have managed to destroy the value of people's savings.

The value-destroying list is long, and those interested can go through the business journals of the last 20 years (particularly the cover stories) that detail how these 'whizkids' and 'visionaries' were going to build a modern, industrialised India.

The Savings Data Table — **19.3** suggests that the share market has very little to do with channelling people's savings into productive investment. At best of times (for companies, not investors), the proportion of 'shares and debentures' as a percentage of household financial savings was 5% in 2009. In 2011, it was less than 1%. A large chunk of our investors prefer to invest with banks, post offices, provident funds and life insurance funds. It is suggested by some experts that we are like other Asian countries — a more Bank oriented Economy than Stock market inclined [Gurumurthy S — Clash of Economic Traditions, Business Line, 19-09-2013]

So Proposition 3 is also not self-evident. The stock markets play a very small role in the economy or in funneling savings. The Role of Banks, Insurance and Provident Funds are significant.

Table — 19. 3 Composition of House Hold Savings 2004 to 2012[%]

Item	2004-05	2005-06	2006-07	2007-08	2008-09	2009-10	2010-11	2011-12
GDS to GDP at factor cost	35	36	38	40	34	36	36	33
House hold Savings [HS] to GDS	73	70	67	61	74	75	69	72
Physical Savings [PS] to HS	57	50	51	48	55	53	56	64

Item	2004-05	2005-06	2006-07	2007-08	2008-09	2009-10	2010-11	2011-12
Financial Savings [FS] to HS	43	50	49	52	45	48	44	36
Currency to FS	8	9	9	11	14	10	13	11
Net Deposits to FS	37	46	56	52	58	44	52	59
Shares and Bonds to FS	2	6	7	10	-1	5	0.5	-0.3
Net Claims on Govt. to FS	24	14	3	-4	-4	4	3	-3
Life Insurance to FS	16	15	16	22	23	24	19	19
PF and Pensions to FS	12	10	10	9	9	13	13	14
Total FS	100	100	100	100	100	100	100	100

Note: From currency onwards the percentages are to Gross Financial Savings GDS=Gross Domestic Savings; GDP=Gross Domestic Product; FS=Financial savings ;Net claims on Govt= Small savings in Postal systems; Net deposits to FS= with banks

Source: St. 73, 10 & 18, National Accounts Statistics 2013; CSO New Delhi

Proposition 4: Foreign investments are critical to our growth story.

This is the most accepted wisdom. Look at how P Chidambaram our Finance Minister has been going on road shows to lure foreign investments. But the evidence suggests that our growth is due to our domestic savings, particularly household savings. Our savings rate two years ago was around 34% to 36% of our GDP and more than 70% of this was household saving. FII and FDI inflows were always less than 10% of our investments, and if at all anyone should be appreciated for our growth story it is our households and the average housewife.

There is a story of Lord Ganesha and Subramanya

competing for a mango by trying to go around the world in the shortest time. Subramanya got onto his peacock and went around while Ganesha just went around his parents, Shiva and Parvathi, treating them as the Universe. He was given the mango.

Our Finance Minister knows this story — I am sure — and so, instead of wasting his time in Frankfurt and Tokyo, he should focus on Indian housewives and help them balance their budgets by reducing inflation and the fiscal deficit. Unfortunately, our housewives do not have access to the Nashik note printing press like our FM. The solution to India's problems lie inside, not in wooing FII and FDI inflows.

But as long as our economic thinking is tied to Oxford/ Harvard/Yale/Chicago 'wisdom' we will continue to call the largest segment of our economy — namely partnership and proprietorship firms — as 'residual' and go around the world with a begging bowl to request companies to invest to India.

The stock market is important to 10% of the economy and it cannot be categorised as a barometer of the economy. Unfortunately, the focus of media and experts is on the stock market only. Perhaps it is more 'attractive' compared to dhoti-clad English-ignorant pan chewing India Uninc!

In that case, how do we assess growth in the economy? Quite simply, you should peep out of the window. I mean the real one. If you find lots of economic activity thriving and flourishing, then the economy is growing!!

CHAPTER 20

The Indian Financial Markets: A *Cul-De-Sac?*

The Indian financial markets are a virtual cul-de-sac today, which offer investors and lenders multiple entry points but virtually no scope for exit. With contract enforcement a long drawn out process, the domestic financial sector needs a thorough overhaul to facilitate both entry and exit, before there are any further attempts to integrate them with the global markets.

The facility to enter and exit at all points of time is one of the critical parameters by which markets are measured for their efficiency and effectiveness. Here, we are not talking about making a gain or loss, but of the liquidity of the market and widespread participation. Entry barriers can be overcome by regulations and sometimes even by 'reservations', but the ability to exit the market is not easy to achieve by dint of a government fiat, alone. What the experts otherwise call market timing may not be possible if exit is not easy due to any reason.

Our financial markets, particularly the stock markets and the unorganized credit market, suffer from what I call the Abhimanyu syndrome. The former relates to investors and the latter to lenders.

Small investors are now the cynosure of all eyes. Tomes have been written on how to woo them to the share market. Many industry associations have offered a plethora of ideas on how stock markets could attract small investors, and continue to do so. As a result of this dissemination of awareness about the stock markets, the interest and participation of small investors has grown manifold.

The so-called small investors are the children of the Controller of Capital Issues (CCI) *raj*. Till the early nineties, the CCI used to fix share prices and allow FERA companies to offer stock in the market at those artificially fixed low prices. Investors used to apply for these shares under different names, only to offload them in the market at exorbitant prices after listing. In the process, several fly by night operators also floated companies and took advantage of the boom of the early '90s.

The Harshad Mehta affair was only a part of that story. An important feature of the period was that the stock exchanges took into account only the listing fees while listing companies, and not the due diligence factor and other fundamentals. Later of course, SEBI formulated guidelines governing the listing of new and existing companies in terms of their track record and other parameters.

Investors who entered the market during those halcyon days are unfortunately not in a position to exit now, even at a loss. As many of us are aware, in the Mahabharata during the Great War, Abhimanyu, the son of Arjuna, knew how to enter the *Chakravyuha*. Abhimanyu met his nemesis because of his inability to come out of the *Chakravyuha* formation made by the Kauravas even though he could enter it. For the benefit of the MTV generation, let me explain by saying that Abhimanyu, the son of Arjuna in Mahabharata, learnt the art of entering the *Vyuha* when he was in his mother's womb. But before he could be taught the exit technique, he was born. He could not double-click on a mouse then!

The plight of these investors is due to a four-fold problem in our markets. The stock markets are very illiquid. This means that there are no takers for most shares at any price. Though nearly 9,000 scrips are listed in all our exchanges, nearly half were not quoted or traded last year [see Table — 20.1]. Another 25% were quoted only a couple of times during the last year. The shares of only 25 securities commanded more than 40% of the trade turnover. Compare this with the New York Stock Exchange (NYSE), where no single scrip normally enjoys more than 1% of the turnover. Though market players and exchanges blow their bugle about India having the largest number of scrips listed, only around a hundred scrips are active. Actually, last year, only 3700 scrips out of 9000 scrips were traded at least once. So, if you hold the wrong scrip, you can only use it as cattle feed!

Table — 20. 1 Liquidity in the Market

		2004-2005	2012-13
1.	Shares Traded [BSE] In Lakhs	477174	654137
2.	Shares Delivered [BSE] in Lakhs	189077[40%]	255999[39%]
3.	Shares Traded [NSE] in Lakhs	787996	1616978
4.	Shares Delivered [NSE] in Lakhs	202277[26%]	443232[28%]
5.	Share of Top five securities*	26%	16%
6.	Share of Top ten securities*	42%	26%
7.	Share of Top 25 securities*	58%	44%
8.	Share of Top 50 securities*	72%	61%
9.	Share of Top 100 securities*	84%	77%
10.	Share of Top 25 members*	35%	47%
11.	Share of Top 100 Members*	65%	77%
12.	Share of Mumbai/Thane**	56 %	56.4%
13.	Number of stocks Traded Above 100 days@	2368	3203(2011-12)
14.	Number of Stocks traded at least once in 2011-12@	2906	3752(2011-12)

Note: * Pertaining to NSE ** Pertaining to NSE & BSE; @ Pertaining to BSE

Source: (1) Rows 1&2, Table 8&20, SEBI Bulletin April 2005 & 2013, Rows 3 &4 :Table 9 & 21, SEBI Bulletin, April 2005 & 2013, Rows 5 to 14, Table 19, SEBI Bulletin April 2005 and April 2013, Row 15, Table 16, SEBI Bulletin April 2005 & 2013, Row 16 and 17, Table 2.20, p 58, SEBI Annual Report 2010-11

We notice from Table — 20.1 that around 28% of the trade at National Stock Exchange NSE has resulted in actual delivery of shares in the last year. This implies in a sense that a substantial amount of transactions are for squaring off on the same day. Day traders practice this. One can infer that there is a high level of speculative activity in the market. Even the remaining portion of the delivery is mainly by institutional investors, since they have to take delivery or make payments.

Small investors do not figure in all this. Exchanges should publish detailed and separate statistics on a daily basis about trade done by brokers on their own accounts and trading by them on behalf of clients. This will be very revealing. It will lay bare the fact that most of the trading is being done only on their own accounts by brokers.

In well-organized markets, there is a system of market makers who offer two-way quotes on any scrip so that continuous liquidity is provided to all scrips. We do not have this facility. Our merchant bankers and brokers are significantly under-capitalized, and therefore, cannot perform this role effectively. A company should not get listed unless market making is assured for its scrip. The lack of this facility is the noose around the neck of our small investors.

Several expert groups from SEBI, Bombay Stock Exchange [BSE], Institute of Company Secretaries, Department of Company Affairs etc., are now searching for companies, which are not traceable. Photographs of Directors of these companies may be put up in railway stations and other public places! But these Directors are also Directors of many other companies that are thriving! These gentlemen are very much part of the dining and 'wining' circuit in Bombay and Delhi. Taking investors for a ride is the national pastime of India Inc.!

Above all, small investors do not have timely protection against non-payment or non-delivery of shares by brokers. If a broker defaults, then the matter has to go through the process of being heard by an investors' grievance committee, then an arbitration committee, a default committee, and finally, there is the process of the auction of the defaulting broker's membership card. This rigmarole can take two to three years if the investor is lucky. Justice hurried is justice buried all right. But the harried investor gets buried much earlier.

There are other twists to the tale. If the broker has shown the amount received from a client as a loan and not as an advance for buying certain shares, then the stock exchanges will not even hear the investor's grievance — justifiably so — since that transaction is outside their purview. Contract enforcement is cumbersome and time-consuming in the Indian context.

Why do we enthusiastically lure small investors to such a speculative, illiquid, unprotected and opaque den? Why encourage small investors and give them false hopes? Of course, the goat is always well fed and treated with care before it is sacrificed. But to add insult to injury, it is also not afforded the luxury of free expression of its opinion on the matter!

Credit Market
In the unorganized credit market, the lenders are like Abhimanyu. They are not in a position to re–possess the

unsecured loans they have advanced for any trade or other businesses.

It is mentioned in the Kamba Ramayana that Ravana was feeling depressed like an indebted person on being asked by Rama to come back next day to fight the battle, since Rama did not want to fight with Ravana who had lost his weapons, horse, chariot etc. If Kambar were to write it today, he would probably write that Ravana was as depressed as a person who had lent money in the credit market in India. If the lender is an unincorporated body, then he does not have the protection of recovery tribunals or asset reconstruction agencies.

Lending in the market is based on the 'relationship' with the borrower rather than on detailed legal documentation. Under the circumstances, the lender tries to take recourse to extra-legal mechanisms including engaging 'collection agents' to get his money back.

In such a situation, the capability of the lender is eroded and recovery mechanisms distort risk–return relationships. Evolved credit rating mechanisms coupled with active participation of the commercial banker in accommodating the Unincorporated Business [UIB] Entities as channel partners could, to some extent, ameliorate the situation.

It is important that we rework our financial architecture to reform our illiquid stock markets and integrate domestic credit markets, evolve a single yield curve and enhance the capability of participants to enter and exit the market at all times.

Such a reworking is required before we talk in terms

of integrating our domestic markets into global financial markets or chanting the mantra of making Mumbai the global financial hub. A financial market with a million Abhimanyus is a poor model to showcase for global participants to view. Global players may even try to take advantage of such a market, which might only create larger issues for household investors and other unincorporated lenders in the years to come.

Caste and India Uninc.

Chapter 21	Reservations: Strong Policy and Weak Data Base
Chapter 22	Job Reservations: Make them Entrepreneurs instead
Chapter 23	India Growth: The untold story — Caste as social capital

Reservations: Strong Policy and Weak Database

There is a move on the part of the Government to introduce reservations in the private sector. This is to enhance social justice and also social equity by facilitating increased and statutorily enforced participation of the socially and educationally disadvantaged sections in the private sector. This is considered all the more important in the context of withdrawal by government from various economic activities. But the data available to formulate meaningful policies in this important area has been 'Pulled Out of Thin Air' — what we call POTA data. It is unfortunate that policy formulations with such far-reaching implications are to be considered with an unreliable and suspect database. The data on the supply side as well as on the demand side is neither reliable nor useful.

1931 may not reflect the reality of 2006

Many of us may not be aware that the Mandal formula of the eighties allocating fifty per cent of the seats in Government service and educational institutions is based on the Census data of 1931. The Census was affected due to World War II in the year 1941 and from 1951 onwards, collection of caste data [except that pertaining to SC/ST data] in our Census count was stopped since it was felt that such data might not be appropriate in achieving our aim of creating a casteless society.

The assumption made by the Mandal commission based on the 1931 Census and other parameters that more than 50% of the population belongs to Other Backward Castes (OBC) may not be true any longer. On that assumption the figure of 27% reservation for OBCs was arrived at which along with 22.5% reservations for SCs and STs adds up to 49.5% reservations which is lower than the suggested ceiling of 50% by the Supreme Court. National Sample Survey 2003 Round suggests that the OBCs may be around 36 % of the population and not 50% [Household Assets Holding, Indebtedness, Current Borrowings and Repayments of Social Groups in India (as on 30.06.2002) All-India Debt and Investment Survey NSS 59th Round — January–December 2003]. If one excludes Muslim OBCs then the figure falls to 32 % according to the NSS. The earlier National Family Health Statistics [NFHS] conducted in 1998 suggests that the population of OBCs [Non-Muslims] is around 30 % which is fairly close to the NSS figures.

Hence the earlier assumption regarding OBC population being around 50% may be a substantial over-estimation.

In other words, we do not have a reliable head count for the 'Other Backward Communities' except some count made by state level Backward Class Commissions which are also not Census in nature. It may be useful to have a detailed caste–wise census to look at the actual numbers.

Organized and Unorganized Sector Work Force

The discussion of having reservations in the private sector presumably pertains to the organized or perhaps more specifically to the corporate sector. Individual companies need not and do not provide data in their Annual Reports regarding the number of employees leave alone caste wise categorization. But we have some aggregate data for the private organised sector. In the case of manufacturing activities, organised sector consists of a facility employing ten or more with power or twenty or more without power and in the case of services, it is mainly company forms of organizations.

Table — 21.1 details the employment in the Private organised sector.

Table — 21. 1 Employment in the Private Organised Sector [Lakhs]

Year	Employment
1990	75.82
1995	80.59
2000	86.46
2005	84.52
2010	107.87
2011	114.22

Note: Non-Agricultural employment in the Private sector employing 10 or more persons

Source: Table3.3 ; Page S-50, Economic Survey 2005-06 & 2012-13 Table 3.1, pp-A-56 Ministry of finance, GoI

We find that as of end March 2011 there were in all 114 lakhs employed in the private organised sector. This is out of a total workforce of around 40 crore. Hence the policy of reservation will impact in creating a maximum of some twenty lakh or so jobs if we assume for the sake of argument that no SC/ST is employed currently in the private organised sector. This number is very small in relation to the total demand. In the case of the unorganized sector, legislated reservation will not help since we are not able to enforce even our Minimum Wages Act in that sector. Also, a substantial number of them are partnership and proprietorship firms and legislation of this nature will increase Inspector Raj and corruption. We should also recognize that substantial portion of SCs and STs are self-employed. An Economic Census of the Central Statistical Organization in 2005 reveals that out of 42 million enterprises, more than 50% of the enterprises were owned by SC (8.8%) ST (3.6%) and OBC (38.1%) social groups.

Creamy Layers Exclusion

The debate also does not take into account that backwardness is not a static phenomenon but a dynamic one. The late great sociologist, M.N.Srinivas said, "An important feature of social mobility in modern India is the manner in which the successful members of the backward castes work consistently for improving the economic and social condition of their caste fellows. This is due to the sense of identification with one's own caste, and also a realization that caste mobility is essential for individual or familial mobility." [Collected Essays; pp196-197 OUP 2005]

For instance, data pertaining to Medical College admissions in Tamil Nadu, which has reservations, practised for decades reveals that substantial number of 'open seats' are obtained by students nominally belonging to 'backward communities'.

In addition, according to a report in The Hindu in 2004, students belonging to the Backward Class (BC) or Most Backward Classes (MBC) have taken 952 of the total 1,224 seats in 12 government medical colleges in the State (77.9%). The first 14 ranks in medical admissions went to BC and MBC students. Even in the open competition category, five Scheduled Caste (SC) candidates have got into the MBBS course in 2004.

In Tamil Nadu, BCs get 30% reservation in educational institutions, MBCs 20%, SCs 18% and Scheduled Tribes (ST) one per cent. The 1,224 medical seats are thus divided into 354 for BCs; 247 for MBCs; 226 for SCs; and 13 for STs. The rest of the 384 seats are allowed as open competition, where everyone competes, regardless of community. The final tally (original list with 69% reservation) released by the Directorate of Medical Education however shows that only 28 students from the 'non-reserved' or Forward Castes (FC) have got into government medical colleges, representing about 2.3%. In fact, in the top 400 rank holders only 31 are from FC. In the top 100 rank holders only six are from the FC, 79 from BC and 13 from MBC. [Source: The Hindu dated 23-08-2004]. The situation in recent years have become more favourable to SC/BCs

Unless continuous data collection and revision of the groupings are done, the reservation formulations may not achieve their desired objectives. Hence assuming that the caste situation is static is not appropriate and there is a need to have a time series data on the nature of mobility, which is taking place across castes both in employment and in business particularly from the non-corporate to corporate business. Unfortunately, political parties are not interested in excluding any category as was seen in the prolonged agitation by advanced Backward Castes after their exclusion for reservation by the Second Backward Class commission in Karnataka based on its exhaustive survey. Many state governments have denied the existence of any creamy layer in their state.

The Drop Out rate is an important issue

Not only that, the drop-out rate at the Elementary level [Class 1 to 8] is very large among all and more so among SC and ST students, more particularly among girls as seen in Table — 21.2.

Table — 21. 2 Drop-out Rate among Class 1 to 8 students [%]

Year	All Boys	All Girls	SC Boys	SC Girls	ST Boys	ST Girls	Total
1990-91	59.1	65.1	64.3	73.2	75.7	82.2	60.9
2002-03	52.2	53.5	58.2	62.2	66.9	71.2	52.8
2007-08	43.7	41.3	53.6	51.1	62.6	62.3	42.8

Source: Select Education Statistics, Ministry of HRD, Govt. of India, IndiaStat.Com, statistics of school education Ministry of HRD, Govt. of India.

Hence the battle is to be fought at the primary and secondary school level for the weaker sections in order to make them entrepreneurs or self-employed rather than chase the mirage of jobs in the corporate sector. The policy of 'Where is a problem, then legislate' may not be appropriate particularly when the data base is weak and expectations are strong particularly pertaining to votes. That is why the Supreme Court, as reported widely, while hearing a batch of petitions challenging the validity of the 77th, 82nd, 83rd and 85th amendments to the constitutions expanding the scope of job reservations asked the pertinent question, "Where is the data regarding the entry of OBCs in the open quota?" [28th April 2006, The Telegraph, Calcutta].

It is easier to stoke passions based on Pulled Out of Thin Air [POTA] data but much more difficult to douse it with facts since to be a statesman is far more complicated and time consuming than to be a politician.

CHAPTER 22

Job reservations: Make them Entrepreneurs instead

The government should concentrate more on developing the entrepreneurship skills of Scheduled Castes and Scheduled Tribes rather than trying to replicate the existing public sector reservation system in the private sector, which anyway has only limited job opportunities.

As discussed in the previous chapter, a debate is currently raging in the polity regarding reservations for Scheduled Castes and Scheduled Tribes (SC/ST) in the private sector, similar to the one that is provided in the government and the public sector. As stated earlier, the private corporate sector constitutes a relatively small portion of the national income, namely, around 18-20%.

Let us look at the employment statistics pertaining to the private sector. We do not have separate statistics on the number employed by the private corporate sector and proprietorship and partnership [P&P sector] forms of organizations. Many companies do not provide information on the number of people employed by them since it is not required to be given in their Annual Reports.

First, the facts. We have provided in Table — 22.1 (for select years) the number of persons employed in government and semi-government organizations. We find that the employment in the government and the public sector has stagnated in the nineties and has actually shown a decline in the last two years. The reasons are two-fold. One pertains to the non-expansion of governmental activities, particularly pertaining to the public sector, compared to the socialistic approach of the sixties when everything from bread to rockets was made by the government. The second reason is that the government is broke, and more so, at the state level. Salary, wages and pensions constitute more than 50% of the expenses of many state governments. The Government (both Centre and states) have shifted from defined benefit to defined contribution pension schemes. The dependency ratio [namely, the number retired to number currently employed] is increasing at an exponential rate for most governments/government departments. Hence, the opportunity for employment in the government has been significantly reduced and this impacts SCs/STs, also.

Table — 22. 1 Employment in Government
[Lakhs Persons as on 31st March]

Year	1981	1990	1995	2000	2005	2010	2011
Central Government	31.95	33.97	33.95	32.73	29.38	25.52	24.63
State Governments	56.76	69.79	73.55	74.60	72.02	73.53	72.18
Quasi Government	45.76	61.73	65.20	63.26	57.48	58.68	58.14
Local Bodies	20.37	22.23	21.97	22.55	21.18	20.89	20.53
Total	154.84	187.72	194.67	193.14	180.07	178.62	175.48

Source: Table3.1 Page S56, Economic Survey—2012-13, Ministry of Finance GOI.

Table — 22.2 gives employment data for the private sector for select years. According to the Government of India, as claimed in the Economic Survey, there were 5.5 lakh persons employed in trade activities [wholesale and retail] in 2011 in the whole country. This presumably includes hotels and restaurants also, since they are not separately provided and they come under the trade category in our statistics. Also, the number of people employed by the construction industry is stated to be 1 lakh in the whole country during 2011. This number seems incredibly low! In a city like Bangalore itself, there are probably more than 1 lakh people working in construction activities. According to the figures, in the transport, storage and communications sector, only 1.9 lakh persons were employed in the whole country in the year 2011.

Major debates are conducted on television using such

unreliable data. It is unfortunate that major national policies are being formulated using such fiction.

The government and private organized sector has only a small share [8% to 9%] of the total workforce of the country. The organized private sector employs a total of 114 lakhs, which is around 3% of the total workforce [nearly 400 million]. Under the circumstances, even if the entire organized private sector is reserved for the SC/ST/OBC, the gains from employment will be very meagre.

Table — 22. 2 Employment in organised Private Sector by Industry [Number in lakhs]

Year	1981	1990	1995	2000	2005	2010	2011
Manufacturing	45.45	44.57	47.06	50.85	44.89	51.84	53.97
Construction	0.72	0.68	0.53	0.57	0.49	0.91	1.02
Wholesale, retail trade	2.77	2.91	3.08	3.30	3.75	5.06	5.46
Transport, storage	0.60	0.52	0.58	0.70	0.85	1.66	1.89
Finance and Insurance	1.96	2.39	2.93	3.58	5.23	15.52	17.18
Community, social services	12.22	14.60	16.03	17.23	18.20	21.40	23.50
Total — [including others]	73.95	75.82	80.59	86.46	84.52	107.87	114.22

Note: Refers to establishments in the Private sector employing ten or more persons. Coverage in construction, particularly is known to be inadequate

Source: Table 3.1 page S-56, Economic Survey, 2012-13, Ministry of Finance, GOI

But the perspective needs to be different. The more pertinent issue is the share of the SC/ST/OBC in the ownership of the private sector.

We have the exhaustive Economic Census 2005, conducted by the Central Statistical Organization [CSO] which covers 41.83 million enterprises engaged in different economic activities other than crop production and plantation. It deals with own account enterprises as well as establishments, an enterprise run by employing at least one hired worker. It covers private profit and non-profit institutions, co-operatives, and all economic activities including *dharamshalas*/temples.

Table — 22.3 provides the salient findings pertaining to ownership of enterprises.

Table — 22. 3 Social Group of Owners of the Enterprises [%]

Item	Rural	Urban	Combined
SC	10.0	6.9	8.8
ST	4.6	2.1	3.6
OBC	40.6	34.2	38.0
Total of above	55.2	43.3	50.5

Source: Table 2.5,Economic Census, and CSO, 2005

We find that nearly half of all enterprises are owned by SC/ST/OBCs. In the rural areas, it is 55%. This encompasses manufacturing, construction, trade, hotels, restaurants, transport, finance, business and other services.

The Enterprise Survey reveals that out of the total of 41.83 million enterprises in the country, 37.63 million [90%] were found to be self-financing. This speaks volumes about our credit delivery systems. What is required to be debated is the enhancement of credit systems for the enterprises, and more so to those owned by the SC/ST and other backward communities. In other words, the focus should be on the *'Vaishya–visation'* of large segments of our civil society, instead of creating a large number of 'proletariat' in the fashion of nineteenth century economic models.

There are inter-state variations in terms of industry focus among these social segments which also requires a closer study to encourage and enhance entrepreneurial activities by these social groups in different states.

Incidentally, one of the arguments given is regarding the enhancement of the 'Social Status' of these segments. Social backwardness, it is pointed out, is a valid reason for caste-based reservations compared to reservations based on, say, economic criteria. In today's context, politics, cricket and cinema/TV provide substantial social status and hence, maybe the demand should be in these areas, as compared to corporate keyboard punching!

The Marxist postulate is that, it is 'inevitable' that the 'petite bourgeoisie' becomes a proletariat in the process of the growth of capitalism. The corporate Globalizer, who belongs to the Metropolitan Elite, also argues about 'scale efficiency' and 'modernization' and feels that the 'rational route' is for all these small *Vaishyas* to disappear and become blue/white-collar workers for the cause of 'global efficiency'. Both the theories are based on nineteenth century experiences.

Policy planners and experts need to work on a road

map to calibrate changes in our current context. Already, we find that it is difficult to locate a tailor or a cobbler in many towns. Let us remember that Wal-Mart was built in rural America by liquidating thousands of mom-and-pop stores which are equivalent to our street corner *kirana* shops.

The arrival of the Internet and cell phones present opportunities to innovate in the linking of millions of small 'Vaishyas' to create scale economies. Indian civilization, over the centuries, has always been innovative and creative in finding solutions to social problems. Maybe, the time has come for the government to perform mainly the task of a *Kshatriya* [internal and external security] and encourage large segments of our society to become *Vaishyas* through instrumentalities of credit delivery, taxation, social security and development of regional and community based clusters. This may go a long way in enhancing the social status of the SC/ST/OBCs rather than providing some limited job opportunities in listed companies.

CHAPTER 23

India Growth: The untold story — Caste as social capital

The metropolitan elite and rootless experts have concluded that caste is bad. They have made it a 'four letter' word and so every Indian is expected to feel guilty whenever caste is mentioned and talked about. But caste has played an important role in the consolidation of business and entrepreneurship in India particularly in the last fifty years or so. We also find that caste in politics divides but caste in economics unites. Not only that, castes which have used business as a route for upward mobility have succeeded much better than those who tried to use politics. Caste has been a major social capital in our growth process and it has not been adequately recognized. This chapter explores the economic growth constituents and catalytic components. It also identifies the role of caste in the growth process among the emerging entrepreneurial groups.

The Indian economy has been growing at a Compounded Annual Growth Rate [CAGR] of more than 8% in the last decade. The largest segment of the economy namely, the service sector accounts for nearly 65% is also the fastest growing sector. We find that the share of the non-corporate sector namely, partnership and proprietorship firms in the service sector is significant. It is more than 70% in activities like trade, hotels and restaurants, transport and other areas like plumber, carpenter, painter, mason, priest etc. Domestic savings have been the primary source of funding for this growth. They constitute nearly 90% and the role of Foreign Institutional Investments [FII] and Foreign Direct investments [FDI] has never been more than 10%. Of this domestic savings, the role of Household savings is phenomenal and it constitutes nearly 75% of the domestic savings. Hence the growth is due to households in the service sector facilitated by self-financing or financing by extended families and communities. Different castes and communities have played an important role in this growth in terms of capital formation, market access, risk mitigation and diversification etc.

The Role of OBC's/SC/ST in Enterprises

The exhaustive Economic Census 1998 and 2005, conducted by the Central Statistical Organization [CSO] which covered 30.35 million and 41.83 million enterprises engaged in different economic activities respectively, other than crop production and plantation was something of an eye-opener. It dealt with own account enterprises as well as establishments, an enterprise run by a person by employing at least one hired worker. It covered private profit and non-profit institutions, cooperatives, and all economic activities including *dharamshalas and* temples. In 1998, it revealed that more than 50% of all enterprises were owned by SC/ST/OBC's in the rural areas and it was around 45% in the total. In 2005, the percentages were 55% for rural areas and 50% of the total. This encompasses manufacturing, construction, trade, hotels and restaurants, transport, finance and business and other services.

The Enterprise Survey also revealed that 90% were found to be self-financing. Much of it is likely to have come from informal caste networks. The number of establishments financed by financial and non-financial institutions were only 4%. The remaining was financed by voluntary organizations, government etc. What is required to be debated is the enhancement of credit systems for the enterprises and more so to those owned by SC/ST and other backward communities. In other words the focus should be on *'Vaishya–visation'* of large segments of our society. In that context, one needs to look at the past to identify the nature of 'discrimination' practised.

Was there discrimination in Education?

The renowned Gandhian, Dharampal visited British and Indian archives and reproduced reports which were undertaken by the British in Madras, Punjab and Bengal

Presidency for 1800 to 1830. According to a detailed survey done during 1822-25 in the Madras Presidency [that is, the present Tamil Nadu, the major part of the present Andhra Pradesh, and some districts of present-day Karnataka, Kerala and Orissa] it was discovered that 11,575 schools and 1094 colleges were in existence in the Presidency and that the number of students in them were 1,57,195 and 5431 respectively. [Dharampal, 'Beautiful Tree–Indigenous Indian Education in the Eighteenth Century; Vol-3 of Collected writings'; Other India Press Goa 2000]

Much more important in view of our current debates and assumptions is the unexpected and important information provided with regard to the broad caste composition of the students in these institutions. Table — 23.1 provides the relevant data. We find that the position as early as the first part of nineteenth century was significantly in favour of the backward castes as far as secular education was concerned.

Hence the British inspired propaganda that education was not available to the so-called backward castes prior to their efforts is not valid. Education always played a major tool in social transformation prior to British rule.

Table — 23.1 Survey of Madras Presidency on Education during 1822-1825

Share of Sudras in schools	Percentage
Tamil speaking areas	70-80 %
Oriya Areas	62%

Share of Sudras in schools	Percentage
Malayalam Areas	54%
Telugu Areas	35-50%
Share of Brahmins in Tamil Speaking areas	
South Arcot	13%
Madras	23%

Source: Dharampal; Beautiful Tree–Indigenous Indian education in the Eighteenth Century; Vol-3 of Collected writings; Other India Press Goa 2000

Hence the foundations of modern education were very much present even in the beginning of the19th century and this facilitated growth of entrepreneurship in the later period.

Social Capital

Sociologists underline that a nation can be maintained successfully only when people are able to live with each other as groups. The French sociologist Durkheim had earlier noted *"A nation can be maintained only if between the state and the individual there is interposed a whole series of secondary groups near enough to the individuals to attract them strongly in their sphere of action and drag them, in this way, into the general torrent of social life... Occupational groups are suited to fill this role, and that is their identity... community orientation creates trust among the members of the society."* [Emile Durkheim — 'The Division of Labor in Society', pp liv; The Free Press New York 1997]

Fukuyama notes that trust has an economic value. He

says, *"The ability to associate depends, in turn on the degree to which communities share norms and values and are able to subordinate individual interests to those of larger groups. Out of such shared values comes trust and trust as we will see has a large and measurable economic Value and trust results in social capital."* [Francis Fukuyama — 'Trust' pp 10; The Free Press Paperbacks, New York 1996]

Aiyar defines Social capital in the following way: *"From time immemorial groups of people have created strong communities based on commonly observed rules and mutual self-help. These social links discourage deviant behavior through ostracism and other social penalties, create a climate of trust in which agreements are honoured and grievances redressed and facilitates collective action against threats from outsiders and risks from natural disasters. This is social capital. Unlike financial or human capital it cannot be owned by individuals, only by social groups. Being less tangible than financial or human capital it is difficult to measure and so has been ignored in the past. Yet it is an invaluable asset."*[Swaminathan S Aiyar — 'Social Capital — An idea whose time has come' — Times of India — 28 May 2000]

He also stresses the significance of social capital for the economic development of nations. He says, *"But neither human nor financial capital can adequately explain why some nations succeed and others fail. A third element called social capital has long been emphasized by sociologists and is now increasingly recognized by economists. Sociologists like Robert Putnam have demonstrated that enormous economic benefits flow from social capital. Contrasting the huge economic success of northern Italy with the relative failure of the southern part, he finds that the mafias have eroded social capital and hence stalled economic development in the south. High levels of trust greatly reduce risks and costs and so encourage enterprises and innovation while reducing the costs of redress. So social capital ultimately translates into financial capital."* [Swaminathan S Aiyar 'Harness the caste system'— Times of India — 4 June 2000]

Mr. Gurcharan Das the corporate chief turned author and analyst says, *"In the nineteenth century, British colonialists used to blame our caste system for everything wrong in India. Now I have a different perspective. Instead of morally judging caste, I seek to understand its impact on competitiveness. I have come to believe that being endowed with commercial castes is a source of advantage in the global economy. Bania traders know how to accumulate and manage capital. They have financial resources and more important, financial acumen. They have an austere lifestyle and the propensity to take calculated risks. They have proven their flexibility of mind as they graduated from trading to industry. These constitute significant strengths. Joel Kotkin demonstrates these strengths in the case of Palanpur Jains, who have used their castes and family networks in wresting half the global markets for uncut diamonds from the Jews."* [Gurcharan Das — 'India Unbound — From Independence to the Global transformation Age'; pp 150 Penguin Books, New Delhi 2002]

Role of Caste: An Illustration

The World Bank suggests that the remarkable growth of Tirupur in Tamil Nadu is due to the co-ordinated efforts of a caste group known as the Gounders, many of them not even matriculates.

"Since 1985 Tirupur has become a hotbed of economic activity in the production of knitted garments. By the 1990s, with high growth rates of exports, Tirupur was a world leader in the knitted garment industry. The success of this industry is striking. This is particularly so as the production of knitted garments is capital-intensive, and the state banking monopoly had been ineffective at targeting capital funds to efficient entrepreneurs, especially at the levels necessary to sustain Tirupur's high growth rates.

What is behind this story of development? The needed capital was raised within the Gounder community, a caste relegated to the land-based activities, relying on community and family network. Those with capital in the Gounder community transfer it to others in the community through long-established informal credit institutions and rotating savings and credit associations. These networks were viewed as more reliable in transmitting information and enforcing contracts than the banking and legal systems that offered weak protection of creditor rights." [World Development Report, pp175; The World Bank.2002]

The same is true regarding the Nadar community in the Virudhunagar area, again in Tamil Nadu and an area associated with the match-box and printing industry. The amount of networking and contract enforcement mechanisms available with caste institutions are not fully appreciated.

Clusters and Caste

Clusters occupy a significant place in the economic scene in India. They play a crucial role in the development of the Indian businesses. Their contributions to the national income, employment, exports and innovation is very significant. The United Nations Industrial Development organization [UNIDO] had noted that in India, *"It is estimated that there are approximately 350 small scale industrial clusters and around 2000 rural and artisan based clusters contributing almost 60% of the manufacturing exports and 40 % of the employment in the manufacturing industry."* [UNIDO Case studies: Fabio Russo: Strengthening Indian SME clusters UNIDO experience US/GLO/95/144 — July 1999]

The Ministry of Small-scale Industries, Government of India has estimated that there are 2042 clusters of which 1223 are in the registered sector in 26 states and another 819 in the unregistered sectors in 25 states and union territories. They constitute significant portions in output, employment and exports in different states. [Third All India Census of Small Scale industries — Final results Pp 83-85; 2001-2002] Also, the study of several clusters spread across several regions of the country points to the role of community in the emerging entrepreneurial development. [Kanagasabapathi, 'Indian Models of Business and Economics' pp176-189;PHI;India; 2010 New Delhi.]

Clusters are promoted and run by ordinary persons, many of whom are first generation entrepreneurs. In the Sankagiri transport cluster of Tamil Nadu which has second highest truck traffic in the country, more than 80% of the truck owners were earlier drivers and cleaners. Similarly, in the knitwear industry in Tirupur, more than 90%are from agricultural backgrounds. Descendants of farmers from Palanpur and Kathiawar have created the diamond hub in Surat which provides employment to large numbers in Antwerp and New York. Clusters tend to breed entrepreneurs with less formal education and more practical knowledge. There are studies to show that *Tirupur Gounders* [knitwear exporters] and *Sivakasi Nadars* [matches/crackers and printing] usually have less than high school education but significant shop floor experience. This experience is gained in units run by other family members or community members. Hence, the community becomes a crucible for gaining practical knowledge.

Entrepreneurs build clusters as is seen by Morvi clocks and Surat diamonds, both of which have benefitted by the presence of clusters. Jamnagar brassware is another example. Actually, clusters are not anonymous group of individual entrepreneurs but interconnected extended families/castes and communities.

The important aspect of clusters are that they are relationship based businesses rather than rule based. They are also not state dependent but self-funded and developed. Once clusters develop, entrepreneurs establish schools, colleges, and other common facilities like marriage halls required for their communities. In almost all the clusters one sees educational institutions established by the local communities. Clusters develop as full-fledged centres of economic, social and religious activities.

Another important characteristic is the generation of funds and mobilization of resources from close and local sources. As is evident from our earlier arguments, a significant portion of economic activity is self-financing or funded by extended families and community networks. This also facilitates dealing with failures due to risk taking. Actually there is risk sharing and failure is not looked down upon. The extended family/community extends its help in the context of distress and failures and this act as a major cushion in undertaking risky activities like exploring newer markets or innovating new product lines. Clusters act as drivers of economic activities facilitated by family/extended family/caste networks.

A lot of literature is available on *Marwaris*, *Sindhis*, *Kutchis*, *Bohras*, *Patels*, etc. and the nature of the global networks some of them have created. In a financial sense, caste provides the edge in being a risk taker since failure is recognized and condoned and sometime encouraged by the group. Instead of creating large numbers of 'proletariat' in the fashion of nineteenth century models, we need to recognize caste as the natural social capital present in our system.

Incidentally one of the arguments given in favour of reservation pertains to enhancing the 'Social Status' of the backward segments of our society. Social backwardness, it is pointed out, is a valid reason for caste based reservations compared to reservations based on economic criteria. But as M.N. Srinivas, the doyen of sociologists points out , *"An important feature of social mobility in modern India is the manner in which the successful members of the backward castes work consistently for improving the economic and social condition of their caste fellows. This is due to the sense of identification with one's own caste, and also a realization that caste mobility is essential for individual or familial mobility"* [M.N. Srinivas — Some reflections on the nature of Caste hierarchy; Collected Essays; pp196-197, OUP 2005]

It is also assumed that caste is a rigid hierarchical system which is oppressive. But it has been pointed out by the renowned sociologist Dr. Dipankar Gupta that *"In fact, it is more realistic to say that there are probably as many hierarchies as there are castes in India. To believe that there is a single caste order to which every caste, from Brahman to untouchable, acquiesce ideologically, is a gross misreading of facts on the ground. The truth is that no caste, howsoever lowly placed it may be, accepts the reason for its degradation."* [Dipankar Gupta; Interrogating Caste; pp1; Penguin Books 2000].

Caste and New Capitalists

In his pioneering work on New Capitalists and Caste, Harish Damodaran elaborates on the emerging trends of new businesses and castes. He delineates three general trajectories of industrial transition by communities. *"The first is the conventional Bazaar-to-Factory route involving the various Bania and Vaishya groups. The second from office to Factory, route taken by Brahmins, Khatris, Kayasthas, The Bengali bhadralok, and other scribal castes with a distinct urban middle class orientation. These sections traditionally dominated the bureaucracy and white collar professions and their entry into business in phenomenal proportions was essentially a post–independence development. The third pathway; from Field to Factory covering those communities classified as shudras in the classical Hindu chatur varna scheme. This wide–ranging category included land owning peasant castes like the Kammas, Reddys, Gounders, Jats, Patidars and Marathas and also lower shudras such as Nadars, Ramgarhias, and assorted rural service provider communities. They may be viewed as constituting 'rural middle class' whose political, social and economic empowerment was one of the epochal features of last century. Their journey into corporate boardrooms howsoever uneven across regions paralleled a similar transition achieved by the urban scribal castes. Both these urban and rural middle class led trajectories have undermined the time honoured association of 'business communities' with an exclusive Vaishya [Bania] order. "* [Harish Damodaran — 'India's New Capitalists' — pp 315; Permanent Black — New Delhi; 2008.]

Recent studies by journalists from Mint newspaper [Mint: Changing role of Caste: 4 articles, June 4-16, 2010] bring out the issue of caste facilitating the emergence of newer businesses in different locations of the country. The role of extended family and caste has been recognized in the upward mobility of middle castes in commerce and business.

Dalit Entrepreneurship

We also find that Dalits are increasingly getting into businesses and entrepreneurship. The Dalit Indian Chamber of Commerce and Industry [DICCI] is playing an important role in this. [http://www.dicci. org/en/] Members of this body have been consulted by the Planning Commission as part of their pre-budget consultation. It marks the emergence of a nascent trend in India of enterprising Dalits choosing to create independent businesses instead of depending on quotas in government jobs to get ahead. Some of them have built impressive empires like Kalpana Saroj who heads Kamani Tubes with an estimated turnover of Rs. 500 crore and Ratibhai Makwana whose Rs. 300-crore Gujarat Pickers is one of the country's largest polymer distributors. [http://articles.timesofindia.indiatimes.com/2010-12-31/india/28230674_1_dalit-entrepreneurs-dalit-indian-chamber-chandrabhan-prasad]

We find that caste in politics divides but caste in economics unites. Not only that, castes which have used business as a route for upward mobility have succeeded much better than those who tried to use politics. The examples which come to mind are *Nadars* and *Gounders* in the former category and *Vanniars*, *Thevars* and *Dalits* in the latter category in Tamil Nadu. It is required for policy planners and experts to work on a road map to calibrate changes in our context.

Conclusion

In international forums caste is used as a stick to beat anything connected to Indian religions, customs and culture. In other words, caste has been made to be for Indians what 'holocaust' is for Germans and Austrians.

We have an uncanny ability to be masochistic. But more tragic is our enthusiasm to convert all our strengths to weaknesses since some white men started to abuse Indians for having the caste system. We fail to recognize that it is a valuable social capital, which provides cushion for individuals and families in dealing with society at large, and more particularly the State. The Anglo-Saxon model of atomizing every individual to a single element in a rights-based system and forcing him to have a direct link with the State has produced disastrous effects in the West wherein families have been destroyed and communities have been forgotten. Every person stands alone there, in a sense stark naked with only rights as his imaginary clothes to deal directly with the State. The State also does not have the benefit of concentric circles of cushions to deal with individuals. The State has taken over the role of father and mother as well as spouse in terms of social security, old age homes and rights of children to sue and divorce parents!

Caste has been made a curse by the intellectuals

based on half-baked knowledge and acceptance of the Eurocentric model of the individual, which is a rights based system rather than a duty based system. Hence one way to overcome it is to have reservations since the Euro-centric model suggests that. If you decide to carry the cross or burden which others impose, then you begin to impose the solution provided by them. In a sense, the debate does not distinguish between caste discrimination and caste as a social capital. The cry to abolish caste is to homogenise Indian society which has been attempted by many reformers but has not been successful.

Swami Vivekananda in his address at Jaffna in 1897 says *"The older I grow, the better I seem to think of these [caste and such other] time-honored institutions of India. There was a time when I used to think that many of them were useless and worthless, but the older I grow, the more I seem to feel a diffidence in cursing any one of them, for each one of them is the embodiment of the experience of centuries."* [http://en.wikisource.org/wiki/The_Complete_Works_of_Swami_Vivekananda/Volume_3/Lectures_from_Colombo_to_Almora/Vedantism (1)]*

Caste has played an important role in the consolidation of business and entrepreneurship in India particularly in the last fifty years. The economic development that has taken place in India Uninc. or the partnership and proprietorship activities has been financed by domestic savings and facilitated by clusters and caste and community networks.

---

* Note: An earlier version of this was published in Handbook of Hindu Economics and Business : Edited by Prof. Hrishikesh D Vinod— ISBN/EAN13: 148398088X/9781483980881 Mar 2013 Amazon/Create Space

Miscellaneous Musings & Conclusions

Chapter 24	The NGO Sector
Chapter 25	Decline of the West
Chapter 26	Art of Giving: Warren Buffet to be told
Chapter 27	Leveraging on the Mobile Phone Revolution
Chapter 28	Time to say Good-bye to the World Bank
Chapter 29	Sports in India — BCCI the largest Uninc.
Chapter 30	Bollywood as Uninc.
Chapter 31	Conclusions

The NGO Sector

The NGO Sector or what is known as the Third Sector [other than Government and Private] in academic circles is a fairly significant actor on the economic stage and in particular in the Uninc. sector. A Non-Governmental Organization [NGO] is any voluntary, non-profit, citizens' group which is organized at a local, national or international level. They are one of the largest non-corporate sectors in India. As of now, many NGOs are registered under the Foreign Contribution Regulation Act [FCRA] Act and get huge amount of funds from abroad. With the new Companies Act which provides for compulsory allocation of profits by companies for Corporate Social Responsibility [CSR] activities, perhaps the time has come to scrap FCRA in terms of NGOs getting money from abroad.

NGOs could be registered as a society, trust or as Section 25 companies even though some co-operatives also claim this label. Two important criteria are that they are supposed to be independent of the government and they are supposed to be organizations not meant for making profit. They are also expected to be 'value based' organizations.

The type of activities they are involved in is mind boggling as is apparent from Table — 24.1. It indicates that the range of concerns of these Uninc. organisations and their activities are as wide as that of a sovereign state.

Table — 24. 1 Type of Activities of NGO's

Age Care	Environment
Agriculture	Health
Animal Welfare	HIV/AIDS
Art & craft	Housing and Slums
Caste	Micro Finance
Children	Population
Cities	Poverty
Community Development	Rural Transformation
Culture and Heritage	Tribals
Disability	Waste Management
Disaster Management	Water
Education	Women
	Others

Source: Indianngos.com

The list is indicative and not exhaustive and it reveals the range of activities in which NGOs are involved.

Since NGOs are involved in different types of activities, correspondingly the type of organization could differ as indicated in Table — 24.2.

Table — 24. 2 Typical Forms of NGOs

Item	Type of NGO's
1	**Advocacy:** These NGO's advocated or campaign on issues or causes. They do not implement programmes /projects. For instance, PETA advocates the cause of ethical treatment of animals
2.	**Consultancy/Research organizations:** They work on Social and Developmental Research and Consultancy
3.	**Training/Capacity Building organizations:** Training is called capacity building by NGO's and some NGO's work on capacity building for other NGO's
4	**Networking organizations:** They provide network for other NGO's in specific fields. AVARD works on networking NGO's in rural development
5.	**Mother NGOs:** These are recipients of funds as well as givers. They have a work focus but instead of implementing projects they identify projects and monitor, evaluate and build capacities of other participating NGO"s. CRY is one example.
6.	**Grassroots organization:** They directly work with the community. In a sense, all Mahila Mandals fall in this category.
7.	**City Based organizations:** They restrict their focus to cities. AGNI in Mumbai could be an example.
8.	**National organizations:** They have a national presence: CRY, Concern India etc.
9.	**International organizations:** They are part of an international NGO. Like a mother NGO, they receive and disburse grants. CARE and Oxfam could be examples.
10.	**Self-help Groups:** They are formed by beneficiary communities. Typically women form these groups of ten plus members. In rural AP and TN they are increasing in numbers. They are funded even by commercial banks for productive activities. In a sense, they are not typical NGO's.
11.	**Religious NGO's:** Religion based organizations; many affiliated to international Church groups.

Source: Indianngos.com

The funding for these NGOs could be domestic or international. The international flow of funds is regulated by the Foreign Contributions Regulation Act [FCRA Act] of the Central Government which the Ministry of Home Affairs has re-formulated now. In the period from 2001 to 2010 [9 years], such organizations received more than Rs. 80000 crore and in the year 2010-11 [for which data is available] it was Rs. 10334 crore. [http://www.mha.nic.in/fcra.htm] [Also see Table — 24.4]

Salient Features for the year 2010-2011 [the year for which latest data is available]

I. A total of **40575** Associations were registered under the Foreign Contribution (Regulation) Act up to 31.3.2011. During the year 2010-11, **2139** Associations were granted registration and **393** Associations were granted prior permission to receive foreign contribution.

II. **22735** Associations reported a total receipt of an amount of **Rs. 10,334.12 crore** as foreign contribution.

III. Among the States and the Union Territories, the highest receipt of foreign contribution was reported by **Delhi (Rs. 2016.63 crore),** followed by **Tamil Nadu (Rs. 1557.40 crore)** and **Andhra Pradesh (Rs. 1176.79 crore).**

IV. Among the districts, the highest receipt of foreign contribution was reported by **Chennai (Rs. 772.67 crore),** followed by **Bengaluru (Rs. 774.09 crore)** and **Mumbai (Rs. 643.73 crore).**

V. The list of donor countries was headed by the **USA (Rs. 3260.22 crore)** followed by **UK (Rs. 1065.35 crore)** and **Germany (Rs. 1007.39 crore)**.

VI. The list of foreign donors is topped by the **Compassion International USA (Rs. 99.2 crore)** followed by **HCL Holdings Ltd. Mauritius (Rs. 69.98 crore)** and **Action Aid UK (Rs. 62.66 crore)**.

VII. Among the Associations which reported receipt of foreign contribution, the highest amount of foreign contribution was received by the **World Vision of India, Chennai, Tamil Nadu (Rs. 233.74 crore)**, followed by the **Believers Church India, Kerala (Rs. 160.72 crore), Rural Development Trust, Ananthapur, A.P. (Rs. 135.38 crore)**

VIII. The highest amount of foreign contribution was received and utilized for Establishment Expenses **(Rs. 1337.15 crore),** followed by Rural Development **(Rs. 863.12 crore)**, Welfare of Children **(Rs. 746.24 crore)**, Construction and Maintenance of schools/colleges **(Rs. 681.40 crore)** and Grant of Stipends, scholarships and assistance in cash and kind to poor and deserving children **(Rs. 458.13 crore)**.

We have provided some salient statistics from the Home Ministry web site in Tables 24.3 to 24.8.

Table 24.3 reveals that there are more than 40000 associations registered under FCRA and during the last ten years they have received more than Rs. 80,000 crore from foreign countries/donors.

Table — 24. 3 Number of Associations and Amount of money received

Year	Associations Registered under the Act [End March]	Amount of Foreign Contributions Received [Rs Crore]
1993-94	15039	1865
1998-99	19,834	3402
1999-00	21244	3924
2000-01	22924	4535
2001-02	24563	4872
2002-03	26404	5047
2003-04	28351	5105
2004-05	30321	6257
2005-06	32144	7878
2006-07	33937	11007
2007-08	34803	9663
2008-09	36414	10803
2009-10	38436	10338
2010-11	40575	10334

Source: http://mha.nic.in/fcra/annual/summary_2010-2011.pdf

We find from Table 24.4 that major donors are USA and other European countries like Germany, UK, Italy etc.

Table — 24. 4 TOP FIFTEEN DONOR COUNTRIES [Rs. Crore]

2009-10		2010-11	
Country		Country	
USA	3105.73	USA	3260.22
Germany	1046.30	UK	1065.35
UK	1038.68	Germany	1007.39
Italy	583.47	Italy	490.01
Netherlands	509.46	Netherlands	468.81
Spain	437.25	Spain	351.41
Switzerland	302.06	Canada	299.95
Canada	297.98	Switzerland	286.24
France	189.12	France	190.89
Australia	148.28	Australia	159.44
UAE	133.15	Austria	132.66
Belgium	122.05	Belgium	111.05
Austria	112.10	UAE	109.32
Sweden	105.79	Sweden	97.20
Mauritius	101.02	Mauritius	72.89

[Source: http://www.mha.nic.in/fcra.htm]

We observe from Table 24.5 that most of the major donors are Church related organizations from the West for the purpose of charity work to be undertaken by Indian Church related organizations.

Table — 24. 5 TOP FIVE DONOR AGENCIES
Foreign contribution (Rs. in crore)

| S.No. | 2009-10 | | 2010-11 | |
	Donors name & country	Amount	Donors name & country	Amount
1.	Gospel For Asia Inc., USA	232.71	Compassion International, USA	99.2
2.	Fundacion Vicente Ferrer, Barcelona, Spain	228.6	HCL Holdings Private Ltd., Mauritius	69.98
3.	World Vision Global Centre, USA	197.62	Action Aid UK	62.66
4.	Compassion International, USA	131.57	Population Service International, USA	48.91
5.	HCL Holdings Private Ltd., Mauritius	94.28	Bill & Melinda Gates Foundation, USA	48.37

[Source: http://www.mha.nic.in/fcra.htm]

We also find from Table 24.6 that the recipients are mainly Church related organizations like Rural Development Trust in AP; Believers Church in Kerala and Karuna Bala Vikas in TN and there is criticism in some quarters that these funds are used for conversion activities.

Table — 24. 6 TOP FIVE RECIPIENT ASSOCIATIONS Foreign Contribution (Rs. in crore)

S.No.	2009-10		2010-11	
	Name of the Associations	Amount	Name of the Associations	Amount
1.	World Vision of India, Tamil Nadu	208.94	World Vision of India, Tamil Nadu	233.74
2.	Rural Development Trust, A.P.	151.31	Believers Church India, Kerala	160.72
3.	SSNEC Trust, Tamil Nadu	94.28	Rural Development Trust, A.P.	135.38
4.	Believers Church India, Kerala	88.45	Caruna Bal Vikas, Tamil Nadu	96.44
5.	Karuna Bal Vikas Tamil Nadu	82.6	Women Devl. Trust, A.P.	72.75

[Source: http://www.mha.nic.in/fcra.htm]

From Table 24.7, we find that Establishment expenses consist of buying land, buildings, jeeps, setting up offices, mobiles, laptops, cameras, salaries, consultancy fees, honorarium and foreign travel etc., and this constitutes nearly 50% of the expenses and in some cases, it is as high as 70%. This goes against the grain of service motto where the ultimate recipient is supposed to get the maximum. Now, such organizations even recruit executives from management institutions. Most of the top recipients are Church or Church related organizations. They use the funds for service as well as religious purposes.

Table — 24. 7 Receipt/Utilization of Foreign Contribution Towards Major Five Purposes During The Year 2009-10 & 2010-11

S. No.	2009-10		2010-11	
	Purpose of utilization	Amount	Purpose of utilization	Amount
1.	Establishment Expenses	1482.58	Establishment Expenses	1337.15
2.	Rural Development	944.13	Rural Development	863.12
3.	Welfare of Children	742.42	Welfare of Children	745.24
4.	Construction and maintenance of School & college	630.78	Construction and maintenance of School & college	681.4
5.	Grant of stipend/ scholarship assistance in cash and kind to Poor/ deserving children	454.7	Grant of stipend/ scholarship assistance in cash and kind to Poor/ deserving children	458.13

[Source: http://www.mha.nic.in/fcra.htm] Some Concerns about these types of Uninc. organisations

They are not covered by Right to Information Act as they are not part of the government. For instance, this writer has tried unsuccessfully to get the annual accounts from the web site of the top 25 recipients, many of whom are often reported in newspapers and TV as stressing the importance of 'transparency' in the functioning of the government. Many do not have any information on their web sites. Some of the web sites contain nothing on finances. These Civil society groups who day in day out harangue us on TV talk shows about transparency and disclosures for the government and corporate sector etc., should practice what they preach.

There is a long list of illustrative programmers/activities to be carried out by these associations receiving foreign contributions. This is given in the web site http://www.mha.nic.in/fcra.htm

More importantly, the amended act suggests that acceptance of foreign contributions should be within the broad parameters as listed in the MHA guidelines. For instance, the money received should not be used for political activities nor for proselytization. But the punishment for violating the act is paltry.

Nature of Use of Funds

As stated earlier, a significant portion of the received funds are used for 'Establishment Expenses' which is against the basic canon of charity work. It is expected that charity involves lesser fixed assets creation particularly of the flamboyant nature. Also the jet setting aspect of NGO's provides clues to the nature of expenditure. Whether it is New York or Geneva we find members of the Indian NGO community lobbying for some cause mostly to do with human rights. This creates a closed loop wherein they receive money to further an agenda and on doing so, they receive even more money.

Religious Conversion

A large amount of funds go to Christian organizations whose purpose is conversion. This act of 'soul harvesting' or 'planting of the Church' is an anachronistic practice of the nineteenth century which is totally incongruous in the twenty first century where faith based political movements like Church movements are disappearing from Europe, their cradle of growth. Europe which has given up on the Church is trying to overcome its guilt by exporting Christianity to India. The recipient organizations may argue that they are serving the poor but do they need European money to serve Indian poor.

Also some organizations like World Vision appear to be secular or non-denominational in India. But the fact of the matter is that they are Christian in origin and membership. This has been affirmed by the Supreme Court of USA. We can take them as a representative example wherein they do not mention much about their exclusive Christian identity when campaigning for funds within India.

[http://www.worldvision.org/content.nsf/learn/christian-identity-hiring-practices?Open]

There were also concerns that the anti-nuclear activities conducted at Kudankulam in Tamil Nadu were supported by some NGO's with foreign funding support. The debate is not yet settled.

Employment

The number of persons employed in NGOs is not separately available. One estimate by PRIA Research published by Indiangos.com indicates the figure at 19.4 million with West Bengal [1.52mn] Tamil Nadu [1.49mn] and Delhi [1.03mn] leading the pack. These figures imply that the total number of Government employees at nearly 20 million [Central, State and Local bodies] and the number employed by NGO's are comparable.

By definition, NGO activity is voluntary and hence one expects that the overheads of the organizations are lean. In financial parlance, the fixed cost is expected to be relatively very small. Contrary to this belief, we find that the Establishment Expenses are the major reasons for receiving donations from abroad. In other words, NGOs are perhaps becoming like top heavy government departments wherein substantial portion of developmental expenses are spent on salary wages and other expenses like telephone, travel [both domestic and international] etc.

Another important aspect is the funding and functioning of NGOs who get funds from domestic sources. Unfortunately, we do not have a full picture of the financing namely, the Sources and Uses of Funds of the entire spectrum of NGOs.

Other Countries

For instance, a few years ago Russia approved a bill that introduced stringent control over the activities of foreign funded non-government and non-commercial organizations in a move designed to pre-empt any 'colored revolution' in the country.

It says, *"The Kremlin has learnt its lessons from a string*

*of 'colored revolutions' in the former Soviet Republics —
the 'Rose Revolution' in Georgia, the 'Orange Revolution'
in Ukraine and the 'Tulip Revolution' in Kyrgyzstan — all
inspired and orchestrated by western funded NGO's. The
bill allows NGO's to be shut down if they threaten the
country's 'sovereignty, independence, territorial integrity,
national unity and originality, cultural heritage and
national interests'. There are 450,000 NGO's in Russia
representing religious organizations, charities, think tanks,
and professional groups. The US Congress has allocated $
85 million for the support of democracy in Russia in 2006."*
[The Hindu Dated 26-12-2005].

Incidentally, there is an act in the USA called Foreign
Agents Registration Act [FARA] and it provides for
penalties up to ten years in jail for anyone acting as a foreign
agent without notification to the Attorney General. The
FARA was originally passed in 1938 to prevent the spread
of Nazi ideas and propaganda.

Hence regulations of NGOs operating within a country
are neither new nor something that curtails their freedom.
Their activities have grown manifold and hence the
issue of accountability becomes very important. This in
no way minimizes their importance nor questions their
functioning. One can argue that they are accountable to
their donors but it is not like a corporate situation where
the company is accountable to its shareholders. They
have a large impact on our civil society and hence their
role is more than that of giving details to their donors.
Particularly in our civil society, which places importance

on voluntary efforts and appreciates it, their responsibility is much more.

To start with they must publish their annual reports including accounts on their web sites on a regular basis. It would also facilitate domestic individual donors make decisions regarding providing funds to them based on their effectiveness as measured by overheads. They should agree to be covered under the RTI since they insist that Political parties etc. be covered.

NGOs can create a self-regulatory body, or the community creates a body, which is a creature of their own and to which they are accountable. They can co-opt eminent citizens in this body. This becomes important since it is perceived that some NGOs are engaging in religious conversions in a rather aggressive fashion and some others are using the NGO banner to blackmail well-functioning corporate and Government entities. Social cohesion may be affected by the activities of some NGOs particularly those which are active in proselytizing.

Of course, the nature and dimension of such activities may be considered 'small' today, but it would be prudent to be proactive and generate credible self-regulating systems to enhance the effectiveness of the third sector. It would not be appropriate to suggest that everything is fine with every NGO in the country. Their numbers are growing, their causes are increasing in scope and funding particularly from abroad is increasing. Hence perhaps, the time has come for them to be more transparent and enhance disclosure practices to be like Caesar's wife i.e., above suspicion. Transparency and regulation and full disclosure are what they demand from corporates and the government. Hence it might be appropriate to expect the same from them.

In the light of the new Companies Act which specifies a sum of 2% of the profit to be distributed for Corporate Social Responsibility [CSR] activities, they may not require FCRA anymore since domestic donations will be more than adequate for meeting the requirements of genuine NGOs.

It is important that the Government of India bans foreign funding of civil society groups and NGOs who want to reform India or use it for conversion. We are no more the 'white man's burden'. Scrap the FCRA and save the republic should be the call of our times by policy makers and other concerned citizens.

CHAPTER 25

Decline of the West

We should recognize that for most of the Indian elite, their umbilical cords are linked to the west. Many of them are/ were educated in the US or Europe, and most of them have their children studying or working there. Due to colonial genes, acceptance/recognition by the west is critical for average middle class Indians. The reality, that the west is in decline and many of its institutions are failing, has still not struck us and we will continue to try and imitate them — including dysfunctional family systems. The danger is that we are going to buy their failed models when they are in decline. They will try to sell us everything they have, and we will buy because of our colonial genes.

Ten years ago, America had Steve Jobs, Bob Hope and Johnny Cash. Now it has no Jobs, no Hope and no Cash. That pretty sums up the situation in the USA. The less said the better about Europe. I was asked by a business channel in 2008 about recovery in USA. I mentioned 40 quarters and after that I wasn't invited for discussion. Recently, another media person asked the same question and I answered 80 quarters. He was shocked since he had been told that some sprouts were visible. It is important to recognize that the dominance of the West has been so only for the last 200 plus years. As per Angus Maddison's pioneering OECD study, India and China had nearly 50% of the global GDP as late as the1820's. Hence, India and China are not emerging or rising powers. They are merely retrieving their original position. In 1990 the share of G-7 in world GDP [on PPP base] was 51% and that of the emerging markets was 36%. But in 2011 it is the reverse.[See Chart 25.2] So the dominant west is a myth. Similarly, the crisis. It was a US-Europe crisis and not a global one. Like the two wars — which were essentially European wars — were made out to be world wars with one English leader commenting that we will fight the Germans to the last Indian. In this current economic scenario countries like India are also being made to feel that they are in a crisis. Since the white man says it, we swallow it hook, line and sinker. At no point of time in the last twenty years have FDI and FII put together exceeded 10% of our domestic investment. Our growth is due to our domestic savings which is again predominately household savings. Our housewives require awards for our growth, not any *Gora* fund.

The crisis faced by the West is primarily due to forgetting a six letter word called 'saving' which is a result of forgetting another six letter word called 'family'. The West has nationalized families over the last sixty years. Old age, ill health, single mother, everything is the responsibility of the State. When family is a 'burden' and children an 'encumbrance', society can be said to be in a state that should cause concern. Actually, for long household savings has been negative in the USA.

Table — 25.1 Overall Debt And Components as % of GDP

Country	Overall Debt	Govt Debt	Household
UNITED STATES	289	90	83
CANADA	273	69	91
BRITAIN	494	92	96
GERMANY	287	86	60
FRANCE	349	91	49
SPAIN	366	75	81
ITALY	310	104	46
RUSSIA	72	7	9
BRAZIL	148	66	15
JAPAN	511	227	67
SOUTH KOREA	315	32	82
CHINA	184	28	28
INDIA	122	55	10

Source: IMF, World Economic Outlook-2012

We find from Table — 25.1 that the Debt to GDP ratio is above 300% in many developed countries. Importantly, the Household Debt to GDP ratio is significantly high in many G-7 countries like US, UK, Canada etc. and comparatively low in countries like China and India. Saving is still not forgotten in these countries. Also, the credit card culture could be a major reason for such high levels of indebtedness in the developed countries

Not only that, the West is also facing a severe demographic crisis. The population of Europe at the time of the First World War was nearly 25% of the world's population; today, it is around 11% and is expected to become 3% in another twenty years. [See Chart — 25.1] Europe will disappear from the world map unless migrants from Africa and Asia take it over. The demographic crisis impacts them in other ways too. The Social Security system goes for a toss since people are living longer and there aren't sufficient numbers to contribute towards the Social Security fund or pay taxes. So the nationalization of families becomes a burden on the state. European work culture has deteriorated with even our own Tata complaining about the work ethics of British managers. In France and Italy, the weekend starts on Friday morning itself. The population has become lazy and state dependent.

In UK, the situation is worst with alcoholism becoming a common problem. The Chief Rabbi of the United Hebrew Congregation in London says, *"There are all signs of arteriosclerosis of a culture and a civilization grown old. Me has taken precedence over We and pleasure today over viability tomorrow."* [The Times, 08-09-2011]. Married couples make up less than half [45%] of all households in the USA says the recent data from the Census Bureau.

Also, there has been huge growth in unmarried couples and single parent [mostly poor black women] families. Society has become dysfunctional or disorganized in the West. The Government is trying to be organized. In India, society is organized and Government is disorganized. Because of the disorganized society in the West, the state has to take care of families. The market crash is essentially due to the model of consumption with borrowings and no savings.

Chart 25.1

World Population By Region

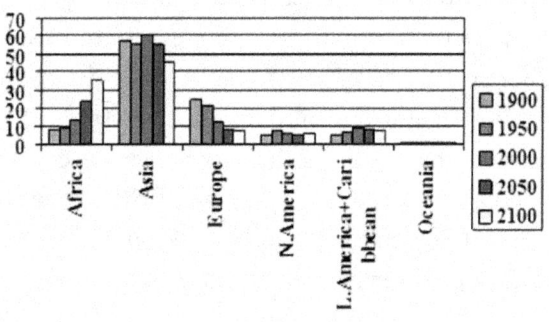

Source: United Nations Dept of Economic and Social Affairs - Population Division. World Population Prospects - The 2010 Revision, accessed from http://esa.un.org/unpd/wpp/Other-Information/wallchart.htm

According to a recent report [Wall Street Journal, 10-10-2011], nearly half of the U.S. population lives in households receiving government benefits like food stamps, subsidized housing, cash welfare or Medicare or Medicaid (the federal-state health care program for the poor) or Social security etc. The US is also a stock market economy where half of the households are involved in the stock market and bank and corporate failures have hit them the most. Even now less than five per cent of our household financial savings goes to the stock market. It's the same case in China and Japan.

Declining empires are dangerous. They will try to peddle their failed models to us and we will swallow it since colonial genes are still present here. You will find more Indians heading global corporations since India is a very large market and one way to capture it is to make Indian sepoys work for it.

A declining West is best for the rest and also for the West. It's good for the West since it needs to rethink its failed models. For the rest like us, that the West has failed has to be told to us by some white 'scholars'. Till then, we will try to imitate it and create more dysfunctional families. The need is to recognize that Big Government and Big Business are twin dangers for average citizens. India faces both and they are two *asuras* we need to guard against. NAC leftists want all families nationalized and governed by a Big State and reform marketers of the CII and CNBC variety want Big Business to flourish under crony capitalism. Beware of these twin evils since both look upon India as a charity house or as a market and not as an ancient civilization.

Two reports released in December 2012 in the US will have significant and far-reaching implications for countries like India. These reports are: **Global Trends 2030: Alternative Worlds**, by the US National Intelligence

Council, and **US Strategy for a Post-Western World: Envisioning 2030**, by the Atlantic Council.

These reports should be read and digested by countries like India as we need to prepare strategies to deal with the post-Anglo-Saxon era.

Earlier in the chapter, we had recalled the pioneering study of Angus Maddison for the OECD, in which he demonstrated that till 1820 India and China had nearly 50 per cent of the global GDP before their decline started. From that point of view, we are 're-emerging markets' and not emerging markets. Nearly 200 years of western dominance are coming to a close, and, as predicted by Sri Aurobindo, *"India will rise from the ruins of the western civilisation."*

The above mentioned two reports tell us something we always hesitate to believe till someone from the West confirms it for us. The reports indicate how China and India will be more powerful than the US by 2030. One of the reports also suggests that Asian cultures will superede America's and Europe's in 20 years as the global middle class grows. But it also predicts that competition for resources, including food, space and water, will be fierce.

Five trends which will have far-reaching implications for the west and us are the following:

- The West's problems are related to the decline of the family as an institution and household savings.
- Demography is increasing the proportion of old people in the population.
- Rising longevity is leading to a social security crisis

which will bankrupt governments.

- The decline of the Church and belief systems — both in Europe and US — could have major implications.
- The Westphalia Consensus about the sovereignty of nations which are not western/white is over.

These trends have not been adequately dealt with in the main reports possibly because they are focused more on economics, energy etc. But the building blocks of any civilization start with the family, and this has become an issue in the western world, without alternate institutions emerging.

Chart — 25.2

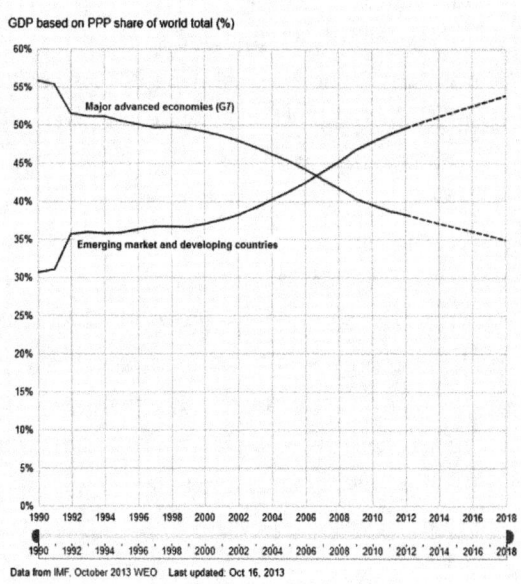

GDP based on PPP share of world total (%)

Major advanced economies (G7)

Emerging market and developing countries

Data from IMF, October 2013 WEO   Last updated: Oct 16, 2013

During the early nineties, more than 50% of global GDP, adjusted for Purchasing Power Parity [PPP] was with the G–7 countries (predominantly white/western), with the major emerging markets like India and China accounting for 36%. But as stated earlier, this has already been reversed. It is expected that the original G–7 countries will have less than 35% of global GDP by 2020 [See Chart 25.2]. Also, the forecast of their growth rates in the coming years is either negative or a very low number.

The unemployment rate in many European countries like Spain and Greece is more than 20% and among youth (aged 16 to 24 years) it is nearing 50%.

Britain has fallen out of love with marriage. The 2011 Census shows that the number of married people has fallen to 20.4 million, nearly 200,000 less than a decade ago. A quarter of the people in England and Wales are single, while the number of those cohabiting has risen from 9.8% of the population to 11.9%. Growing numbers of people are also choosing to divorce.

The breaking up of the family has put tremendous pressure on the state to sustain single parent/single women families and also the elderly. This has put their social security schemes — if at all funded — under strain.

Europe has become secular, which is a euphemism for renouncing or ignoring the church. For instance, the recent census in the UK has revealed that there has been a decline of 12% in people belonging to Christianity and 25% of the population said they had no faith — an increase from 15% a decade earlier.

The UK is also exhibiting tendencies in societal behavior more typical of third world countries. For instance, urinating in the streets is becoming a major issue and the town of Chester is using innovative ways to punish offenders like asking them to maintain local heritage sites.

The French are grappling with the issues of illegitimacy and a failure of the family system. An ex-French law minster had simultaneous relationships with eight men and it was difficult to ascertain who the father of her child was. In another decade, many French children may be able to identify their fathers only through DNA tests.

The USA is facing similar issues. In 2010, more than 50% of the children were born out of wedlock and illegitimacy is the new norm. Among blacks, it is 75% and among Latinos, it is more than 55%.

The US faces an unprecedented crisis since families have been nationalized and businesses privatized. Society has become dysfunctional. This year, more than half the births are of non-white children, giving rise to the possibility of the US becoming a non-white majority country in another 30 years where Spanish and Chinese could become major languages. This could have a tremendous impact in Mid-West and give Bible-thumpers like Rush Limbaugh a field day. This could give rise to sharper social conflicts and open up the old civil war fault lines.

Under the circumstances India needs to strategize for the future.

We should recognize that for most of the Indian elite, their umbilical cords are linked to the west. Many of them are/were educated in the US or Europe, and most of them have their children studying or working there. Due to colonial genes, acceptance and recognition by the west is critical for average middle class Indians.

The danger is that we are going to replicate their failed models when they are in decline. They will try to sell us everything they have, and we will buy it because of our colonial genes. They will hire more Indians to head global companies as showpieces in order to penetrate our markets.

The reality that the west is in decline and many of its institutions are failing has still not struck us and we will continue to try and imitate them — including their dysfunctional family systems. We should recognize that we are a civilization and not just a market. Today, funds are in search of markets and not the other way round. Instead of heading global institutions, we should prepare to acquire them.

Civilisationally, we are nearer to the East than the West. We should take the lead along with others in the East to create alternative institutions to the World Bank, the IMF and the UN. The need is to recognize that the old debate about big business or big government is passé. Our ability to look beyond Marx and market into our thriving communities and bazaars will provide us answers to many issues.

Will India, as Aurobindo mentioned, rise from the ruins of the West?

CHAPTER 26

Art of Giving: Warren Buffet to be told

The Indian ethos of giving has been much misunderstood and not stressed on sufficiently enough. Bill Gates and Warren Buffet have been the recipients of much praise, while Indian pioneers like Dyal Singh Majithia are sadly forgotten.

The visits of Bill Gates and Warren Buffet a couple of years ago resulted in copious media columns being devoted to reporting not only their business and investment insights, but also their 'charitable' instincts.

It is important that both of them are educated about our system and the Indian ethos of giving which exists from ancient times and do not require lectures by business channels which live and even die for TRPs.

Buffett should know that the greatest hero of all times in India in our scriptures is Karna who gave away everything he had and his name is interchangeably used for the art of giving in many Indian languages. Harshavardhana, the ancient Indian Emperor was yet another individual fabled for his charity.

Ratan Tata may not want to point out to Bill Gates that the Tata founders bequeathed a considerable portion of their individual wealth to many trusts that they had created for the greater good of Indian society. So is the case with G D Birla and Jamnalal Bajaj. This may not be trumpeted by Kumara Mangalam Birla and Rahul Bajaj. As a perceptive blogger, Sandeep Singh says, as early as 1895 Dyal Singh Majithia bequeathed three million rupees for noble causes including new ventures by Indians. Actually, Majithia was an early 'venture capitalist' in India even though not many know too much about him.

In similar fashion, we find that Swami Vivekananda could not have gone to the USA but for local small business people funding him and medals could not have been won by boxers, weightlifters and wrestlers but for local traders financing their clubs in remote parts of Manipur and Haryana. Many may not have heard about Ekal Vidyalayas which are one teacher schools functioning in remote parts of India particularly in tribal areas. They are in as many as 35000 villages, educating more than one million children. Take the other example of the Satya Sai initiative to bring water to Rayalseema using private donations. The 9th Plan document of the Planning Commission says, *"The Sathya Sai Charity has set an unparalleled initiative of implementing on their own without any budgetary support*

*a massive water supply project with an expenditure of Rs. 3
billion to benefit 731 villages."*

Later this project was extended to Chennai costing
more than Rs. 600 crore. The Ramakrishna Mission
runs around 200 hospitals serving nearly 1 crore people
annually mostly in rural areas. It also runs around 1200
educational institutions serving more than 3.5 lakh
students of which more than 1.25 lakhs are in rural areas.
The Nadar community in Tamil Nadu has funded hundreds
of educational institutions and hospitals and so have the
Marwaris, Chettiars, Kutchis, Bohras etc. all over India.

An enormous amount of our education, health, art and
literature and spiritual pursuits have been financed by
businessmen who are loath to talk about it. Herein lies
the secret to the fundamental ethos of giving in India. It
is done without advertisements and trumpets. Actually
in our tradition the giver is reluctant to talk about it
since it embarrasses the receiver. The fact that it could
demean the receiver is reason enough for the giver to keep
silent. Remember the way Nitish Kumar reacted when
the donation from Gujarat to flood relief in Bihar was
advertised? Nitish recalled our tradition of giving without
revealing.

It is told in our ancient wisdom that one should give
till the hand bleeds and one should not talk about it.
The action will speak even centuries later. The upstarts
of today write on every tube light their names before
donating it to temples or call press conferences to declare
their 'intentions'. That is the US culture. Everything from

love making to charity has to be advertised and shown on prime time television.

But why this sudden wallowing in self-pity and whining about giving? It all started with the Indira Gandhi Prize being given to Bill Gates on July 25th 2009 wherein the Chairman of the National Advisory Council, Ms. Sonia Gandhi read a speech on the need for Indian businessmen to give for charity [like Bill Gates] and it was published in full by the Wall Street Journal and a columnist in that paper prompted the *"rich in India to open their wallets"*. Leaders and the media in India who are clueless about Indian ethos are using Gates and Buffett to further pontificate to our business people. And the Alienated Metropolitan Rootless Wonders in India [AMROWs] are happy to be castigated by white experts!

It is interesting that Bill Gates who has operations in the Cayman Islands and in Reno in the state of Nevada to minimize or evade taxes to be paid to US Government is enthusiastic about 'Giving by India Inc.'. Warren Buffett is planning to give his dollar assets to the Gates Foundation which will reduce his estate taxes in the future. Interestingly, both of them are some of the few US business barons supporting estate taxes.

Somebody should also tell Gates and Buffett that India Inc. constitutes less than 18%of our GDP and the real growth masters are small partnership and proprietorship firms which are deeply involved in giving. Actually, India Inc. in our economy is like an item number in a Bollywood movie! Also can we suggest to Gates and Buffett that they stop investing in firms in tax havens since that sucks away billions of dollars of money from countries like India. If they really want to help India, then they should start a campaign to close down all these tax havens rather than having expensive company paid dinners at the five star hotels of our country urging Indian businessmen to 'give'.

CHAPTER 27

Leveraging on the
Mobile Phone Revolution

The impact of telecommunications on the self-employed and more particularly among the poorer groups has not been fully understood or appreciated. Mobile phones have created a sort of tsunami among lower level entrepreneurial groups like plumbers, carpenters, masons, small time construction contractors, painters, cooks, etc. In the long run, telecommunications will be a major competitor to the financial institutions since already more than 60% of the cost of operations of many global banks is software and telecom cost.

It was just a board hanging on the branch of a tree in a rural part of Bangalore. It was a computer printed sheet of paper, pasted on a cardboard and said, *"Manju the Plumber — Contact...."* followed by a ten-digit mobile number. Professors are supposed to be curious and I decided to reach him. I learnt that his income had trebled in the last few months after the acquisition of the mobile phone [thanks to a loan from a friend at 6% per month]. Manju has been getting calls from many and he was planning to graduate from his cycle to a moped. People who earlier visited his home in the mornings to catch him were now able to reach him at all times. He no longer worried about losing a customer and did not have to rush back home during lunch time to find out if anyone had come to his one room tenement to ask for him.

The impact of telecommunications on the self-employed and more particularly among the poorer groups has not been fully understood or appreciated. Mobile phones have created a sort of tsunami among lower level entrepreneurial groups like plumbers, carpenters, masons, small time construction contractors, painters, cooks, repair mechanics, winders, welders, water suppliers, tea suppliers, vegetable vendors, retail traders, flower vendors, auto drivers, priests, astrologers, etc. Actually, more than hundred categories of self-employed entrepreneurs.

One of the major forces impacting our financial, labour and product markets is information technology and telecommunications. A lot has been written on information technology and it has been subject to lot of analysis. But something more dramatic is taking place due to the mobile phone. In the long run, telecommunications is likely to be a major competitor to the financial institutions since already more than 60% of the cost of operations of many global banks consists of the software and telecom cost.

As previously stated, around 65% of our economy consists of the Service sector and the fastest growing segments belong to this sector. They are Construction, Road transport [both passenger and goods], Hotels and Restaurants [Dhabas], Wholesale trade and Retail trade, and all types of business and other services. Each of these activities is growing at more than 7% Compounded Annual Average Real Growth Rate [Real-CAGR] in the last decade and these are the engines of our economic growth. These are the segments which have started using the mobile phone on a large scale and that is enhancing their market efficiency as well as improving incomes for the entrepreneurs in these segments.

Efficient markets

Markets whether product or labour or financial are expected to have informational efficiency. Mobile phones provide such a facility and it reduces opportunities for arbitrage by re-establishing the basic law of one price — namely assets and services of similar risk characteristics will command the same price excluding the transaction cost. It enables the truck owner to track goods, which are being transported, from Kollam to Kota and provide immediate information on unforeseen events like accidents, fire etc. and other foreseen obstacles like check-post harassments. It facilitates price discovery by small time traders and distributors and make him decide to send the items to the nearest town where prices are slightly more attractive. It helps the self-employed to plan their activities better. A small time contractor contacts his masons and painters at different work–sites and instructs them instead of commuting to the site on his two-wheeler. It helps fishermen in boats to anchor their boats at locations where the prices are attractive. The time value of money has suddenly become the buzzword and time consciousness among the self-employed has been quietly enhanced.

When time is measured in money terms by the poorest category of self-employed, we can be rest assured that process of economic growth has become infectious and all factor markets will soon become efficient.

Service Provider as Banker

The mobile phone is also being used for some financial services like information on prices, billing settlements etc. But the important development, for which existing service providers and bankers should work for, is using it for a retail credit revolution. One observes that in the boat markets in Bangkok either one can pay by the *Baht*, their local currency or one can get charge cards from the service providers and pay through them. The service providers initially give an Over Draft or revolving credit facility to the retail trader, which is adjusted on a daily basis by crediting the retailer for every debit incurred by the buyer. This is one of the interesting possibilities wherein the retail trade network is provided credit facility and which reduces their cost of borrowing. It requires that they have one mobile instrument with them and periodic crediting of their account based on received calls, which are mostly available free in our context.

The share of trade at 18% of the national income (during 2011-12) was Rs. 13.5 lakh crore out of Rs. 75 lakh crore of NDP at current prices. Of this, the share of non-corporate sector [self-employed] was nearly 76%, which implies Rs. 10 lakh crore. On a conservative estimate of 75% of this figure, the trade sector would have needed Rs 7.5 lakh crore as credit requirements (since in trade, a major portion of capital is working capital) in that period.

The combined financing to trade by all banking sources (both food and non-food credit) was of the order of Rs. 2.1 lakh crore. This implies that around 28% of credit requirement is met by banking channels and the remaining by non-banking ones. So, the potential available for mobile phone service providers is a market of the order of Rs. 5.4 Lakh crore for digital based lending. Even assuming only 10% i.e., Rs. 50,000 crore out of this is tapped in the next say five years; at an interest rate of 20% [retail credit to-day in the 'open' market varies from five per cent per month to one per cent per day] the sum to be earned is Rs. 10,000 Crore. **We can call this Digi-financing or Mobile financing**. The amount of paper work will be minimal and credit will be available right at the doorstep. The collection process is through mobile credits and the cost of financing is therefore reduced.

Instead of permanently singing the Wal Mart *Sankirtan*, we should think of innovative ways wherein technology could facilitate the vast mass of self-employed groups.

The millions of entrepreneurs involved in retail trade, instead of being abused, as 'unorganized' can be made more effective by credit enhancement and price discovery process using mobile telephony. It is not required for Wal Mart to come here and squeeze our farmers and small manufacturers and sell it to consumers at 'lower prices'. We can think of leveraging on telecommunication to make all factor markets more efficient and bring down consumer prices.

Literacy no bar

The most important thing about the mobile phones is — unlike computers — even people who are not literate can use it. The only requirement is ability to speak and /or hear. We need not have to worry about language or massive software developments. Due to this, the small box provides phenomenal power unthinkable by economists or financial experts some ten years earlier.

Let A Million Manjus bloom

The appropriate thing to consider is to make the mobile sets as free goods for the poorer self-employed groups. This can be done through SHG's wherever they are active since they may be better is identifying the beneficiaries. The Central and State governments as well as various charity organizations can give it free to these segments. It is a process of asset creation and making markets work and should not be condemned by the metropolitan experts as a populist scheme. Receiving calls is in many cases free.

They need to receive calls rather than make them. If we can have a market of 1 billion sets then the unit cost can be made for even less than ten paise. But the Government seems to think that service sector is the milch-cow rather than engine of our growth. It is to be taxed at 12%, from an earlier 10% and the argument given by the Finance Minister is that their share is more than 50% in our GDP and hence they should contribute more. What about Agriculture, which constitute nearly 20% and the Government, which is also around 20%? How much do they contribute? The former is a vote issue and the latter is the destroyer of the spirit of entrepreneurship. The aim of the predatory and rapacious Government seems to be to destroy the entrepreneurial spirit and growth process of the service sector by expropriating as much as possible from them for unproductive activities of the Government. This is exactly what happened due to the socialist policies of the sixties in the other two sectors namely Agriculture and Manufacturing. Let us not repeat it for the Service sector.

Since the growth in the economy is not due to the government but in spite of it, the least it can do is to allow million Manjus to flourish for a vibrant and sustained growth process.

CHAPTER 28

Time to Say Goodbye to the World Bank

India has been one of the largest beneficiaries of World Bank assisted schemes in the last few decades and due to this, several health and educational schemes were implemented. But in the life of every society and country, there comes a time to say that we can stand on our own legs particularly if the country has ambitions to become an important power. Since India cannot be a supplicant and also a candidate for the high table of global powers, it is perhaps time to say good-bye to World Bank assistance by India.

During the tenure of the National Democratic Alliance (NDA) government, a decision was taken to forgo bilateral assistance from several countries. At that time it was received with scepticism by many. But the burgeoning foreign exchange reserves justified that decision and it also facilitated larger benefits to some poorer countries.

"First, taking advantage of our comfortable foreign exchange reserves and lower domestic interest rates, the Government has effected premature repayment of 'high-cost' currency pool loans of the World Bank, and of the Asian Development Bank totaling around $ 3 billion. We intend to continue with this policy of prudently managing the external liabilities and of proactively liquidating relatively higher cost component of our external debt portfolio. " [From the Budget Speech of the Finance Minister — 2003-2004]

The then Finance Minister Mr. Jaswant Singh initiated the following steps in the light of the above. The Government decided to (i) discontinue receiving aid from other countries except the following nine: Japan, UK, Germany, USA, EU, France, Italy, Canada and the Russian Federation and (ii) to make pre-payment of all bilateral debt owed to all the countries except the ones mentioned above.

Since July 2003, India has become a net creditor to IMF, after having been a borrower in the past. The Government has written off debts of 30 million US dollars due from seven heavily indebted countries as part of the 'India Development Initiative' announced in February 2003. The interest rate continues to be reduced and is around 6%. This is the lowest in the last thirty years and it is stimulating consumption and investment. These initiatives were largely welcomed and did not seem to have had any major impact on our development paradigm. Actually, it helped in India being seen in a positive light by many developing countries. Similar arguments could be considered for loans from World Bank of both the soft and hard variety. Considering our foreign exchange reserves and Balance of payment positions, it may be the appropriate time to forgo loans from the World Bank.

We have provided in Table — 28.1 the overall external assistance authorized and utilized both for loans and grants. We find that the grants portion constitutes around USD 700 million during 2011-12 and the total is of the order of USD 6380 million and in rupee terms it is Rs. 32473 crore. Given our GDP figure of Rs. 84 lakh crore and a savings figure of Rs. 27 lakh crore during 2011-12 this constitutes only a small portion of our national aggregates. We also find that the assistance utilized is lower than that authorized throughout the period, sometimes as much as merely 60%.

Table — 28.1 Overall External Assistance
(US $ Million)

	2000-01		2004-05		2010-11		2011-12	
	Authorized	utilized	authorized	utilized	authorized	utilized	authorized	utilized
Loans	3769.3	2967.2	5212.2	3359.5	7881.0	7866.5	12414.7	5671.7
Grants	206.3	159.5	703.7	570.7	337.4	624.9	229.1	709.5
Total	3975.6	3126.7	5915.9	3930.2	8218.3	8491.4	12643.8	6381.1
Total (in Rs. Crore)	18124.7	14254.3	25817.2	17151.6	37431.6	37905.6	60472.0	32473.6

Source: Table 8.1(A) & 8.1(B); pp S-107 & S-108, Economic Survey 2012-13, Ministry of Finance, Government of India.

We have provided in Table — 28.2 the source wise external assistance, which have been utilized by India. We find that most of the assistance from International Bank for

Reconstruction and Development [IBRD] namely World Bank and other development agencies are in the form of loans and it was of the order of USD 3600 million during 2011-12. This is from World Bank, Asian Development Bank [ADB] and International Development Association [IDA] put together.

Table — 28.2 Utilization of External Assistance by Source (US $ Million)

Country wise Distribution	2004-05			2011-12		
	Loans	Grants	Total	Loans	Grants	Total
1. Consortium Members of which	2856.6	436.9	3293.5	4389.0	511.1	4900.1
Germany	4.1	25.0	29.1	305.9	154.0	459.9
Japan	666.3	14.5	680.9	1665.3	8.5	1673.9
U.K	0.0	345.3	345.3	0.0	332.0	332.0
I.B.R.D	845.7	7.9	853.6	955.4	5.3	960.7
I.D.A	1054.8	6.1	1060.9	1455.3	0.4	1455.7
2. Others of which	502.9	133.8	636.7	1282.7	198.4	1481.1
European Economic Community	0.0	97.7	97.7	0.0	40.9	40.9
ADB	492.3	0.0	492.3	1251.6	0.0	1251.6
3. Grand Total (1+2)	3359.5	570.7	3930.2	5671.7	709.5	6381.2
4. Grand Total (in Rs. Crore) [1+2]	14660.9	2490.7	17151.6	28863.1	3610.5	32473.6

Note: * an amount of 28.5 million USD from Russia is included in this.

Source: Table 8.2(A) & 8.2(B); pp S-99 & S-101, Economic Survey 2005-06 &Table 8.3(A) & 8.3(B); pp A-113 &115 of Economic survey 2012-13, Ministry of Finance, Government of India.

If we look at our foreign exchange position as given in Table — 28.3, we find that it is of the order of 290 Billion USD in March 2012 and hence the aggregate assistance from these institutions are not critical from the point of view of our exchange position. We can always acquire technology or other requirements for any project by paying in the international markets.

Table — 28.3 Foreign Exchange Reserves (US $ Million)

Reserves	1990-91	1995-96	2000-01	2004-05	2009-10	2011-12
Gold	3496	4561	2725	4500	17986	27023
RTP@	0	0	0	1438	1380	2836
SDRs+	102	82	2	5	5006	4469
Foreign Currency Assets	2236	17044	39554	135571	254685	260069
Total	**5834**	**21687**	**42281**	**141514***	**279057***	**294397***
Total (in Rs. Crores)	11416	74384	197204	619116*	1259665*	1506139*

Note: @ Reserve Tranche Position; + Special Drawing Rights; * includes Reserve Tranche Position in IMF.

Source: Table 6.1(A) & 6.1(B); pp S-66 & S-68, Economic Survey 2005-06,2012-13, Ministry of Finance, Government of India.

There was a time in the eighties when we needed to get forex loans and support for rupee expenditure. But with our burgeoning forex reserves we need not be constrained by the amount of facility we get from the donors. After all self-help is still a good principle which can be practised particularly when we are aiming for two digit growth rates and keeping more than 290 billion USD as foreign exchange reserves.

There are other important issues, which are linked with our continued dependence on World Bank aid. That is related to our ambition to be considered as a world power. We are interested in being included as a member of groupings like G–8 etc. and this implies that we cannot be a recipient of aid from the others who are sitting on the table. World powers would prefer equals and not supplicants in their midst. In the recent past (in 2010), we have actually provided through IMF, facility-assistance to Euro Zone countries of the order of 1Bn. USD which was nearly 1% of our GDP in 2010

The other dimensions are related to the conditionalities associated with such loans and the hoard of advisors who propagate a particular point of view. It has been reported that the World Bank has withdrawn its assistance in projects related to the health sector on the basis of complaints regarding corruption in procurement practices. It is also suggested that the Finance Minister has written to World Bank for a re-consideration. The pressure of the World Bank on this particular issue might be considered as appropriate but in the overall scheme of things the requirements and conditions of the institution may not be appropriate for a country like ours, which is poised to become a major player in the affairs of the world.

The design of the project, the type of execution and the measure of benefits are all typically in the jargon of the World Bank and slowly, we have lost our ability to think through in an independent fashion on many crucial issues pertaining to development. Actually, it is the Planning Commission, which should play the crucial role of formulating, evaluating and creating standards for projects. As far as the major infrastructure projects are concerned, institutions like the Infrastructure Development Finance Corporation and the Planning Commission should play an important role.

A large number of least developed countries will be thankful to us if we come out of the assistance of World Bank since the pie available to them will be larger.

Of course, there may be protests from those who may become unemployed in Washington and in New Delhi. India is a major client of the World Bank and the 'India Story' is useful to them. If India is not a client, then the India Story will be even more catchy and impressive. It will showcase a borrower who has outgrown the situation of being a borrower and it will also establish the fact that the World Bank has achieved something in developing clients who do not need the Bank any more. The decision to bid good bye to World Bank will also bring smiles on the part of leftists. This is what is called unintended benefit of a major decision.

Poverty alleviation can and should be done by India with its own resources and experts and the expertise and money and expertise available at 1818 H Street, Washington D.C, can be beneficially used in other less developed countries.

India Inc. will have benefits in terms of its ability to

raise loans abroad since we are not going around with a 'begging bowl' any more. More importantly, India Uninc. will also be benefitted since global companies will begin to look at India not only as a market but also as a sourcing point. In other words, the India story will get altered in terms of its ability to stand on its legs. Our providing loans and grants to other less developed countries say in Africa, will help India Uninc. since that would boost trade and exports to those countries. As seen earlier, India Uninc. has a significant share in our export trade.

CHAPTER 29

Sports in India — BCCI the largest Uninc.

The two major obsessions of the Indian masses are Sports, i.e., Cricket and Bollywood films. Both of them are very popular and the middle class is obsessed with them. The personal lives of cricket stars and Bollywood actors are dissected and discussed threadbare far more than their field performance or acting. Both of these represent the quintessential India Uninc. even though recently some attempts have been made to produce films under corporate banners.

Indian sports can be alternatively called Cricket since all focus and money is on this game. We do not have listed companies conducting sports activities or even training sports persons.

As of now the government is major provider of funds to non-cricket sports in India. For instance, financial assistance provided to National Sports Federations in India by Government was Rs. 103 crore in 2010-11, Rs. 136 crore in 2011-12 and Rs. 115 crore in 2012-13 (till Feb 2013) [Rajya Sabha Unstarred question no. 3096 dated 20-12-2012 and Lok Sabha starred question no. 556 dated 06-05-2013 as quoted in India Stat.com]. These are essentially to sports like Hockey, Chess, Tennis, Volleyball, Wrestling, Badminton, Weightlifting, Kabbadi etc. It is important to note that almost all these sports bodies are headed by political leaders and in some cases, Ministers. All these organizations are associations or charitable trusts or societies from the point of view of income tax. Most are tax–exempt. Some of these sports are becoming popular due to the achievements of sportsmen and women in these. Chess, Badminton, Weight Lifting and Wrestling have got substantial recognition globally and so have gained increased following within the country.

But the king of sports in India is still Cricket which is run by the Board of Cricket Control of India [BCCI] which is one of the richest sports bodies in the world. Earlier the game — brought to India by Britishers — used to be a five day test affair having its own followers and admirers. But things changed drastically when the shorter one day version and the 20-over speed versions were introduced in a league pattern of the game. The Franchises were up for bidding and the total base price for eight franchisees was fixed at USD 400 million and the auction fetched approximately USD 724 million in 2010.

This electrified the game in terms of broadcasting

rights, advertisements, prize money etc. The Board [BCCI] is controlled by industrialists and political leaders — Cabinet Minister of Agriculture, Sharad Pawar has been President in the past, N. Srinivasan of India Cements is the current President and the Leader of Opposition in the Upper house of Parliament, Arun Jaitley is an important member of the BCCI. According to its Balance Sheet, the BCCI had an income of Rs. 849 crore in 2011-12 and Rs. 756 Crore in 2012-13 and after meeting expenditures had a surplus of Rs. 382 and Rs. 322 crore in respective years. [http://www.bcci.tv/bcci/bccitv/modules/includes/content/ROOT/media/releases/document/treasurer/BCCI%20Treasurer%20Report%202011-12.pdf]

Recently, *Forbes* magazine attempted a valuation of the different cricket boards. According to its calculations, the BCCI was worth $1.5 billion, the England & Wales Cricket Board $270 million and Cricket Australia $225 million. The International Cricket Council [ICC] was pegged much lower at $200 million. The others were Pakistan ($100 million), South Africa ($65 million), Sri Lanka ($14 million) and Bangladesh ($5 million). *"There are 10 full members of ICC, but in terms of revenue India contributes more than 70% to the game,"* the magazine wrote. *"Most sponsorships and broadcast rights come from India, and Indian tours make foreign boards rich."*

The BCCI's finances, meanwhile, leave many questions unanswered. *"The BCCI behaves like a private club,"* say many critics. There is, of course, no reason why it shouldn't, because the BCCI is a club (It is a society under the Tamil Nadu Societies Registration Act). Squabbles often break out among different factions. Office bearers sometimes make more news than the cricketers do.

In spite of thousands of fans thronging the stadiums and million more tuned to television, the management of the game is still in the hands of a registered society. The BCCI is neither a listed company nor a closely held private company. It is now waging a battle with the Income Tax Department since the Department has withdrawn the tax exemption granted to BCCI.

"The Board of Control for Cricket in India (BCCI), which is no longer considered a 'charitable organization' for assessing income, owes over Rs. 371 crore as tax to the government. And this figure could be even higher as the Income Tax Department is yet to assess the income of one of world's richest sporting bodies for the last two fiscal.

For assessment year 2009-10, the BCCI's income stood at over Rs. 964 crore on which the IT Department demanded a tax of over Rs. 413 crore. But the BCCI paid only Rs. 41.91 crore. As a result, the BCCI still owes over Rs. 371.67 crore to the government as tax for 2009-10, reveals the information gathered under the Right to Information by activist S.C. Aggarwal.

Notably, the BCCI used to get income tax exemption as a 'charitable organization' but now the government has withdrawn this exemption and the cricketing body's earnings now come under the head 'business income'.

The assessee (BCCI) used to claim exemption under Section 11 of the I-T Act 1961, available for charitable organizations. The department has withdrawn registration under Section 12 of the IT Act 1961 and rejected assessee's claim for exemption under Section 11 of the I-T Act 1961.

The department has assessed the BCCI's income under the head 'Business Income, the department said in its reply."[http://www.thehindu.com/sport/cricket/bcci-not-a-charitable-organisation/article2910033.ece]

The board has recently been enmeshed in controversies pertaining to match–fixing and some cases are pending in the Supreme Court pertaining to the role of its members. Because of the nature of the organization, there is lack of transparency and accountability. Actually in a technical sense, the teams sponsored by BCCI are not 'Indian' or National teams since BCCI is only a society under the Tamil Nadu Societies Registration Act and as such does not have powers to sponsor 'National Teams' recognized by the Government of India. The mechanics of neither player selection nor their remuneration is done in a transparent fashion. This in a game with which millions of Indians are obsessed speaks volume about the power of India Uninc. which is relationship focussed rather than rule based.

There have been periodic demands to convert BCCI into a corporate form of organization, even get it listed and become more stake holder friendly. But BCCI refuses to change since it is advantageous for administrators, players, sponsors, advertisers and broadcasters to have the present veil of secrecy in functioning and the associated benefit of lack of accountability.

Sports are the largest Uninc. in India but without the nimbleness and efficiency of the Uninc. in the manufacturing and service sector.

CHAPTER 30

Bollywood as Uninc.

As stated previously, the two major obsessions of the Indian masses are Sports, i.e., Cricket and Bollywood films. The latter includes films made in Hindi and other major regional languages like Telugu, Tamil, Bengali, Malayalam etc. The actors in films are closely followed for their attire, personal life and other idiosyncrasies. The daily city edition supplements of major print media newspapers have news only on cine stars and their exploits.

The name 'Bollywood' which was created by combining Bombay and Hollywood came in to existence somewhere in the 1970s for the Hindi film Industry based in Mumbai.. The other regional language movie centres correspondingly took on names like Kollywood [Tamil movies which are centred in Chennai in an area called Kodambakkam] and Tollywood for Bengali Films since they are produced in the Tollygunge area of Kolkata.

The film industry has played a very large role in the politics of Tamil Nadu and Andhra. In Tamil Nadu, at least three chief ministers have come from the film industry [one script writer — Karunanidhi and two actors, namely MG Ramachandran and Jayalalithaa] and in Andhra, one actor namely, N T Rama Rao has become the chief minister. It reveals to us the power of the media and its reach and influence.

India has the world's biggest movie industry in terms of number of movies produced — above 1200 movies annually. In the year 2011, the film industry generated Rs. 9300 crore revenue (this figure includes domestic and international box office receipts, revenue from cable and satellite rights, home video etc.) which went up to Rs. 11240 crore in 2012 [27-08-2013 Business Standard]. In the early 21st century, Indian cinema became a global enterprise. At the end of 2010, it was reported that in terms of annual film output, India ranks first, followed by Hollywood and China. Indian film industry reached overall revenues of $1.86 billion (Rs. 93 billion) in 2011. This is projected to rise to $3 billion (Rs. 150 billion) in 2016. The industry is expected to grow at a compounded annual growth rate of more than 12%.

Some of the Bollywood films are multi-million dollar productions, with the most expensive productions costing up to Rs. 100 crore (roughly USD 15 million). The Science fiction movie Ra.One was made at an immense budget of Rs. 135 crores (roughly USD 23 million), making it the most expensive movie ever produced in Bollywood.

Sequences shot overseas have proved a real box office draw, so Mumbai film crews are increasingly filming in Australia, Canada, New Zealand, the United Kingdom, the United States, continental Europe and elsewhere. Funding for Bollywood films often comes from private distributors and a few large studios. Until the late 1990s, it was not even recognized as an 'industry'. Even though it has since been recognized as an industry, banks and other financial institutions avoid funding the industry due to the enormous risk involved in the business. Two banks namely, Canara Bank and Indian Bank have reportedly lost heavily by financing films. The industry is significantly dependent on private financiers and there are allegations of black money playing an active role in the industry. As finances are not regulated, some funding also comes from illegitimate sources, such as the Mumbai underworld. The Mumbai underworld has been known to be involved in the production of several films, and is notorious for patronizing several prominent film personalities. Dawood Ibrahim, currently holed up in Karachi was known to have had a grip over the industry. He is wanted for terrorist activities by the Indian Government. On occasion, they have been known to use money and muscle power to get their way in cinematic deals. In January 2000, Mumbai mafia hitmen shot at Rakesh Roshan, a film director and father of star Hrithik Roshan. In 2001, the Central Bureau of Investigation seized all prints of the movie *Chori Chori Chupke* after the movie was found to be funded by members of the Mumbai underworld [Rediff. com. 1-10-2003].

Another problem facing Bollywood is widespread copyright infringement of its films. Often, bootleg DVD copies of movies are available before the prints are officially released in cinemas. Manufacturing of bootleg DVD, VCD and VHS copies of the latest movie titles is a well-established 'small scale industry' in parts of South Asia and South East Asia. The Federation of Indian Chambers of Commerce and Industry (FICCI) estimates that the Bollywood industry loses $100 million annually in loss of revenue from pirated home videos and DVDs. Besides catering to the homegrown market, demand for these copies is large amongst some sections of the Indian diaspora too. (In fact, bootleg copies are the only way people in Pakistan can watch Bollywood movies, since the Government of Pakistan has banned their sale, distribution and telecast). Films are frequently broadcast without compensation by countless small cable TV companies in India and other parts of South Asia. Small convenience stores run by members of the Indian diaspora in the US and the UK regularly stock tapes and DVDs of dubious provenance, while consumer copying adds to the problem. The availability of illegal copies of movies on the Internet also contributes to the piracy problem.

The provision of 100% foreign direct investment has made the Indian film market attractive for foreign enterprises such as 20th Century Fox, Sony Pictures, Walt Disney Pictures and Warner Bros. Indian enterprises such as Sun Network's Sun Pictures, Zee, UTV, Suresh Productions and Adlabs also participate in producing and distributing films. Tax incentives to multiplexes have aided the multiplex boom in India. Around 30 film production companies had been listed in the Stock Exchanges of India, making the commercial presence of the medium felt.

On the exhibition side many single theatres are being demolished and multiplexes are becoming popular. Some of these Multiplexes are owned by company forms of organization.

The industry by and large is in the grip of what is called 'star status' where the actors demand astronomical sums to act in a movie. Their argument is regarding the short life span of their career and the need to earn during the 'prime part of their career'.

Satellite TV, television and imported foreign films are making huge inroads into the domestic Indian entertainment market. In the past, most Bollywood films could make money; now fewer tend to do so. However, most Bollywood producers make money, recouping their investments from many sources of revenue, including selling ancillary rights. There are also increasing returns from theatres in Western countries like the United Kingdom, Canada and the United States, where Bollywood is slowly getting noticed. Bollywood movies have huge markets in Middle East and USA where the Indian diaspora is present. Even in Africa because of its music and dance sequences it is becoming popular. Similarly, Tamil Movies of Rajnikanth have become very popular in Japan. As more Indians migrate to these countries, they form a growing market for upscale Indian films.

For a comparison of Hollywood and Bollywood financial figures, we use tickets sold in 2002 and total revenue estimates. Bollywood sold 3.6 billion tickets and had total revenues (theatre tickets, DVDs, television and so on.) of US$1.3 billion, whereas Hollywood films sold 2.6 billion tickets and generated total revenues (again from all formats) of US$51 million.

A substantial portion of the industry is unincorporated, in the form of proprietorship or partnership firms even though recently company forms of organization are slowly gaining ground in production as well as distribution. The Uninc. model helps the small budget producer and a significant portion of the activities like lighting, make up, dance sequences, crowd gathering, editing, music, outdoor shooting are outsourced. In the process, an enormous amount of people get employed in the production and distribution process of a film.

Whether in the long run big corporates will begin to play a dominant role in this industry is a debatable issue. As of today, Bollywood and its various sisters in regional languages represent India Uninc. in its glory as well as warts in the form of the role of underground mafia and unaccounted money in running the industry.

CHAPTER 31

Conclusion

The role of India Uninc. or the non-corporate sector consisting of proprietorship and partnership firms in our economy is very significant. Its share in national income, savings, capital formation, exports, employment and also the growth rate of our economy has not been adequately recognized. Major reforms at State level are needed to facilitate this sector. The financing of this sector requires special attention. Caste has acted as a social capital in the growth of India Uninc. and its role in the growth of our economy. It is now time to understand this sector and formulate policies so that India comes up Indian answers to its growth paradigm and provides answers to the west which is on the cusp of an economic reversal.

As a Professor of Finance in a Management Institute, I have been teaching and researching Corporate Finance, Capital Markets and other related issues for a number of years. I am also on the board of many large listed companies and also in various committees of regulatory bodies like SEBI, RBI, IRDA, PFRDA etc. It is my view that the corporate India considered in all these fora does not reveal the full picture about India. Hence my interest in India Uninc. On researching India Uninc., I found that there was a huge gap between the India that is functional, operative and growing and the India which is discussed and feted.

There are two issues in our discourse about Indian economy. One is that it assumes that the Sensex Economy — for want of a better name let us call our corporate economy by that name — is the major actor and the main driver of growth. Business experts and the media assume that stock markets represent the health of our economy. As made clear in our discussion, only about 15% to 18% of the national income comes from corporate sector and more importantly less than 5% of our household financial savings go into the stock markets. Asian families save through banking and the Postal system rather than in share markets.

The second issue is more insidious in that Anglo-Saxon economic models are assumed to be true and people are blamed for not acting according to these models. A substantial amount of our academic literature is about testing models which are generated in the West to Indian data and offering elaborate explanations if it is not 'statistically' significant. In other words, Western models are assumed to be the eternal truth and people's behaviour is labelled 'irrational' if it is not as per the model. It is my view that we should construct models based on our data or our own empirical behavior. People will not act as per models, models need to be built on people's behaviour.

Interestingly, the two major obsessions of the middle class namely, Bollywood and Cricket are in the hands of India Uninc. even though in recent years some corporates have entered the film industry.

Already sectors like construction, trade, restaurants, transport and business services where Uninc. is dominant, are growing at more than the 8% real growth rate. Actually what is required at this point are substantial reforms at the State level to remove several constraints on India Uninc. which will then enhance our growth rate.

But most of our 'experts' are obsessed with the 30 to 40 companies listed in the stock market and the flow of FII and FDI in order to make conclusions about the Indian economy. FII and FDI have never exceeded more than10% of our domestic capital formation and the fact that our domestic savings — more so household savings — are the primary driver of our growth is ignored. FII and FDI which are akin to pickles served with curd rice are discussed as the main dish.

A word about our employment scenario. More than 85% of our working population is self-employed or contract and partially employed. Less than 15% are government or private corporate sector employed. But all discussions revolve round this 15%. Actually in the context of the declining joint family, a huge social security crisis looms large for the more than 80% self-employed people who are not covered by any mandatory pension system.

NGOs which are playing an active role in policy formulations as well as project implementation in hills and river beds are one of the major groups of India Uninc. Unfortunately, they are not covered by Right to Information Act [RTI] and they need to be more transparent in their functioning particularly in revealing the sources and uses of funds. The Companies Act 2013 makes Corporate Social Responsibility [CSR] compulsory for companies wherein 2% of the profit has to be disbursed for charity activities. In that context, the FCRA act by which NGOs collect huge funds from foreign donors can be scrapped since we are not the 'White Man's Burden' anymore.

We also find that caste is a major social capital in the development of India Uninc. And there is a process of *'Vaishya-visation'* taking place in the economy wherein every caste group is becoming *Vaishya-like* or a business group to control the organs of power. The castes which entered into business seem to have done much better than those which entered politics as primary activity.

The global economy is undergoing significant changes with a large part of the West in terminal decline. Many major areas of their 'economic assumptions and models' have failed. Banks are in crisis and so are the markets. Their society is in turmoil with 'nationalization of families' and privatization of business. Old age care, single parent care, child-care, health care etc. have all become the responsibility of the state and in many places, the State has broken down. The entire West is on the cusp of change with violence threatening their peace due to the many austerity measures that have been imposed.

The late eighties saw the fall of the Berlin Wall and the demise of the ideology of Marx which was a dominant ideology for several decades in countries like USSR and China. But that era has ended. The era of markets is also showing signs of decline with substantial scandals and wrong practices in LIBOR fixing to FOREX manipulations to Tax Havens.

It is required that India go beyond Marx and Markets and think up a paradigm which accommodates the primacy of families and communities. We are a relationship-based society and to destroy it to make a fully rule based society may not work. We are an adaptive society since we are heterogeneous. We need to re-work our idea of India to suit our own ethos and thousands of years of culture and civilization. We all carry a heavy burden on our shoulders since India needs to show a third way to the world in the coming decades.

The world is eager to listen — Are we ready to offer something new? Or are we going to give them back their own failed recipes?

Acknowledgements

A book of this nature owes its gratitude to many. The seeds of this book were sown as early as the seventies when Dr. K.N.Raj in one of his convocation addresses at IIM Calcutta pointed out the issues of separating savings data between 'pure consuming household' and 'mixed or producing households'. That address inspired me to think about the interesting and unique aspects of our economy.

I wish to thank ICSSR for providing the National Fellow facility to pursue research in the area of the non-corporate sector and their role in our economy. My sincere thanks to the then Chairman, ICSSR, Prof. V.R. Panchamukhi for his constant encouragement and comments. I would also like to thank CRISIL for providing me the opportunity to study the database for the non-corporate sector, which provided rich clues to me in understanding the nature of our database. In particular, I would have liked to thank Mr. Ravimohan, the then chief of CRISIL for his insightful observations and comments, but he is no more.

I would like to thank Mr. N. Rangachary, former Chairman of IRDA for providing deep insights into the social security aspects of the unorganized sector. He also kindly consented to provide the introductory note to this book.

Special thanks to Mr. R. Thiagarajan, Founder of the Shriram Group. He was gracious enough to assist me at various times with his insightful comments and also agreed to write the Foreword to the book. This book has been re-worked from different articles written by me in several publications like Eternal India, The Hindu — Business Line, DNA, The New Indian Express and web Publications like First Post, Niti Central, Centre Right India etc. during a period of several years and I would like to thank all of them.

I have benefitted immensely by discussions with academic colleagues at various institutions and my students of different batches who underwent my courses at IIM Bangalore. Also, special thanks to all my Twitter followers for their encouragement and interesting inputs. My special thanks to Mr. S. Gurumurthy from Chennai for many of his insightful articles on economics and society from which I have learnt a lot. I also would like to thank Ms. Vani and Ms. Aparna, Research Associates at IIM-B for their excellent and patient assistance in going through several versions of this book. Shriram Properties and its MD, Mr. Murali requires special mention for constant encouragement and assistance.

I should mention Mr. Karthik Venkatesh of Westland

Books for editing the book with a sharp eye and patience. I would also like to thank Mr. Gautam Padmanabhan, CEO, Westland Books for his constant encouragement.

Needless to add, the errors and omissions are mine alone.

References

1. All India Income Tax Statistics — Directorate of Income Tax — New Delhi — 2001[Now Discontinued]

2. Annual Survey of Industries [ASI] — Factory Sector — Central Statistical Organisation[CSO] — various issues

3. Dharampal, 'Beautiful Tree — Indigenous Indian Education in the Eighteenth Century; Vol-3 of Collected writings'; Other India Press Goa 2000

4. Durkheim Emile — 'The Division of Labor in Society', pp liv; The Free Press; New York 1997

5. Economic Census, Central Statistical Organisation [CSO], 1998;2005

6. Economic Survey — various issues — Ministry of Finance [MoF] Government of India [GoI]

7. EPW Research Foundation, Mumbai "Scheduled Commercial Banks in India — A 30 year Data Base"

8. Fukuyama Francis — 'Trust' pp. 10; The Free Press Paperbacks, New York 1996

9. Gupta Dipankar; Interrogating Caste; pp1; Penguin Books 2000].

10. Gurcharan Das — 'India Unbound — From Independence to the Global transformation Age'; pp. 150 Penguin Books New Delhi 2002

11. Gurumurthy S — Clash of Economic Traditions Business Line 19-09-2013

12. Handbook of Hindu Economics and Business :Edited by Prof Hrishikesh D Vinod — ISBNISBN/EAN13: 148398088X/9781483980881 Mar2013 Amazon/ Create Space

13. Hand book of Statistics on Indian Economy — Reserve Bank of India, Ministry of Finance; Various issues

14. Harish Damodaran — 'India's New Capitalists' — pp. 315; Permanent Black -New Delhi; 2008.]

15. IMF: World Economic Outlook–Oct 2013

16. India Stat.com

17. Indianngos.com

18. Kanagasabapathi, 'Indian Models of Business and Economics' pp176-189;PHI;India;2010 New Delhi

19. Mint, Live: Changing role of Caste: 4 articles, June 4-16, 2010

20. National Accounts Statistics [NAS] Central Statistical Organisation [CSO] — Ministry of Statistics & Programme Implementation [MOSPI] Government of India [GoI] — various issues.

21. National Accounts Statistics — Sources and Methods 1980;1989;2007;2012

22. National Sample Survey Organisation — NSSO — CSO — Various Surveys/Reports

23. OASIS Report, January 2000

24. OECD fact book — Household Savings — Different Issues

25. Planning commission reports

26. Reserve Bank of India [RBI] bulletins — Several Issues

27. Report of the National Statistical Commission [NSC] — Aug 2001 — Ministry of Statistics and Programme Implementation, New Delhi.

28. Srinivas M.N — Some reflections on the nature of Caste hierarchy; Collected Essays; pp196- 197, OUP 2005

29. Survey of Current Business, Bureau of Economic Analysis — US Department of Commerce — various issues

30. Swaminathan S Aiyar. 'Social Capital — An idea whose time has come' — Times of India — 28 May 2000

31. UNIDO Case studies: Fabio Russo: Strengthening Indian SME clusters UNIDO experience US/GLO/95/144 — July 1999

32. US Bureau of Census

33. Vaidyanathan R — Eternal India — India First Foundation- April 2009 — New Delhi

34. World Bank; pp175 World Development report 2002

35. World Gold Council — Gold Demand Trends — Various issues

Index

A

Abhimanyu 225, 226, 229, 231
All India Income Tax Statistics (AIITS) 53,63,157,193
All Time Money (ATM) 176
Anglo-Saxon Model 263
Annual Survey of Industry (ASI) 17,21
Asian Development Bank (ADB) 306, 308

B

Backward Class (BC) 236,238,239
Bank Deposits 59,126,148
Barings Bank 114
Barometer 62, 216, 219, 220, 223
Board of Control for Cricket in India (BCCI) 314, 315, 316, 317,
Bollywood 177, 296, 313, 319, 320, 321, 322, 323, 324, 327,
Bombay Stock Exchange (BSE) 228
Bureaucracy 100,261

C

Central Statistical Organisation (CSO) 11,12,23,68,107,192,237,250
Centre for Monitoring Indian Economy (CMIE) 18
Chakravyuha 226
Chicago Board of Trade (CBOT) 216
Chit Funds 92, 138, 139, 141, 142, 143, 144, 145, 146
Client Account 161,162,163,166
Colonial Gene 282,287,292
Compunded Annual Growth Rate (CAGR) 72,124,300,320,

Confederation of Indian Industries (CII) 109,287
Consumerist Culture 64,206
Controller of Capital Issues (CCI) 225
Corporate Social Responsibility (CSR) 266, 281, 328,
Credit Rating 92,150,230
Current Account Defecit (CAD) 174

D
Department of Company Affairs (DCA) 18,228
Deposit Insurance and Credit Guarantee Corporation (DICGC) 148
Dharampal 251,252
Digi Cash 179
Due Diligence 225
Durkheim Emile 253

E
Economic Census (EC) 23,45,107,108,237,246,250
Economic Survey (ES) 23,89,137,166,244
Ekal Vidyalayas 294
Employees' Provident Fund (EPF) 70,196,212
Employment Guarantee Scheme (EGS) 110
Establishments 21, 23, 24, 25, 26, 27, 30, 31, 32, 33, 89, 107, 246, 251
Euro Centric Model 264

F
Fast Moving Consumer Goods (FMCG) 123
Federation of Indian Chambers of Commerce & Industries (FICCI) 109,322
Fiscal Deficit 102,223,
Foreign Agents Registration Act (FARA) 279
Foreign Contribution Regulation Act (FCRA)
Foreign Direct Investment (FDI) 53, 85, 89, 99, 100, 109, 210, 222, 223, 250, 283, 327,
Foreign Institutional Investors (FIIs) 53, 210, 222, 223, 250, 283, 327
Forward Caste (FC) 239
Fukuyama Francis 253, 254

G

Gates, Bill 293, 294, 296
Globalisation 144
Gross Domestic Capital Formation (GDCF) 68, 71, 174
Gross Domestic Product (GDP) 18, 35, 59, 83, 86, 154, 191, 194,
Gross Domestic Savings (GDS) 59, 83
Gupta Dipankar 260
Gurcharan Das 255
Gurumurthy S 221, 332

H

Harish Damodaran 260, 261
Hindu Undivided Families (HUFs) 12, 52
Housing and Urban Development (HUD) 203
Hrishikesh D Vinod 264

I

Income Tax (IT) 52, 53, 63, 74, 80, 156, 161, 191, 193, 195, 198,
    314, 316,
Incremental Capital Output Ratio (ICOR) 54,
Inflation 62, 102, 111, 159, 160, 195, 208, 223,
Informal Sector 9, 10,
Information and Communication Technology (ICT) 41, 77, 121,
International Bank for Reconstruction and Development (IBRD) 307
International Development Association (IDA) 308
Insurance Regulatory and Development Authority (IRDA) 326, 332
International Cricket Council 315
International Monetary Fund (IMF) 160, 292, 306, 310, 336,

K

Kanagasabapathi 257, 336
Karmic Cycle 113,
Kirana Shops 91, 97, 248,
Know Your Customer (KYC) 92,
Kshatriyas 248,

L
Labyrinthine 111, 112,
Leeson, Nick 114,
LIBOR 329,
Life Insurance Corporation (LIC) 7, 67, 196,

M
Mehta, Harshad 114, 225,
Micro Small and Medium Enterprises (MSME) 23, 37, 38
Minimum Wages Act 237,
Ministry of Statistics and Program Implementation (MOSPI) 27, 336,
Mint, The 261, 336,
Most Backward Classes (MBC) 238, 239,
Multinational Corporations (MNCs) 47, 82, 95, 96, 148,

N
National Accounts Statistics (NAS) 4, 5, 6, 10, 19, 21, 35, 59, 68, 122, 192, 217, 336,
National Family Health Statistics (NFHS) 235,
National Rural Employment Guarantee Act (NREGA) 73, 102, 168,
National Sample Survey (NSS) 10, 22, 27, 94, 107, 235,
National Sample Survey Organization (NSSO) 23, 27, 37, 45, 89, 337,
National Statistical Commission (NSC) 8, 22, 23, 43, 44, 45, 46, 337,
National Stock Exchange (NSE) 227
Nationalization 64, 126, 285, 328,
Negation 4,
Net Domestic Product (NDP) 16, 17, 18, 44, 71, 72, 87, 302,
National Pension System (NPS) 196,
New York Stock Exchange (NYSE) 216, 226,
Non Banking Financial Companies (NBFC) 131, 132, 133, 134, 136, 137, 138, 149,
Non Banking Financial Sector (NBFS) 119, 122, 128, 129, 130, 131, 138, 148, 151, 204,
Non Governmental Organizations (NGO) 265, 266, 267, 269, 276, 277, 278, 279, 280, 281, 328,

Non-Performing Assets (NPAs) 133, 136, 138,
Non Resident Indians (NRIs) 173,

O

OASIS 59, 175
OECD 207, 283, 288
Organized Sector 4, 5, 6, 8, 9, 10 , 11, 17, 18, 19, 21, 22, 44, 45,
    70, 71, 79, 106, 122, 126, 129, 137, 190, 196, 197, 218,
    236, 237, 245, 332
Own Account 24, 25, 26, 29, 37, 107, 161, 162, 163, 164, 165,
    168, 169, 228, 246, 251

P

Partnership and Proprietorship (P&P) Economy 15, 40, 50, 58, 66,
    70, 74 , 85, 103, 115, 116, 122, 123, 194, 243
Pension Fund Development and Regulatory Authority (PFRDA) 204,
    326
Petite Bourgeoisie 56, 97, 109, 178, 247
Planning Commission 262, 294, 311
Poverty 49, 83, 110, 169, 206, 311
Prime Lending Rate (PLR) 149
Proprietorship Firms 58, 59, 66, 70, 72, 77, 83, 85, 87, 93, 103,
    115, 121, 146, 149, 163, 181, 203, 207, 210, 217, 219, 223,
    237, 243, 250, 264, 296, 324
Public Sector 5, 6, 8, 11, 12, 17, 28, 45, 110, 127, 148, 149, 159,
    242, 243
Pulled Out of Thin Air ("POTA") 13, 234, 241

R

Re-Possession Agents 115, 116
Reserve Bank of India (RBI) 18, 55, 64, 96, 123, 130, 133, 136,
    137, 139, 174, 204
Reverse Annuity Mortgages 201

S

Samskaras 60, 63, 64, 163, 212

Scheduled Caste (SC) 33, 238, 242

Scheduled Commercial Banks (SCBs) 126

Scheduled Tribe (ST) 33, 239, 242

Securities and Exchange Board of India (SEBI) 225, 228, 326

Self Help Groups (SHG) 28, 303

Sick Companies 110

Social Security 48, 59, 60, 63, 95, 101, 160, 172, 175, 177, 184, 185, 190, 196, 198, 200, 209, 212, 214, 248, 263, 285, 287, 289, 290

Social Capital 116, 169, 249, 253, 254, 255, 259, 263, 264, 325

Srinivas M. N. 238, 260, 315

Swaminathan S. Iyer 254, 255

T

Tax Deduction at Source 196

Time Value 111, 113, 117, 301

Triple Nodes 147

U

Un-Incorporated Business (UIBs) 122, 132, 136, 150, 151, 230

UNIDO 257

US Security Cleared (USC) 187

V

Vaidyanathan R. 167

Vivekananda, Swami 264, 294

Vaishya 247, 248,, 251, 261, 328

W

World Bank 160, 256, 292, 305, 306, 310, 311

World Gold Council (WGC) 173